T0305760

World Scientific Book Series in Marketing – Volume 2

# New Directions in Behavioral Pricing

# World Scientific Book Series in Marketing

**Series Editor: Chezy Ofir**
*(The Hebrew University of Jerusalem, Israel)*

*Published:*

Vol. 2:  *New Directions in Behavioral Pricing*
edited by Chezy Ofir

Vol. 1:  *Finding Wisdom in Brand Tragedies: Managing Threats to
Brand Equity*
by Robert J Thomas

World Scientific Book Series in Marketing – Volume 2

Series Editor

**Chezy Ofir**
*Hebrew University of Jerusalem, Israel*

# New Directions in Behavioral Pricing

Editor

**Chezy Ofir**
*Hebrew University of Jerusalem, Israel*

**World Scientific**

V JERSEY · LONDON · SINGAPORE · BEIJING · SHANGHAI · HONG KONG · TAIPEI · CHENNAI · TOKYO

*Published by*

World Scientific Publishing Co. Pte. Ltd.

5 Toh Tuck Link, Singapore 596224

*USA office:* 27 Warren Street, Suite 401-402, Hackensack, NJ 07601

*UK office:* 57 Shelton Street, Covent Garden, London WC2H 9HE

Library of Congress Control Number: 2024011394

**British Library Cataloguing-in-Publication Data**
A catalogue record for this book is available from the British Library.

**World Scientific Book Series in Marketing — Vol. 2**
**NEW DIRECTIONS IN BEHAVIORAL PRICING**

ISBN 978-981-12-9222-4 (hardcover)
ISBN 978-981-12-9223-1 (ebook for institutions)
ISBN 978-981-12-9224-8 (ebook for individuals)

For any available supplementary material, please visit
https://www.worldscientific.com/worldscibooks/10.1142/13814#t=suppl

Desk Editors: Aanand Jayaraman/Sandhya Venkatesh

Typeset by Stallion Press
Email: enquiries@stallionpress.com

Printed in Singapore

# About the Editor

**Chezy Ofir** is the Kmart Chair Emeritus Professor at the School of business Administration, The Hebrew University of Jerusalem. He received his B.Sc. and M.Sc. in Engineering from Ben-Gurion University and M.Phil. and Ph.D. in Business Administration from Columbia University as a Fulbright Scholar. His research is in the areas of marketing, consumer behavior, and judgment and decision-making. His research has been published in journals including *The Journal of Consumer Research, Journal of Marketing Research, Journal of Marketing, Management Science, Journal of Personality and Social Psychology, Journal of Consumer Psychology, Psychometrika, International Journal of Research in Marketing, Organizational Behavior and Human Decision Processes, Journal of Retailing, Multivariate Behavioral Research, British Journal of Mathematical and Statistical Psychology, Journal of Forecasting, Marketing Letters, Journal of Economic Psychology, etc.*

He has been invited as a Visiting Professor and/or research partner to many top universities, including University of California Berkeley, New York University (NYU), Stanford University, Georgetown University, University of Florida at Gainesville, Bocconni University (Milan, Italy), and others.

# About the Contributors

**Ajay T. Abraham** is an Associate Professor of Marketing at the Albers School of Business and Economics, Seattle University. His primary expertise lies in the area of Pricing and in methodological approaches such as Meta-Analysis and Eye-Tracking, and he is also interested in Morality and Corporate Social Responsibility. He has published in outlets such as *Journal of Marketing Research*, *MIT Sloan Management Review*, *SAGE Research Methods Cases*, *Journal of Business and Industrial Marketing*, and *Journal of Management for Global Sustainability*. He teaches in-person and online MBA and undergraduate classes on Introduction to Marketing, Marketing Management, Personal Selling, and Creating Value Through Marketing and Operations.

Ajay is actively involved in university service, and he has served as an ad hoc reviewer for multiple journals including *Journal of Marketing Research*, *Journal of Consumer Research*, and *Journal of the Academy of Marketing Science*. He has a Ph.D. in Marketing from the University of Maryland; a PGPM from the Indian School of Business; and a B.Tech. in Computer Science and Engineering from Mahatma Gandhi University. Prior to joining academia, he has worked at multiple organizations including Microsoft, Wipro Technologies, and UST Global, in roles spanning marketing, program management, pre-sales, research, content development, technology, and technology evangelism.

**Lisa E. Bolton** is a Professor of Marketing and Anchel Professor of Business Administration at the Pennsylvania State University. Her Ph.D. is in Marketing from the University of Florida. She has a Master's degree in Clinical Engineering from the University of Toronto and a Bachelor's degree in Engineering Physics from the Royal Military College of Canada. Her research focuses on judgment and decision-making by managers and consumers, with substantive interests in pricing, new products and technology, cross-cultural marketing, and consumer welfare (e.g., spending and finances, health, sustainability). She has published in leading marketing journals, including the *Journal of Marketing Research, Journal of Consumer Research, Journal of Marketing & Public Policy, Journal of Service Research, Journal of Consumer Psychology, and Journal of Retailing.* She serves on the editorial review boards of the *Journal of Consumer Research* (AE), *Journal of Marketing* (AE), *Journal of Marketing Research* (AE), *Journal of Service Research* (AE), *Journal of Public Policy & Marketing (AE), Journal of Retailing* (AE), *Journal of Consumer Psychology,* and *Journal of Consumer Affairs.* She teaches marketing courses, with an emphasis on consumer insight, in undergraduate, MBA, and Ph.D. programs in the Smeal College of Business.

**Haipeng (Allan) Chen** is Professor, Gatton Endowed Chair in Marketing, and University Research Professor at the University of Kentucky. He received his Ph.D. in Business Administration (Marketing concentration) from the University of Minnesota (Twin Cities), his M.A. in Applied Linguistics from Zhejiang University (Hangzhou, China), and his B.Eng. (with honors) in Mechanical Engineering from Shandong University of Technology (Zibo, China). He conducts research in the areas of Behavioral Decision Theory (BDT) and pricing. He has published in the *Journal of Consumer Research, Journal of Marketing, Journal of Marketing Research, Marketing Science, Management Science, Strategic Management Journal, Information Systems Research, Journal of Consumer Psychology, Journal of Academy of Marketing Science, Journal of Retailing, Journal of Monetary Economics,* and *Review of Economics and Statistics,* among other journals. He is currently serving as an Associate Editor for the *Journal of Consumer Research,* a DE for *Decision Sciences,* and an Associate Editor for the *Journal of Retailing,* and is on the editorial review board of the *Journal of Marketing, Journal of Consumer Psychology,* and *Journal of the Academy of Marketing Science.* He is a Co-editor of the JACR special issue on Behavioral Pricing, and a co-chair of the 2022 ACR Conference (Denver) and SCP Boutique Conference on the Global Consumer (Singapore).

**Sergei Graguer** is a Lecturer at the Ashkelon Academic College. He received his BA, MBA, and recently his Ph.D. from the Hebrew University of Jerusalem. His current research focuses on behavioral pricing and judgement and decision-making of consumers and managers. He was a finalist in the dissertation competition of the European Marketing Association and the winner of the best case study competition by Eli Hurvitz Institute for Strategic Management at Tel-Aviv University.

**Ori Grossman** is a Lecturer at the School of Business Administration, Bar-Ilan University. His research includes pricing, consumer decision-making, and consumer behavior. He is a Doctoral graduate from the faculty of Business Administration, The Hebrew University of Jerusalem. Dr. Grossman holds an MBA and BA in economics and accounting from The Hebrew University of Jerusalem and BA in political science and communication from Bar-Ilan University.

**Rebecca W. Hamilton** is the Michael G. and Robin Psaros Chair in Business Administration, Senior Associate Dean for Faculty Affairs and Professor of Marketing at Georgetown University's McDonough School of Business. She received her Ph.D. from the MIT Sloan School of Management in 2000 and was on the faculty at the University of Maryland's Robert H. Smith School of Business from 2000–2014. Professor Hamilton's research examines the effects of contextual factors — including the social environment, stage of decision-making, and presentation format — on consumer decision-making. She served as Co-Editor of the *Journal of Marketing Research* from 2016–2020, and has served as Associate Editor for the *Journal of Consumer Research, Journal of the Academy of Marketing Science,* and *International Journal of Research in Marketing,* and on the Editorial Review Boards of the *Journal of Marketing,* and *Journal of Interactive Marketing.* Professor Hamilton enjoys teaching consumer behavior classes to undergraduate, MBA, and executive MBA students.

**Arnaud Monnier** is an Assistant Professor of Marketing at EDHEC Business School (France), and a recent Ph.D. graduate from Cornell University. He studies how people assess the value of products and its consequences for market prices, brand positioning, consumer behavior, and well-being. His research has been published in the *Journal of Consumer Research* and the *Journal of the Association for Consumer Research.*

**Kent B. Monroe** (BA, Kalamazoo College 1960, MBA Indiana University 1961, DBA University of Illinois, 1968) has pioneered research on the information value of price and has authored: *Pricing: Making Profitable Decisions*, 3rd ed. McGraw-Hill/Irwin, 2003. Dr. Monroe has presented papers before several international associations in Asia, Europe, and North America. His research papers have been published in the *Journal of Marketing Research, Journal of Marketing, Journal of Consumer Research. Journal of Consumer Psychology, Management Science, Journal of the Academy of Marketing Science, Journal of Retailing* and other journals. He has served as a consultant on pricing, marketing strategy, and marketing research to business firms, governments, and the United Nations.

He has conducted executive training programs for business firms, non-profit organizations, and universities in North and South America, Europe, Asia, Australia, and Africa. He was the Founding Editor of *Pricing Practice and Strategy* (1993–2003). He received the American Marketing Association/McGraw-Hill Irwin Educator of the Year award, February 2005. He is a Fellow of the Decision Sciences Institute, Association for Consumer Research, and American Marketing Association.

**Matti Rachamim** is a member of the faculty at the School of Business Administration, Bar-Ilan University. Matti received her Ph.D. in Marketing from the Hebrew University Business School. She also holds a B.Sc. in Chemistry and an MBA from the Hebrew University of Jerusalem. Matti currently serves as Chair of the Executive MBA Programs at the School of Business Administration, Bar-Ilan University. Her research interests focus on advertising, consumer behavior, social marketing, and consumer decision-making. In her work she has examined the influence of subliminal marketing content on consumer decision-making; factors shaping advertising's effectiveness; negative advertising's impact on consumer behavior; and the effect of ethnic identity on consumer preferences.

**Priya Raghubir** joined NYU Stern School of Business in July 2008. She is the Dean Abraham L. Gitlow Professor of Business. She is the past Editor of *JCP-Research Reports* and is an MSI Academic Fellow. Prior to joining NYU Stern, Priya was at the Haas School, University of California, Berkeley (1997–2008) and HKUST (1994–1997). Priya's research interests are in the areas of consumer psychology, including psychological aspects of prices and money; memory and context effects; health risk; and visual and sensory information processing. She has published over 75 articles and book chapters in journals such as the *Journal of Marketing Research (JMR), Journal of Consumer Research (JCR), Journal of Consumer Psychology (JCP), Journal of Marketing (JM), Journal of Personality and Social Psychology (JPSP)* and *Marketing Science* and has over a dozen other working papers. She has delivered over 100 invited presentations at major universities, symposia, and conferences around the world, and her work has been presented a similar number of times at schools and conferences by her co-authors, students, and herself.

Priya received her undergraduate degree in Economics from St. Stephen's College, Delhi University in 1983; her M.B.A from the Indian Institute of Management, Ahmedabad in 1985; and her Ph.D. in Marketing from New York University in 1994. She worked with Tata Administrative Services (India), Citibank, N.A. (India and Hong Kong), and Jardine Fleming (Hong Kong) between 1985 and 1990.

**Aner Sela**, Ph.D., is a Professor of Marketing at University of Florida's Warrington College of Business. He received his Ph.D. in Business from Stanford University. Dr. Sela is an expert on how people make choices and form preferences. His work highlights how everyday decisions are shaped by people's momentary experiences, their intuitions, and seemingly unimportant features of the decision context. He has been repeatedly ranked among the top 50 most productive marketing authors and recognized as a leading scholar by the Marketing Science Institute.

**Martin Spann** is a Professor of electronic commerce and digital markets and Dean of the LMU Munich School of Management at the Ludwig-Maximilians-Universität München (LMU Munich), Germany. His research focuses on digital markets and the impact of information technology on consumer behavior. He is particularly interested in questions pertaining to mobile commerce, interactive pricing mechanisms, virtual stock markets, and social networks. His work has been published in leading international journals such as *Management Science, Marketing Science, Journal of Marketing, Information Systems Research, MIS Quarterly* and other journals.

**Lucas Stich** is an Assistant Professor at the Institute of Electronic Commerce and Digital Markets at the Ludwig-Maximilians-Universität München (LMU Munich), Germany. His research focuses on issues in quantitative marketing, electronic commerce, and behavioral and experimental economics. He is particularly interested in questions related to the digital economy, specifically pricing and auctions, transparency as a marketing strategy, and social networks and online crowdsourcing markets. His research has been published in the *Journal of Decision Systems*, *Journal of the Academy of Marketing Science*, *Journal of Economic Behavior & Organization*, *Communications of the ACM*, *Business Information Systems Engineering*, and other journals.

**Manoj Thomas** is Nakashimato Professor of Marketing and Senior Director of Executive MBA and MSBA programs. Thomas is a behavioral scientist who trains MBA students and executives to be customer-centric leaders and encourages them to build meaningful and purposeful connections with customers. His lectures on consumer insights are available online through eCornell's certificate program on Consumer Behavior. Thomas has received the Apple Award and the Stephen Russell Family Teaching Award for excellence in teaching.

Thomas has published several research papers on the psychology of price evaluations. By characterizing irrational responses such as the left-digit effect, the price precision effect, and the mode of payment effect, Thomas has demonstrated the pervasive influence of heuristics and biases on price evaluations. He also studies how political identity and moral beliefs influence consumer behavior. His recent research with Shreyans Goenka explains why some consumers consider conspicuous consumption immoral while others happily engage in such consumption. He is the Co-author of the book *Why People (Don't) Buy: GO and STOP Signals*. He is an Associate Editor for the *Journal of Marketing Research* and the *Journal of Consumer Research*.

# Contents

# Introduction: New Directions in Behavioral Pricing

## Matti Rachamim, Sergei Graguer, Ori Grossman and Chezy Ofir

One of the main objectives of behavioral pricing research is to investigate how consumers perceive, evaluate, and integrate prices with other factors to make value and fairness judgments and product and brand choices. Encompassing customer price-related attitudes, knowledge, cognitive processes, and behaviors, it seeks to predict and explain customers' reactions to price strategies and associated psychological, physiological, and emotional processes. Behavioral pricing research is viewed as central to academic marketing research as well as to strategic pricing by executives. The objective of this book is to introduce new research trends in this domain. The following is a brief overview of the work presented herein.

This Introduction is followed by Priya Raghubir's "Valuing New Currencies: A Framework for Future Research," which delineates how

Matti Rachamim, Graduate School of Business Administration, Bar-Ilan University, Israel (Matti.rachamim@biu.ac.il); Sergei Graguer, Ashkelon Academic College, Ashkelon, Israel (Sergeig@edu.aac.ac.il); Ori Grossman, Graduate School of Business Administration, Bar-Ilan University, Israel (Ori-avraham.grossman@biu.ac.il); Chezy Ofir, School of Business Administration, The Hebrew University of Jerusalem, Israel (Chezy.Ofir@huji.ac.il).

alternative currencies (e.g., airline miles) are priced, and how consumers make pricing decisions concerning them. Prior research has examined how payment modes, such as cash, credit cards, debit cards, and gift certificates, affect price-related behavior, including likelihood of purchase, amounts spent, and quantity and variety of items purchased. Raghubir suggests that the findings and conclusions of these studies may be contingent on product price as expressed in money-based currency, and that when prices are expressed instead in alternative currencies (e.g., airline miles), previous behavioral pricing research findings are likely to be cast into doubt. The author subsequently develops a set of propositions while shedding light on alternative payment modes and bargains. In the discussion, emphasis is laid on different aspects of airline miles rewards and redemption, and how they compare with traditional money-based payment formats.

In Chapter 2, "Affective Price Evaluations: How Pain, Pleasure, and Metacognitive Feeling Influence Price Evaluations," Thomas and Monnier show that while the role of affect in behavioral pricing literature has tended to be overlooked historically, in the last two decades it has gained attention primarily due to notable advancements in the social cognition and decision-making research fields. This recent work has demonstrated that emotions elicited by prices, products, and the shopping context, as well as the metacognitive feelings elicited by the process of price evaluation, have a significant role in explaining price-related consumer behavior. The authors present a conceptual framework for affective processes in price evaluations that includes three types of consumer affective response influencing price assessments and further purchase decisions and spending behaviors: pain of paying, metacognitive experiences, and hedonic price evaluations. The "pain of paying" principle refers to consumers' affective responses to price based on their perception of relative price magnitude (e.g., current versus previous price) and mode of payment (e.g., cash versus card), and the negative effects of the act of parting with money. In the context of metacognitive experience, three main effects are discussed: the ease-of-recall effect (i.e., judgments based on feelings of ease in recalling task-related information), the ease-of-computation effect (i.e., the reliance of customer judgments on the ease with which a number-based task is performed), and the feeling-of-not-knowing effect (i.e., making customer judgments based on a subjective sense of whether the knowledge generated is veridical or reliable). Affective responses of the latter type are labeled hedonic price evaluations, and refer to evaluations stemming from the product itself, the situational context, or the customer's personal issues. In reviewing previous theorizations, the authors explain that two processes are likely to drive a hedonic mindset: valuation by feelings (i.e., sensitivity to the nature of the product) and valuation by calculation (i.e., scope sensitivity or the willingness to pay for a greater amount of product). Valuation by feelings and valuation by calculation are presented as two poles of the same continuum, where increasing emotional sensitivity decreases scope sensitivity and vice versa.

Bolton and Chen's contribution, "Behavioral Pricing and Price Fairness" (Chapter 3), uses as a theoretical base Kahneman *et al.*'s (1986) principle of dual entitlement, which refers to the fairness perception of pricing during buyer–seller transactions. According to the theory, buyers are entitled to a reference price, and sellers to a reference profit. The authors describe two main currents in subsequent research. The first is dedicated to revealing and testing the antecedents of the reference transaction as a key determinant of entitlement and fairness; for example, customers tend to judge costs and prices as unfair if they are not in line with past or competitor prices. In addition, scholars have demonstrated that consumers are highly susceptible to the price paid by other consumers for the same products or services. The second current attempts to go beyond the reference transaction, including individual and contextual factors as additional determinants of price fairness. Among these factors are firm motive and reputation, cultural belonging, and consumer power. Based on previous suggestions that collectivist consumers are guided by communal norms and individualist consumers by exchange norms, the authors examine cross-cultural (collectivistic versus individualistic) and industry differences in fairness judgments regarding asymmetric pricing.

In Chapter 4, "Communicating Price Changes and Price Differences," Kent Monroe focuses on how price changes are conveyed to consumers. Price change messages, he notes, are significant in marketing activities and assume myriad forms, including absolute monetary discount or percentage-off, bonus packs, free samples, coupons, refunds, etc. The multiplicity of alternative forms adds to the challenge of understanding these processes. The chapter outlines an array of theories and paradigms and their implications, with a focus on three main research domains: (1) the asymmetry of gains and losses due to price changes, (2) processes associated with internal norms (e.g., reference price, price thresholds, comparative processes, etc.), and (3) theories and findings in the numerical cognition domain. Monroe then specifies four main variables influencing consumer's perception of and response to price change messages: (1) the perceived price difference between the new price and (internal or external) reference price serving as a stimulus, (2) the individual, (3) the numbers in the price message, and (4) the relationships between these numbers. Finally, these research domains and variables, and the interactions between them, are discussed.

Stich and Spann's "Buyer Behavior in Pay-What-You-Want Pricing" (Chapter 5) refers to a relatively new pricing phenomenon that delegates complete control over price to potential customers. The authors demonstrate that notwithstanding the intuitive belief that applying pay-what-you-want (PWYW) pricing leads customers to possess the goods without paying, consumers in most instances willingly opt to pay favorable prices. In reviewing selected research in the PWYW field, Stich and Spann cite three theoretical domains that potentially explain consumer behavior given the PWYW pricing mechanism. The first of these, the social preferences domain, is based on game theory and considers outcome-based theories (i.e., people's tendency toward unselfish behavior and consideration of the well-being of others) and intention-based models of reciprocity (i.e., a phenomenon whereby people's behavior is influenced by other people's actions), either of which could account for customers' positive payments under PWYW pricing. The second one, the strategic considerations domain, refers to reputational models of finitely repeated games with incomplete information, and maintains that given a repeated task, people will prefer to cooperate rather than choose a one-time dominant strategy. In a similar manner, repeated interactions between customers and firms could be viewed through the prism of the longitudinal relationship, a perspective that might help to explain buyers' motivation to pay more under PWYW pricing, for example, to prevent a firms' closure or relocation. The third and final domain is signaling. The signaling mechanism assumes that people benefit from prosocial behavior, with signaling occurring on both a personal and social level. Thus, people may be inclined, on the one hand, to incorporate self-perceptions into their customer experience in various market contexts and wish to pay more in terms of PWYW in order to justify an image they created for themselves (e.g., altruism, high morality, sustainability, etc.). On the other hand, consumer behavior under PWYW pricing could have more to do with social signaling, namely, ascription of importance to one's social status (e.g., esteem or popularity) and the judgments of others. Accordingly, customers might be willing to pay higher prices to highlight their wealth, charitable public image, etc.

In Chapter 6, "How Does Partitioning Prices Influence Consumer Responses?", Abraham and Hamilton present the results of a meta-analysis in a partitioned pricing framework. A partitioned price refers to a type of price presentation format in which the overall product/service price is divided into two or more parts: a base price and surcharges. The first is termed the focal component, and the other parts, the secondary components. Although initial research in the domain supplied evidence in favor of using partitioned pricing (e.g., after exposure to partitioned prices, buyers tended to refer the lower focal price component exclusively, ignoring the secondary ones), more recent studies have yielded contradictory findings, thereby rendering the issue more ambiguous for marketers. The authors, consequently, employ a meta-analysis to formulate and classify three mechanisms that might explain why partitioned pricing (versus all-inclusive pricing) elicits more or less favorable consumer responses: the encoding mechanism (namely, the ease of interpretation of surcharge information), the attentional mechanism (i.e., wherever the increase in surcharge magnitude draws more attention to it), and the appraisal mechanism (i.e., based on consumer beliefs concerning the marketer's initial intent in defining the surcharge, wherever the surcharge contributes to enlargement of the seller's profits or simply coverage of fees). The study's findings provide the strongest evidence for the appraisal mechanism, followed by encoding. Finally, the authors discuss some helpful insights for researchers and managers based on their results.

The book concludes with Sela's "Crossing the Efficiency Frontier: A Framework for Understanding Consumers' Responses to Bargains." Here, the author examines the attractiveness of marketing offers, suggesting that simple marketing offers (e.g., promotions or price discount deals) alone usually are not sufficient to impact consumers' perception of bargains. An offer's attractiveness, he argues, depends more on the potential perceived value for the customer than on the marketer's initial intent. Furthermore, customers believe that sellers' offerings in general are aimed at maximizing profits, providing the target consumer with the minimum surplus required to complete a transaction. Therefore, despite the appeal of seemingly attractive deals, consumer perceptions of personal value remain elusive. The chapter offers a basis for understanding consumer responses to marketing offers and the signals they use as indicators of personal value or the lack thereof. Consumers' choices, Sela opines, are based largely on personal beliefs and preferences, as well as idiosyncratic circumstances of which the marketer is usually unaware. Consequently, customers are attracted to more personally distinctive offerings that digress from normal or market-efficient conditions. Assuming that marketers develop proposals that provide a minimum surplus for the intended purposes, those that appear to deviate from this "efficiency frontier," due to factors unconsidered by the marketer, are more likely to be regarded as bargains. The author tests these propositions within the framework of five field studies presented in the chapter.

# Chapter 1

# Valuing New Currencies: A Framework for Future Research*

## Priya Raghubir

Prices are typically expressed in terms of legal tender (e.g., US$). Research in the last two decades has examined how payment modes, such as cash, credit cards, debit cards, and gift certificates, affect consequences such as the likelihood of purchase, the amount spent, and the variety of items purchased. The purpose of this chapter is to suggest that these conclusions may be contingent on the price of the item/service being expressed in legal tender. When prices are expressed in alternative currencies (e.g., airline miles), then there could be a variety of follow-up consequences that would lead to limiting boundary conditions on previous findings in the domains of behavioral pricing research. The new currency that I focus on is airline miles. This new currency is becoming ubiquitous with the growth of airline loyalty programs. It is unclear how consumers who are endowed with them value them and how they relate them to legal tender. It is equally unclear how managers of loyalty programs should price products/services in these currencies and what array of products they should make available, so as to

---

*In *New Directions in Behavioral Pricing*, Chezy Ofir Ed., 2024, World Scientific Publishing Company.

Priya Raghubir, Stern School of Business, New York University, New York, NY 10012, USA (raghubir@stern.nyu.edu).

1

encourage/discourage consumers to use their unspent balances or let them lapse. This chapter starts off with examples from popular airline loyalty programs that demonstrate their heterogeneity across time, across offerings, and across programs. From this discussion, I summarize some of the dimensions of money and ways in which the new currency of airline miles differs from the traditional legal tender (e.g., US$). I then build on a series of testable propositions regarding how miles are valued, with implications for how they will be spent depending on different types of communication appeals. I end with implications for managers as to how to design loyalty programs with a specific focus on how to price products using miles. Theoretical implications for behavioral pricing are discussed as are managerial implications for loyalty programs.

The purpose of this chapter is to introduce how our understanding of pricing as developed in the domain of legal tender may need to be modified when applied to new modes of payment and currencies. One example of a new currency that is ubiquitous is airline miles. Broadly applied, loyalty currency, such as "miles," exists in all loyalty programs: credit cards, hotels, retail, travel sites, and others. While developing ideas in the domain of miles as an exemplar, within the larger domain of virtual currencies (cf. Scheidegger and Raghubir 2022), the hope and expectation are that the ideas in this chapter as applied to miles will be transferable to other domains where a loyalty program is in existence or is being planned. From a theoretical perspective, the purpose of this chapter is to encourage original empirical research into the domain of loyalty programs (including airline miles and credit card points) to better understand how customers value them, what will make them likely to save or spend them, and how doing so will translate into customer satisfaction, loyalty, and long term customer lifetime value.

I start off with illustrative examples of mileage programs and two hypothetical customers who belong to these loyalty programs that lead to a number of unanswered questions as to why the two loyalty programs that I focus on are structured in the manner that they are. This leads to questions surrounding how customers value their miles. That is, how do miles function as an alternate currency? Are they treated the same as payments in cash or credit cards or gift cards, or do consumers feel, think about, and act differently when they pay with loyalty currencies, such as airline miles? Examining this question is the primary purpose of this chapter.

To summarize, how newer currencies, such as loyalty points, are priced and how consumers respond to those pricing decisions are both understudied in the domain of behavioral pricing. This chapter proposes testable propositions to guide future research and assist in the design and implementation of loyalty programs, in general, and airline loyalty programs, in particular.

## The Case of Renny and Suzanne: United and Delta

Renny has 363,000 miles in her United MileagePlus frequent flyer account,[1] and Suzanne has 142,000 in her Delta SkyMiles account. They use them to buy flights and upgrade, and, occasionally, for a special hotel room, but rarely for anything else. If you ask them, they will tell you that it is difficult to get an upgrade with their miles, and most of the time they need to travel, the cost of the price of a ticket using miles is prohibitive, so they don't end up using their miles. In fact, Hlavinka and Sullivan (2011) report how mileage memberships and mileage balances have been growing exponentially over the last many years, with US consumers earning approximately \$50 billion in loyalty currencies per year. The stockpiling of loyalty points is an issue more recently examined by Stourm *et al.* (2015).

For example, in 2019, Renny paid almost \$1,000 to rent a car for a week on the Big Island in Hawaii, rather than using her frequent flyer miles to rent the car. Suzanne could buy magazines with her miles using their Mags for Miles program (see Figure 1), and she reads magazines but ends up buying them at the local store.

Suzanne could buy gift cards for her nieces and nephews, especially for their Christmas Gift Exchange, using her miles (see Figure 2). A \$25 gift card would have cost her 6,350 miles in 2019, an exchange rate of 1 mile = .3937¢ (2,500¢/6,350 miles), whereas she would have got a volume discount if she purchased a \$100 gift card as it would cost her only 24,350 miles, an exchange rate of 1 mile = .4107¢.[2] If she plumped for a \$500 gift card, she would have paid 120,350 miles or 1 mile = .4155¢. At this exchange rate (\$500 Amazon gift card), her balance of 142,000

---

[1]All examples are based on true stories. Names have been disguised to preserve anonymity.

[2]All exchange rates were taken from the different programs at the time of writing this chapter: February 3, 2019. Exchange rates may have changed over the last three and a half years.

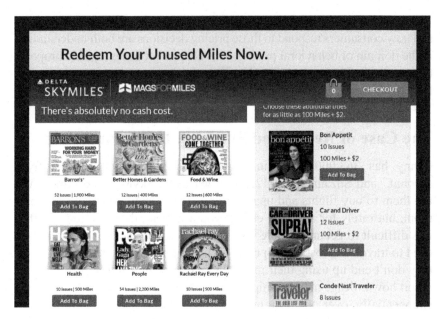

**Figure 1.**   Delta's MagsforMiles screenshot (retrieved February 3, 2019).

is approximately equal to $590. Said differently, if Suzanne purchased a single $500 gift card, she would have 21,650 miles left in her account (142,000 miles–120,350 miles), but if she bought twenty $25 Amazon gift cards worth a total of $500, she would only have 15,000 miles (142,000 miles–127,000 miles [20 × 6,350]). This is a difference of 6,650 miles and could have purchased a backpack, wine glasses, a coffee maker, a toaster, or a bathrobe with miles to spare (see Figure 4)!

   Why are Amazon and Delta pricing the different denominations of Amazon gift cards differently? Could this be due to processing costs, i.e., shipping and handling costs of the physical gift cards? Or could they be an incentive to get customers to spend more or let their miles lapse? If they are designed to get customers to spend down their balances, how many of their customers would do the math and, even if they did, would find the difference worth it? Said differently, is the volume discount for buying a $500 gift card versus 20 × $ 25 gift cards a noticeable and substantial difference in the customer's eyes?

   Supposing Suzanne did not want to make a purchase at Amazon but at Best Buy instead, how could she monetize her Delta SkyMiles? The price of Best Buy gift cards is cheaper than those of Amazon gift cards:

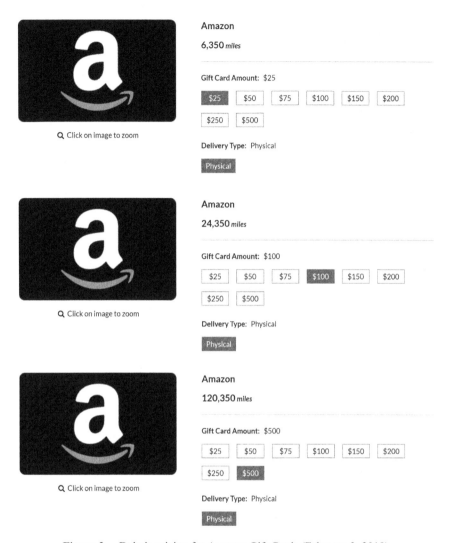

**Figure 2.**   Delta's pricing for Amazon Gift Cards (February 3, 2019).

6,250 miles for a $25 gift card (instead of 6,350 miles), and there is a further discount of 150 miles if the delivery of the gift card is digital, to make the price 6,100 miles or an exchange rate of 1 mile = .4098¢ (see Figure 3). The exchange rate is even more favorable for a digital gift card of $500 at 118,200 miles or .4230¢, making her 142,000 miles balance equivalent to approximately $600. Why is Delta pricing Amazon and

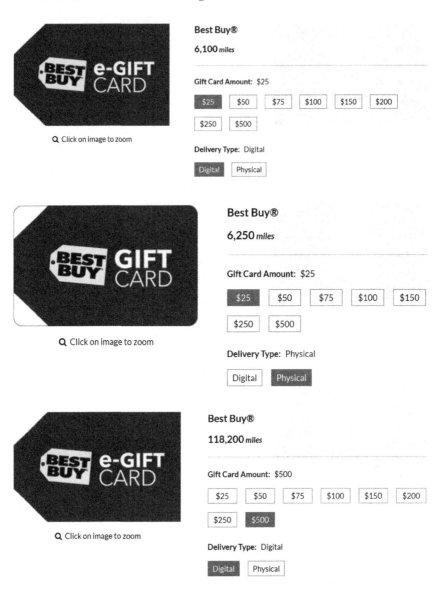

**Figure 3.**   Delta's pricing for Best Buy Gift Cards (February 3, 2019).

Best Buy gift cards differently? Could this be due to the differential fungibility of the gift cards of these two retailers with Amazon offering a wider array of products than Best Buy?

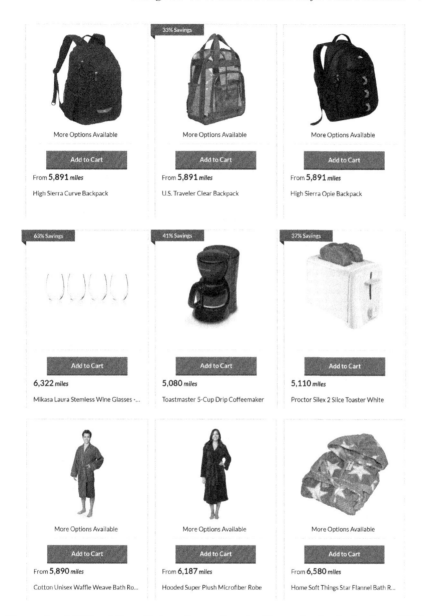

**Figure 4.** Additional items that can be purchased with saved miles by buying a $500 Amazon gift card versus twenty $25 Amazon gift cards on Delta (February 3, 2019).

Now, let's move to Renny and the United MileagePlus frequent flyer program to examine their pricing of gift cards. United does not offer Amazon or Best Buy gift cards. However, both United and Delta offer Starbucks gift cards. A $10 gift card is priced on United for 1,562 miles (1 mile = .64¢), whereas on Delta SkyMiles, the same $10 gift card costs 2,550 miles (1 mile = .39¢), a difference of 988 miles or 63% more (see Figure 5). Why this price disparity? Clearly, United miles are worth more than Delta's for a Starbucks cup of coffee, but why? Are they more difficult or expensive to earn? Do Delta customers value Starbucks coffee more than United's customers? Or, are these idiosyncratic differences that have not been carefully thought through because managers are unaware of how consumers think of miles as currencies?

The programs also differ in terms of the range of denominations available. On United, the three denominations available for Starbucks gift cards are $10, $25, and $50, whereas on Delta, the gift card values can go up to $500. Why this difference in range?

The same higher pricing for Delta miles is evidenced with a $100 Bath and Body Works gift card. On United, the cost of the gift card is 10× the cost of the $10 Starbucks card (15,625 miles), whereas on Delta, it is 8.9× the cost of a $10 Starbucks gift card (22,700 miles). Why this differential pricing across denominations in one program and not the other?

Both programs differ in terms of whether the value of each mile depends on what gift card you will purchase. For example, in United's MileagePlus program, the gift cards are now priced at a standard $100 = 15,625 miles (or 1 mile = .64¢) for all 270 gift cards that they offer. This was not the case in 2016, three years ago, as they priced different gift cards at different mile prices (see Figure 6, Panel A). At Delta, on the other hand, a $100 TGIF gift card costs 22,500 miles, a $100 Nordstrom gift card costs 23,600 miles, and an Amex $100 gift card costs 25,350 miles, with a Red Door Spa $100 gift card only 21, 850 miles and a big bargain for a Delta $100 gift certificate at 11,100 miles (or 1 mile = .90¢; see Figure 6, Panel B).

These examples give rise to a host of research questions surrounding how managers design their mileage programs. To answer these questions, it is important to understand how consumers feel, think, and behave with miles. We turn to the little literature that has addressed this topic in the following section.

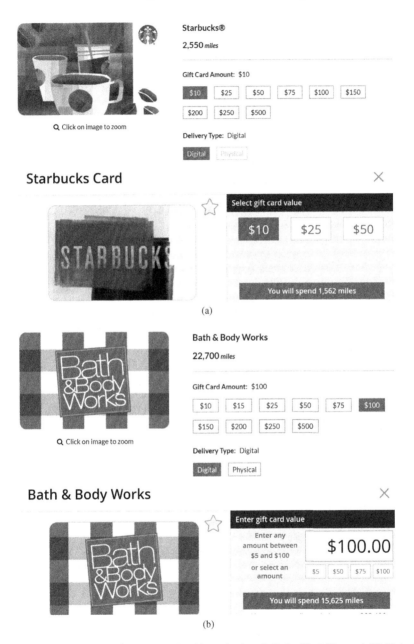

**Figure 5.** (a) Price of a $10 Starbucks gift card using (i) Delta SkyMiles and (ii) United MileagePlus Miles (February 3, 2019) and (b) Price of a $100 Bath and Body Works gift card using (i) Delta SkyMiles and (ii) United MileagePlus Miles (February 3, 2019).

**Panel A: United 2016**

**Panel B: Delta 2019**

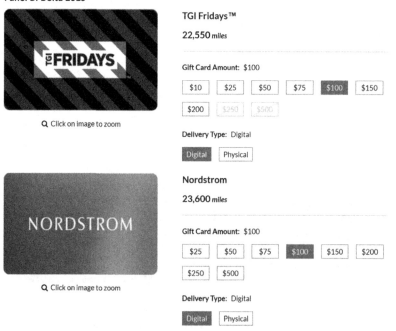

**Figure 6.**   Differential prices for a $100 gift card: Panel A — United in 2016, and Panel B — Delta 2019.

*Source*: https://www.thepointcalculator.com/Airline/United/united-miles-value#cashvalue.

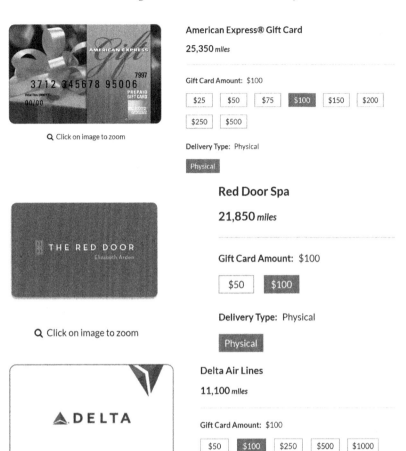

American Express® Gift Card

**25,350** *miles*

Gift Card Amount: $100

| $25 | $50 | $75 | $100 | $150 | $200 |

| $250 | $500 |

Delivery Type: Physical

Physical

## Red Door Spa

**21,850** *miles*

Gift Card Amount: $100

| $50 | $100 |

Delivery Type: Physical

Physical

Delta Air Lines

**11,100** *miles*

Gift Card Amount: $100

| $50 | $100 | $250 | $500 | $1000 |

Delivery Type: Digital

Digital

Q Click on image to zoom

**Figure 6.** *(Continued)*

| United Miles Redemption Chart | |
|---|---|
| 60000 | 🔽 Miles |
| United Flights<br>1.4 cents on average | $840 |
| Hotels<br>0.68 cents on average | $408 |
| Hertz [Standard and Lower]<br>0.1 cent on average | $600 |
| Hertz [Interm SUV and Higher]<br>0.07 cents on average | $420 |
| Thrifty<br>0.078 cents on average | $468 |
| Cruises<br>0.78 cent on average | $468 |
| All Gift Cards<br>0.64 cents | $385 |

**Figure 6.**   (*Continued*)

# How Do Consumers Feel About, Think About, and Act with Their Miles?

The question of how consumers feel about, think about, and act with their miles can be looked at from two distinct angles: one from the point of view of treating miles as a virtual currency and the other from the point of view of a marketing mechanism to maintain loyalty. Of course, the two are connected.

## *Loyalty program research*

Most research on loyalty programs has focused on the latter question (e.g., the effectiveness of loyalty programs at creating loyalty, Kim *et al.* 2001; Sharp and Sharp 1997; Tammo *et al.* 2011; Verhoef 2003; Yi and Jeon 2003). For example, a review of loyalty programs identified that status, habit, and relationship with the service provider were the three key underpinnings of the effectiveness of loyalty programs in generating repeat purchase behavior (Henderson *et al.* 2011).

The popular press reports that loyalty programs are hugely profitable for airlines. For example, an examination of the frustration consumers feel when they attempt to use their miles reported, *When United Airlines filed for bankruptcy in 2002, it was forced to disclose that its mileage program at the time posted profit margins as high as 45%. Since the airline emerged from bankruptcy, United has stopped reporting such financial details.*[3] Liu and Yang (2009) underlined this conclusion when they proposed and tested a model that demonstrated that large firms benefit more from their loyalty programs than small firms. Voorhees *et al.* (2015) found that loyalty programs did not have a direct effect on the share of wallet of their loyal customer base. They say *The industry should consider their customers' permanent characteristics (i.e., their level of loyalty or willingness to switch brands) and revise these programs to ensure that they continue to deliver value to a firm's best customers rather than just attracting brand switching customers.*

Thus, while some academic research has investigated the effect of loyalty programs on company's profitability (e.g., Bijmolt *et al.* 2011; Stourm *et al.* 2015), few have examined the effect of how the pricing of loyalty programs affects customers' well-being as well as their trust in the company. The only key result from a pricing point-of-view is that combined pricing (miles and cash) reduces consumers' perceived price (Drèze and Nunes 2004), even though the airline pricing policy can erode customers' trust (Nunes and Drèze 2006).

Attesting to this loss of trust, Wallet Hub, that tracks consumers' price-spending decisions, reported that "six of 10 US airlines' reward programs lost value for members in 2017 compared with the year before" and this was due to unexpected and unannounced devaluation of miles. We turn to this question next.

## Miles as a virtual currency

While prior research has examined the effectiveness of loyalty programs in generating loyal customers for the firm, little empirical research has examined how customers value their miles (but see Scheidegger and Raghubir (2022) for a theoretical examination of virtual currencies). That is, no one has yet examined the former question: How do miles function as an alternate currency? To suggest that miles are a currency that consumers feel, think about, and act with differently as compared to alternate forms of payment (such as cash and credit cards) is the primary purpose of this chapter.

---

[3] https://www.latimes.com/business/la-fi-frequent-flier-programs-20170914-story.html.

Previous research has shown that payment modes, such as cash, credit cards, debit cards, and gift certificates, are more likely to be spent and lead to greater spending than payments in cash (Feinberg 1986; Gourville and Soman 1998; Hirschman 1979; Prelec and Simester 2001; Raghubir and Srivastava 2008; Shah *et al.* 2016; Soman 2001). This phenomenon has been termed the "monopoly money" phenomenon (cf. Raghubir and Srivastava 2008) and refers to all forms of payment that do not involve legal tender.

Based on this research, we would expect that airline miles, that are not expressed in the form of legal tender (e.g., US$) but in terms of loyalty points (e.g., miles), should be more likely to be spent than cash and be associated with greater spending. However, it is unclear whether this is, in fact, the case. Twenty-five years after the introduction of the Mileage Plus and SkyMiles programs, in 2005, it was estimated that 14 trillion frequent-flyer points had been accumulated by customers, corresponding to a total value of 700 billion US dollars.[4] Why is it that consumers are willing to pay using a credit card with a lower pain of payment but less willing to liquidate their mileage balances and monetize them? The question is, do consumers even think of their mileage balances as cash balances that they could use for a variety of purchases? The anecdotes at the start of this chapter suggest otherwise.

To summarize, the pricing of miles and how that affects customer use of mileage balances is an understudied domain. This chapter suggests some testable propositions that can help guide future research in this domain.

## *The role of uncertainty in value*

When consumers value a product, service, or even a currency or form of payment, they do so in terms of the utility it provides them. The greater the uncertainty associated with value (in the case of products and services, this could be in terms of confidence in the claims or in the expected variation in quality levels), the lower the mean value associated with the product or the service. What about in the domain of forms of payment or different currencies? Past research has shown that people assess the value

---

[4]"Frequent-flyer miles". *The Economist.* 2005-01-06 as quoted in https://en.wikipedia.org/wiki/Frequent-flyer_program.

of money, for example, a salary raise, based on its nominal rather than real value (Shafir *et al.* 1997), an idea that has been applied to how people assess the value of foreign currencies (Raghubir and Srivastava 2002). This leads to predictable biases: prices that are equivalent are perceived as cheaper when they are presented in a currency where the nominal value of the price is lower (because the foreign exchange rate is a fraction of the "home" currency). This is despite the fact that foreign exchange rates are known and are present in the context where judgments are made.

Now imagine a scenario where the exchange rate was not only unknown but also changing over time and over products. This introduced a further level of uncertainty into the computation of value. If the value of airline miles is contingent on (a) the program they are associated with (e.g., United or Delta), (b) the product they are used to buy and the retailer where it is available (e.g., TGIF meal or Red Door Spa treatment), and (c) the denomination of a gift card ($25 versus $100), as the examples in the previous section demonstrate, then there will be uncertainty associated with the value of a mileage balance. Further, if these exchange rates themselves change over time, then all of these factors will increase the uncertainty associated with how a consumer assesses the value of their mileage balance (or other loyalty currency that is not expressed in legal tender terms).

We propose that the reason that consumers do not use their miles is due to the uncertainty in their value. Note, given the frequent devaluation of miles, it would be rational for consumers to use miles sooner rather than later (as they would be worth less after devaluation), but we propose that consumers are unaware of this and only react to the sticker shock of how many miles it costs to make a purchase, comparing this with what is advertised by the airlines. For example, United will advertise that you can purchase a round-trip domestic airline ticket for 25,000 miles. If a customer sees a mileage price that is higher than this, they are less likely to use their miles, instead they will hoard them and frequently waste them. This would lead to a disappointing redemption experience and undercut customer loyalty as well as brand image and attitudes.

In fact, it is estimated that in 2012, 24% of the mileage balance held by United expired, a phenomenon referred to as "breakage" which costs the airline nothing.[5] This is an estimate that enters an airline's

---

[5]https://medium.com/@dfcatch/loyalty-myths-is-breakage-good-873950da26dc.

calculation for their liability carried for miles for flying. This is a large number. For American Airlines alone, in 2015, it was estimated at $657 million. Given that customers with a positive redemption experience have a higher customer lifetime value, it is in the long-term interests of airlines to respect customers' airline mile balances. The example provided at the start of this chapter suggests this is not always the case.

We now turn to theoretical and managerial questions surrounding the understanding of miles.

# Theoretical and Managerial Research Questions surrounding the Understanding of Miles

There are a number of open questions that we need to answer to help a manager better design the pricing of their offerings for their loyalty-program customer who purchases products and services in the currency of miles. These begin with the most basic understanding of currency and move to the more logistical concerns that face every manager in terms of the decisions that they must make. Some of these questions are as follows and range from a simple question of how consumers evaluate miles to why loyalty programs differ across providers:

1. **How do customers evaluate the currency of miles**? For a customer, is a mileage balance perceived to be a currency at all, or is it perceived to be a free gift for making a purchase? Is it perceived to be a store of value — a basic underlying characteristic of money? Do customers think of miles as a partially fungible instrument that can be monetized and exchanged for another product, i.e., a medium of exchange which is the underlying definition of money? Said differently, to what extent are miles like money? Given that they are virtual (never touched or felt), less fungible and less widely accepted (available for only a limited number of items, albeit that set of items is increasing every day), expressed in different units (miles versus legal tender), not guaranteed by a Central Government (just an airline, that may be private or public), cannot be easily exchanged on a marketplace with another buyer/seller (although there are websites where one can monetize miles, such as cashformiles.com and themilesbroker.com), and less familiar to most than legal tender due to the relatively lower frequency with

which they are acquired and used, it is likely that miles are perceived to be much less like "money" than legal tender.

There is at least one well-researched dimension in the domain of the subjective value of money and prices: that of monopoly money (Raghubir and Srivastava 2008). Monopoly money captures the idea that a form of money does not feel like "real money" and so is more easily spent. It has been applied to understand why people spend more using gift certificates and credit cards as compared to cash. We now propose that on the continuum of monopoly money, we have the following:

I.   *Miles are more like "Monopoly Money" than legal tender.*
     From this, it follows that consumers are likely to display greater price elasticity for an item whose prices are expressed in miles than for a product whose prices are expressed in legal currency.

2.  **What are the dimensions that make miles similar to or different from other forms of money**? Some of the dimensions on which miles differ from legal tender include the following: (a) fungibility, (b) how widely the form is accepted, (c) how easy it is to exchange, (d) how easy it is to monetize into another form of legal tender, (e) familiarity, (f) virtual versus physical form, (g) number of years in existence, (h) the extent to which it is a reward for work or a reward for spending, (i) the extent to which is it guaranteed by a legal institution, (j) the extent to which the price in legal tender is salient at the time of payment, (k) the extent to which products and services are expressed in prices using miles versus legal tender, and (l) the certainty and uncertainty in the value of the balance (due to changes in pricing systems and devaluations).

    On all these dimensions, miles are less like money than legal tender. Given this, one would predict that the pain of payment (cf. Prelec and Loewenstein 1998) associated with paying with miles would be lower than the pain of payment associated with paying with legal tender.

II.  *Miles are associated with lower "pain of payment" than legal tender.*

3.  **Where in a perceptual map of monetary payment forms do miles lie**? As new forms of payment and pricing methods evolve, there is a bewildering array of ways in which products can be priced and

manners in which customers can pay for them. Prices can be in local and foreign currencies, as well as cryptocurrencies, like bitcoin, and methods of payment now include cash (notes and coins), credit cards, debit cards, mobile phone pay apps (e.g., Apple Pay in the US and PayTM in India), gift cards and gift certificates, credit card points (e.g., Citi ThankYou points), and retail loyalty points (e.g., Macy's cash), with new forms coming up on a regular basis. Airline miles are a method of payment, and products and services are also priced in terms of miles, making them comparable to other forms of pricing, such as local, foreign, and cryptocurrencies. What are the dimensions that make prices expressed in these forms different?

One is certainly the familiarity of use. People are more familiar with local currencies than they are with foreign or cryptocurrencies, or airline miles. Local currencies also have many of the other dimensions that differentiate "real" money from "monopoly" forms of payment, such as fungibility, how widely they are accepted, how easily they can be exchanged, how easy they are to monetize into another form of legal tender, with local and foreign currencies being less virtual, around for more years, and guaranteed by government institutions more so than cryptocurrencies and miles. For all of them, however, prices are likely to be salient at the time of payment, albeit in different currencies. Therefore, it is possible that if one of the dimensions that differentiate these currencies is the extent to which they are "real" or "monopoly," another dimension could be the salience of the price in legal tender or the virtual/physical aspect of the money, how trusted they are due to their backing by governments, and/or their mere familiarity. As such, we have the following:

III.   *Miles will be in a different quadrant as compared to legal tender in a perceptual mapping of pricing forms and monetary forms.*

4.   **Mileage Wealth Assessment**: How do customers assess the value of mileage balances? Do they? How accurate are customers in assessing the value of their mileage wealth? Given the virtual nature of mileage wealth and transactions, it is unlikely that consumers will have a well-accepted, easily accessible exchange rate for miles to legal tender. Given that prior research has shown that even with foreign currencies, where the exchange rates are provided, consumers make systematic

errors in price judgments (the "face value effect," cf. Raghubir and Srivastava 2002), it is plausible that these errors would be compounded in the domain of miles to money — leading to customers not accounting for their mileage balances as a source of wealth.

Note that airlines can translate the value of miles into their monetary equivalent which should lead to consumers appreciating the "cash back" reward of their business, which, in turn, should lead to greater loyalty. That is, instead of being told how many miles a particular trip accrued, an airline could inform customers of the cash value of the miles accrued and this would serve as the perfect "silver lining" for customers making a big ticket airline fare purchase (Thaler 1985). However, as the current accrual is typically in a currency distinct from the currency spent (miles versus USD, for example), it is unlikely that they are thought of as part of a single transaction. Therefore, in the absence of such policies at the current moment, we predict the following:

IV. *Mileage balances will not be incorporated into consumers' wealth assessment.*

5. **Mental Accounts and Purchase Patterns**: Do consumers treat mileage balances as part of a separate mental account as compared to other forms of wealth that they possess (cf. Thaler 1985, 1990, 1999)? If so, why? The innate difference in legal tender and mileage accounts (due to fungibility, etc.) is one reason to expect that miles belong to a different "mental account" as compared to legal tender. Items that are in different mental accounts (e.g., mortgage versus vacation account) are treated and spent differently (Thaler 1999). In fact, prior research has demonstrated that payment modes, such as cash and credit cards, affect the variety of items purchased, with credit cards associated with more hedonic purchases than cash (Thomas *et al.* 2011) and similar effects found for gift cards (Reinholtz *et al.* 2015). We predict the following:

V. *Miles will be more likely to be used for hedonic and experiential purchases than cash of the same value.*

6. **Source of the Miles**: Do consumers treat miles accrued through work differently from miles accrued through personal travel? It is possible

that they do, as the miles accrued from work travel could be considered as a "perk" for work. This would imply that they go into a different "mileage mental account." On the other hand, given the difficulty of tracking what percentage of one's balance is due to personal (versus work) travel, it is more likely that they do not. Note, that if the differential component was easy to track, then it is plausible that miles earned through work would be valued as lower than those earned through personal travel as the consumer had not spent any of their own money to earn those miles. This should not be difficult for airlines/hotels/travel sites (such as Expedia) to implement and could lead to a drawdown of mileage balances, thereby indirectly increasing customer loyalty. We propose the following:

> **VI.** *Miles accrued through business or personal travel will not be placed into different account.*

7. **Mileage Goals**: The way in which customers have goals in terms of reaching a particular (mileage) goal during a specified time period, do they also have goals for their total mileage wealth? The structure of mileage programs suggests that they might. For example, Mileage Plus has tiers for Silver (25,000 miles), Gold (50, 000 miles), Platinum (75,000 miles), and 1K (100,000 miles) per year to which they added minimum spend requirements but removed it during their attest revamp of their program which has a new currency called "PQPs" (it is unclear what criteria they use for their "Global Services" category). Over a customer's lifetime, they have the Million Miler program (and then Two Million and Three Million), and with every tier, a customer gets additional benefits (e.g., early intimation of potential upgrades, checked bags, and priority boarding). Based on the work by Kivetz and Simonson (2000, 2002, 2003; see also Kivetz *et al.* 2006), it is plausible that mileage goals work in a manner similar to any other goal with consumers speeding up accrual as they approach a goal.

> **VII.** *The progress to mileage goals will follow the U-shaped curve of a goal gradient with faster progress as the goal is imminent.*
>
> In fact, Hsee *et al.* (2013) suggest that accumulating wealth may become an end in and of itself, leading to inoptimal spending behaviors. If people want to "overearn" miles the

way they do money, then this would be an impediment to their using their miles.

8. **Motivations for Spending and Saving Miles**: What are consumers' motivations for spending their miles and what are their motivations for saving them? Are there particular types of customers who are more likely to spend their miles as compared to saving them? Are these types related to socio-demographic, psychographic, geographic, or other differences? These are empirical questions that are worthy of research to gain a more nuanced understanding of why and when consumers want to spend their miles, and what is their resistance to spending them. Is the construct of likelihood of saving and spending related to the constructs of tightwad and spendthrift as shown in the domain of money (Rick *et al.* 2008)? Given the proposition that miles are not thought of as money, we propose that the two constructs are orthogonal:

**VIII.** *Spendthrifts and Tightwads in the monetary domain will be equally likely to spend or save their miles.*

9. **Awareness**: To what extent are consumers aware of the range of products and services that they can purchase with their miles? It is unclear that consumers have a clear idea of the exchange rates that govern the miles-price exchange for different products and services. It is also unclear that airlines are working to increase that awareness in more than a token manner. If loyalty program managers wished to have their customers take advantage of their loyalty program benefits, the awareness of the range of options that miles could buy should be increased and the value of the miles should be made explicit. For example, providing prices for items in duty-free catalogs in both currencies, or allowing customers to purchase snacks, meals, drinks, and other in-flight services (like Wi-Fi), or baggage charges in miles are likely to increase their usage. Some European airlines (e.g., Lufthansa and Austrian Air) do price their duty-free catalogs in miles and allow in-flight purchases using miles. US airlines are lagging behind in that. However, United has started a push toward pricing a larger range of items in miles. For example, in Newark Airport, a set of new service establishments allow a traveler to purchase food and drinks using their miles. As such, we predict the following:

IX.   *Consumers' awareness of what they can purchase with their miles, and the value of their miles, is low. Offering prices in miles for a wider range of products and services will increase purchase likelihoods of these products and services.*

10. **Choice of Payment Mode**: How do customers decide whether to pay in legal tender or miles when they have the option to do either? This is a big question that would involve not only the actual price (in miles or money) that would affect perceptions of affordability but also the exchange rate which would affect perceptions of fairness and context effects which would determine which form of payment was most salient. Further, if customers were interested in accumulating mileage balances to reach a particular goal or achieve a certain spend amount to achieve a loyalty tier, they would be less likely to use their miles to make a purchase and more likely to use money. Prior research has demonstrated that combined prices (miles and money) are perceived to be cheaper — as the face value of both elements is lower than the face value of any one element (Drèze and Nunes 2004). Accordingly, we predict the following:

X.   *Allowing customers to customize their payment mode with any fraction of miles and money will increase their likelihood of redemption of their miles.*
      While some loyalty programs (e.g., Swiss Air's Miles and More Program) do allow this using a sliding scale that goes from 100% money to 100% miles, many others (e.g., United) do not.

11. **Choice of Products**: Are there particular types of products or services that customers are more likely to purchase with miles than with legal tender? Are mileage balances more likely to be used for self or gift purchases? For hedonic or utilitarian purchases? For experiential or non-experiential purchases? For special or routine purchases? If so, why? Given prior research has demonstrated that payment modes, such as cash and credit cards, affect the variety of items purchased, with credit cards associated with more hedonic purchases than cash (Thomas *et al.* 2011), we predict the following:

**XI.** ***Miles will be more likely to be used for hedonic and experiential purchases than cash of the same value.***

12. **Diversity across Programs**: Why do some loyalty program managers use fixed mileage pricing rates across all program offerings and others use variable prices? Why do some devalue customer mileage balances? Why do some offer a wider range of options to use miles? The answer to these questions may lie in the goal of the loyalty program. If the goal is to increase customer satisfaction, then having customers continue to build and use their miles would appear to be the way to go. If, on the other hand, the goal is to have a short-term gain by having customers' miles expire, then the goal would be to prevent customers from using their miles. We propose the following:

**XII.** ***The greater the transparency, stability, and fungibility of miles, the greater the customer satisfaction with the loyalty program.***

## Theoretical Implications for Behavioral Pricing

Consumers have already been shown to display money illusion in the domain of local and foreign currencies: the face value effect (Raghubir and Srivastava 2002) and the europoly money effect (Raghubir *et al.* 2012). Cognitive complications with multiplication and division are likely to be compounded in the domain of miles where one currency is a 100th of a fraction of the other in terms of exchange rates. Thus, examining the currency of miles can make a contribution to the domain of numerical cognition and behavioral pricing.

The mere numerosity of miles as a function of legal tender may add to the effect of "sticker shock" given the large number of miles required to make a purchase, though the same numerosity is also likely to make people feel wealthier (Pelham *et al.* 1994; Wertenbroch *et al.* 2007).

People are less likely to track the amounts they have in their mileage accounts and be aware of their worth, as also the monetized value of their mileage wealth. Therefore, they do not have readily available reference points for what something should cost, making it difficult for them to assess the value of a deal. If mileage programs were to be designed where the amount paid in miles was not a multiple of a reference number (e.g., "25,000 miles") but in increments tied to the monetary price of the product (e.g., $325 airfare = 24,500 miles and $650 airfare = 49,000 miles), then customers would be more likely to use their mileage balances as the transparency of the prices would be apparent. Overall likelihood of purchase should also increase as the pain of payment with miles should be lower than the pain of payment associated with other legal tender monetary forms. Finally, as these payments would be of different amounts, they would resemble charges adding up to a credit card (even though they are a drawdown of a balance more akin to a gift card), and, accordingly, each instance should be difficult to recall, leading to continued future drawdowns of mileage balances (Srivastava and Raghubir 2002).

The fact that miles are different from money suggests the possibility that customers may be less price sensitive with miles than they are with money as they value miles less than money. Examining the price elasticity of different products and services as a function of mode of payment is offered as an interesting future area of research.

# Managerial Implications for Loyalty Program Managers

From the above discussion, there are a few prescriptive recommendations for loyalty program managers:

1. Recognize that award balances are hard-earned wealth of your customers that you are managing, much like a bank is entrusted with managing the bank balances of its customers.
2. Consistent pricing across merchandise and time. It is the uncertainty associated with what a mileage balance is worth that may be a deterrent to its use.
3. Do not devalue mileage wealth without informing the customers. Be transparent.
4. If you are doing a devaluation, explain why to your loyalty program members along with a clear rationale.
5. Learn from what credit card companies are doing with their points: Translate the value of a customer's mile wealth to them in terms of US$, if you wish the customer to draw it down.

6. Appeals that are likely to work are "merchandise and services are a reward for time spent in the sky."
7. Customize appeals by membership tier. For example, customers who have flown 25,000 miles in the last year as compared to those who have flown 100,000 and those who are sporadic members should get different appeals as they are likely to have not only differential mileage wealth but also differential mileage (and business) potential.
8. Translate the mileage earned into the time and effort the customer has invested in traveling (using averages and estimates) and ask them what they could be worth to them in terms of hedonic and/or experiential gifts for themselves or gift cards for others.
9. Recognize the reality that award flights are rarely available, and customers are increasingly becoming aware of this reality, so advertising award flights as a reason to fly with you or buy more miles is not going to be particularly effective. Instead, consider advertising how they can reach their next desired merchandise/service/experience reward. For example, "You are 2 trans-continental flights away from a free 7-day Mediterranean Cruise."
10. Recognize that as the "perks" associated with higher status become increasingly difficult to attain as the number of customers with "high status" has grown exponentially, the mere status and the benefits it accords (priority boarding and free meal) may not be an adequate method to maintain customer loyalty, especially once a customer has reached a particular goal status level (e.g., United 1K).
11. "Gifts" they can get by using their mileage plus accounts become an effective way to maintain their loyalty willingly, rather than holding them "hostage." As such, a push at typical seasonal gifting times (Valentine's Day, Mother's Day, Father's Day, Graduation, and December), using theme-appropriate products may be effective at getting customers to draw down their balances.
12. Advertise that miles can be monetized. Advertise the range of gift cards available by converting miles into gift cards and redeeming their cash value.
13. Take a leaf out of Amazon's book and create "wish lists" for merchandise, service, and experience awards and then periodically tell customers how much closer they are to their goal.
14. Set up redemption sites so that customers may choose (if they wish) to only look at items for which they have adequate mileage balances.

15. At redemption sites, include prices in both miles as well as legal tender and allow customers to customize what fraction of the price they will pay with miles.
16. When there is inadequate mileage balance for an item, state the difference in the amount that the customer would need to pay in terms of legal tender. This would frame the purchase as almost "free" with a small token payment (as is done when gift cards are redeemed, and, on occasion, miles are redeemed for hotel stays).

## Conclusion

The purpose of this chapter was to introduce the idea of a new currency that is ubiquitous: miles. Broadly applied, "miles" exist in all loyalty programs — credit cards, hotels, retail, travel sites, and others, so the ideas in this chapter as applied to miles should be transferable to other domains where a loyalty program is in existence or is being planned.

From a theoretical perspective, the purpose of this chapter was to encourage original empirical research into the domain of loyalty programs and miles to better understand how customers value them and what will make them likely to save or spend them.

## References

Bijmolt, T. H. A., M. Dorotic, and P. C. Verhoef (2011), Loyalty programs: Generalizations on their adoption, effectiveness and design, *Foundations and Trends® in Marketing*, 5(4), 197–258. http://dx.doi.org/10.1561/1700000026.

Drèze, X. and J. C. Nunes (2004), Using combined-currency prices to lower consumers' perceived cost, *Journal of Marketing Research*, 41(1), 59–72.

Feinberg, R. A. (1986), Credit cards as spending facilitating stimuli: A conditioning interpretation, *Journal of Consumer Research*, 13(3), 348–356.

Gourville, J. and D. Soman (1998), Payment depreciation: The behavioral effects of temporally separating payments from consumption. *Journal of Consumer Research*, 25(2), 160–174.

Henderson, C. M., J. T. Beck, and R. W. Palmatier (2011), Review of the theoretical underpinnings of loyalty programs, *Journal of Consumer Psychology*, 21(3), 256–276.

Hirschman, E. C. (1979), Differences in consumer purchase behavior by credit card payment system, *Journal of Consumer Research*, 6(1), 58–66.

Hlavinka, K. and J. Sullivan (2011), The billion member march: The 2011 COLLOQUY loyalty census: Growth and trends in loyalty program membership and activity. [Technical Report], http://www.colloquy.com.

Hsee, C. K., J. Zhang, C. F. Cai, and S. Zhang (2013), Overearning, *Psychological Science*, 24(6), 852–859.

Kim, B. D., M. Shi, and K. Srinivasan (2001). Reward programs and tacit collusion. *Marketing Science*, 20, 99–120.

Kivetz, R. and I. Simonson (2000), The effects of incomplete information on consumer choice, *Journal of Marketing Research*, 37(4), 427–448.

Kivetz, R. and I. Simonson (2002), Earning the right to indulge: Effort as a determinant of customer preferences toward frequency program rewards, *Journal of Marketing Research*, 39(2) (May), 155–170.

Kivetz, R. and I. Simonson (2003), The idiosyncratic fit heuristic: Effort advantage as a determinant of consumer response to loyalty programs, *Journal of Marketing Research*, 40(4), 454–467.

Kivetz, R., O. Urminsky, and Y. Zheng (2006), The goal-gradient hypothesis resurrected: Purchase acceleration, illusionary goal progress, and customer retention, *Journal of Marketing Research*, 43(1) (February), 39–58.

Liu, Y. and R. Yang (2009), Competing loyalty programs: Impact of market saturation, market share, and category expandability, *Journal of Marketing*, 73 (January), 93–108.

Nunes, J. C. and X. Drèze (2006), Your loyalty program is betraying you, *Harvard Business Review*, 84, 124⁻31.

Pelham, B. W., T. T. Sumarta, and L. Myaskovsky (1994), The easy path from many to much: The numerosity heuristic, *Cognitive Psychology*, 26 (April), 103–33.

Prelec, D. and D. Simester (2001), Always leave home without it: A further investigation of the credit-card effect on willingness to pay, *Marketing Letters*, 12 (February), 5–12.

Prelec, D. and G. Loewenstein (1998), The red and the black: Mental accounting of savings and debt, *Marketing Science*, 17 (Winter), 4–28.

Raghubir, P. and J. Srivastava (2002), Effect of face value on product valuation in foreign currencies, *Journal of Consumer Research*, 29 (December), 335–347.

Raghubir, P. and J. Srivastava (2008), Monopoly money: The effect of payment coupling and form on spending behavior, *Journal of Experimental Psychology: Applied*, 14(3) (September), 213–225.

Raghubir, P., V. G. Morwitz, and S. Santana (2012), Europoly money: How do tourists convert foreign currencies to make spending decisions? *Journal of Retailing*, 88(1), 7–19.

Reinholtz, N., D. M. Bartels, and J. R. Parker (2015), On the mental accounting of restricted-use funds: How gift cards change what people purchase, *Journal of Consumer Research*, 42(4), 596–614.

Rick, S. I., C. E. Cryder, and G. Loewenstein (2008), Tightwads and spendthrifts, *Journal of Consumer Research*, 34 (April), 767–82.

Scheidegger, G. and P. Raghubir (2022), Virtual currencies: Different schemes and research opportunities, *Marketing Letters*, ISSN 0923–0645.

Shafir, E., P. Diamond, and A. Tversky (1997), Money illusion, *The Quarterly Journal of Economics*, 112(2), 341–374.

Shah, A. M., N. Eisenkraft, J. R. Bettman, and T. L. Chartrand (2016), 'Paper or plastic?': How we pay influences post-transaction connection, *Journal of Consumer Research*, 42(5), 688–708.

Sharp, B. and A. Sharp (1997), Loyalty programs and their impact on repeat purchase loyalty patterns, *International Journal of Research in Marketing*, 14, 473–86.

Soman, D. (2001), Effects of payments mechanisms on spending behavior: The role of rehearsal and immediacy of payments, *Journal of Consumer Research*, 27 (March), 460–74.

Srivastava, J. and P. Raghubir (2002), Debiasing using decomposition: The case of memory-based credit card expenses, *Journal of Consumer Psychology*, 12(3), 253–264.

Stourm, V., E. T. Bradlow, and P. S. Fader (2015), Stockpiling points in linear loyalty programs, *Journal of Marketing Research*, 52(2), 253–267.

Thaler, R. H. (1985), Mental accounting and consumer choice, *Marketing Science*, 4 (Summer), 199–214.

Thaler, R. H. (1990), Saving, fungibility, and mental accounts, *Journal of Economic Perspectives*, 4(1), 193–205.

Thaler, R. H. (1999), Mental accounting matters, *Journal of Behavioral Decision Making*, 12, 183–206.

Thomas, M., K. K. Desai, and S. Seenivasan (2011), How credit card payments increase unhealthy food purchases: Visceral regulation of vices, *Journal of Consumer Research*, 38 (June), 126–139.

Verhoef, P. C. (2003), Understanding the effect of customer relationship management efforts on customer retention and customer share development, *Journal of Marketing*, 67, 30–45.

Voorhees, C. M., R. C. White, M. McCall, and P. Randhawa (2015), Fool's gold? Assessing the impact of the value of airline loyalty programs on brand equity perceptions and share of wallet, *Cornell Hospitality Quarterly*, 56(2). https://journals.sagepub.com/doi/10.1177/1938965514564213.

Wertenbroch, K., D. Soman, and A. Chattopadhyay (2007), On the perceived value of money: The reference dependence of currency numerosity effects, *Journal of Consumer Research*, 34(1), 1–10.

Yi, Y. and H. Jeon (2003), Effects of loyalty programs on value perception, program loyalty and brand loyalty, *Journal of the Academy of Marketing Science*, 31, 229–40.

Chapter 2

# Affective Price Evaluations: How Pain, Pleasure, and Metacognitive Feeling Influence Price Evaluations*

## Manoj Thomas and Arnaud Monnier

The pricing literature has largely been tethered to the tenet in neoclassical economics that the price of a good in a market is determined by the forces of supply and demand, and demand, in turn, is influenced by consumers' stable preferences and income levels. In this macro-level model, the consumer is often portrayed as a utility maximizer, making purchase decisions by trading the subjective value of money for the perceived utility of the good. Because of this tethering to neoclassical economics, early pricing researchers largely focused on estimating demand curves and how the demand curves changed with demographic variables, and product-related and category-related factors. They were not very interested in studying the role of affective processes in consumers' price evaluations, mostly because of a lack of appreciation of the role of affect in judgment and decision-making. The literature on theoretical concepts and frameworks required to coherently characterize affective processes is therefore

---

*In *New Directions in Behavioral Pricing*, Chezy Ofir Ed., 2024, World Scientific Publishing Company.

Manoj Thomas, SC Johnson College of Business, Cornell University (manojthomas@cornell.edu); Arnaud Monnier, Nova School of Business and Economics (arnaud.monnier@novasbe.pt).

underdeveloped. Affective responses were not considered an important determinant of consequential economic decisions.

However, in the past two decades, pricing researchers have become more interested in the role of affective responses in consumers' price evaluations. This interest was largely propelled by the findings reported in social and cognitive psychology literature. A burgeoning body of literature in psychology has forcefully demonstrated that affective responses — specific emotions as well as subtle metacognitive experiences — are not only ubiquitous in everyday decisions, but they are necessary for adaptive decision-making (Damasio 1994; Loewenstein 2010; Pham 2007). Inspired by this perspective, in the past five decades consumer researchers trained in the experimental psychology tradition have started developing micro-level models of consumers' responses to prices. Researchers in this stream of research, typically referred to as behavioral pricing research, focus on counterintuitive or so-called irrational pricing phenomena observed in the marketplace, and try to explain these phenomena using psychological principles. This phenomenon-construct mapping approach to pricing has revealed that affective reactions — the specific emotions directly elicited by prices, products, and the shopping context, as well as the subtler metacognitive feelings elicited by the process of evaluating the price — play an important role in consumers' responses to price. In this chapter, we review some interesting findings about the role of affect in price evaluations.

We identify three different ways in which affective responses — affect elicited by the act of parting with money (the pain of paying), affect elicited by metacognitive experiences (processing fluency, feeling of knowing (FOK), and feeling of not knowing (FONK)), and affect elicited by the products and shopping environment (hedonic experiences) — influence consumers' price evaluations and purchase decisions. First, we look at the affective response to the price itself. It has been shown that relative price magnitude (e.g., whether it is higher than past prices) and mode of payment (e.g., cash versus card) can alter consumers' affective responses to price. Researchers have labeled such affective responses to price as the *pain of paying*. Second, we look at the more subtle affective experience evoked by the mental process of price evaluation. Some price evaluations feel difficult and disfluent, while other price evaluations feel easy and fluent. This type of affective response is usually referred to as *metacognitive experience*. We look at the roles of different types of meta-cognitive experiences in price cognition — ease of retrieval, ease of computation, and the feeling-of-not-knowing. Third, we look at how hedonic feelings, specifically the feelings of pleasure induced by the product, the context, or consumers' dispositional states, influence price evaluations. Consumers' price evaluation of a hedonic product can be quite different from that of a utilitarian product. For instance, consumers could be less price sensitive when they are buying a cup of latte from an upscale café, but more price sensitive when they are buying ground coffee for their home, because the two stimuli evoke different types of affective responses. We refer to this type of affective response as *hedonic response*.

To put matters in perspective and to avoid any misunderstanding, it needs to be clarified that affective responses do not operate in isolation. They are always intertwined with cognitive responses. Figure 1 presents a schematic summary of our conceptual framework, clarifying that consumer behavior is influenced by the interplay of affective responses and cognitive heuristics. It might be useful to differentiate heuristics from subjective experiences. A heuristic is a mental shortcut that people use, consciously or unconsciously, to make a judgment. For example, people might decide to quickly judge the magnitude of the difference between two prices by comparing their left-most digits instead of processing all the digits in the two prices. Thus, heuristics are cognitive strategies. Affective

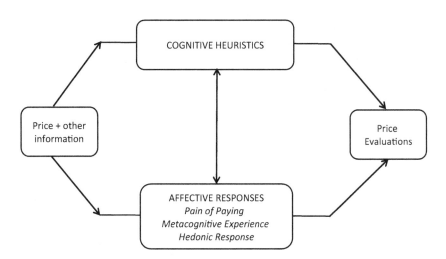

**Figure 1.** The interplay of cognitive and affective processes in price evaluations.
*Source*: Adapted from Thomas (2013).

responses, in contrast, are physiological and experiential states that a person experiences while making a judgment or decision. Affective states can be influenced by the specific heuristics employed, and at the same time, affective states can also influence the type of heuristic that is activated. Thus, cognitive heuristics and affective states have dynamic interdependence; both are intertwined, with each influencing the other. Nevertheless, in this review, we will restrict our attention to the role of affective responses in price cognition, specifically focusing on how pain of paying, metacognitive experiences, and hedonic responses influence consumers' price evaluations. For a discussion on the role of heuristics in price evaluations, we refer the readers to other reviews, such as Raghubir (2006), Thomas and Morwitz (2009), and Santana *et al.* (2020).

## Affect, Emotion, and Subjective Experience

Affect, emotion, and subjective experiences are characterized as often, but not always, as being automatic, fast, and experiential. For example, Paul Slovic *et al.* (2002) proposed that people have intuitive mental representations of stimuli when they encounter them, and that these mental representations are associated with positive or negative feelings. These feelings could be conscious or unconscious. These affect-laden mental representations guide decisions and behaviors more efficiently and sometimes more adaptively than deliberative thinking. Even though judgment and decision-making scholars often characterize affective responses as a source of bias rendering judgments and decisions, less objective, influential scholars (e.g., Damasio 1994; Loewenstein 2010; Pham 2007) have argued that affect is not necessarily a source of bias. Indeed, spontaneous affective reactions can occasionally bias judgments and lead to suboptimal decisions, but more often than not, affect enables people to efficiently direct their attention to motivationally relevant stimuli and avoid getting stuck in the quagmire of deliberative paralysis. Furthermore, scholars have also argued that affective responses and cold calculated reasoning are not mutually exclusive processes, but they co-occur in the brain in an intertwined manner, each influencing and being influenced by the other (e.g., Epstein 1994; Haidt 2012; Zajonc 2001). Additionally, scholars have characterized different types of affective responses — state-dependent affect (e.g., "how do I feel right now?") and stimulus-dependent affect (e.g., "is this product good or bad?"); expected emotions and immediate emotions; conscious emotions and subtle metacognitive experiences (Loewenstein and Lerner 2003; Schwarz 2004; Slovic *et al.* 2002). Building on these perspectives, we characterize affect as an adaptive response that spontaneously orients people to the motivational relevance of spending money, enables them to judge the magnitude of a price even when they do not have all the required information to do so, and informs them whether value should be evaluated only in terms of utilitarian benefits or also in terms of hedonic benefits.

## Pain of Paying

It takes only a little bit of introspection to see that parting with money can elicit spontaneous negative affects. Most people are likely to feel infuriated when the prices of frequently purchased goods go up unexpectedly and conspicuously. In fact, uncontrolled inflation was often the tipping point for the social unrest in many uprisings and revolutions in the past two centuries. Egregious increases in prices have unleashed such fury that it has galvanized peace-loving people to morph into a riotous mob uprooting rulers and governments. However, it is not just high prices that evoke strong negative emotions; several other factors can also elicit similar albeit muted reactions. People feel bad about parting with a hundred-dollar bill from their wallet, but they do not experience such negative feelings when they swipe a plastic card for the same amount. What causes this discrepancy in affective reactions to cash and card payments? Furthermore, this affective reaction to parting with money also varies across individuals — some people are dispositional tightwads while others are dispositional spendthrifts. Why is a tightwad so emotionally attached to his money whereas a spendthrift has no such emotional attachment? To address these tedious questions, behavioral scientists have coined the term pain of paying.

Consumers' evaluations of prices are not based solely on income, price consciousness, and price-quality beliefs.[1] Instead, their responses can be influenced by their affective response to the act of parting with

---

[1]Researchers have suggested that consumers' price acceptability follows an inverted-U shape function, bounded by two price thresholds: a low price threshold under which product quality becomes questionable, and a high price threshold beyond which the product is considered too expensive (e.g., Monroe 1973). Ofir (2004) identified a consumer segment without a lower price threshold who believe that the prices close to zero are most acceptable (a decreasing function). It was also revealed that price consciousness, product

money. People experience a spontaneous instinctive negative reaction when parting with money. Even the mere thought of parting with money, that is, the mental simulation of taking out money from a wallet or purse and handing it over to someone, can generate this negative feeling. This spontaneous negative feeling evoked by the act or the thought of parting with money is called the pain of paying (Prelec and Loewenstein 1998; Rick *et al.* 2008; Zellermayer 1996). The pain of paying is a learned and adaptive emotional response that regulates people's spending behaviors.

Neuroscientific research on brain markers has traced the pain of paying to the anterior insula, the same region in the brain that is implicated in the neural circuitry of physical pain. Brian Knutson *et al.* (2007) invited participants in their study to make shopping decisions in the laboratory. The participants considered several products, one at a time, and decided whether or not to spend their money on the products. The researchers scanned the participants' brains using fMRI while they were making these purchase decisions. Knutson *et al.* observed that an increased activation in the nucleus accumbens, a region associated with the processing of potential gains or rewards, was correlated with greater product attractiveness and purchase intentions. In contrast, they observed increased activation in the anterior insula when shoppers viewed products with very high prices that they did not intend to purchase. This insula activation was not there when they viewed products that they ended up purchasing. These observations led researchers to conclude that the neural activations caused by high price are similar to that caused by physical pain. In other words, a high price can cause negative feelings that are similar to the feelings evoked by physical pain, but at a much lower intensity and sometimes even unconsciously.

Pain of paying can be a situational variable caused by contextual factors such as price magnitude, price framing, and the mode of payment. Rick *et al.* (2008) showed that price framing — presenting a fee as "$5 fee" versus "small $5 fee" — can change the pain of paying and influence purchase decisions.

Pain of paying can also be a dispositional trait, varying across individuals. Some people might experience more intense pain of paying than others. Rick *et al.* (2008) developed a trait scale for pain of paying to identify where people fall on the tightwad–spendthrift continuum. Based

---

involvement, and the belief in price-quality determine consumers responses to price as reflected by these functions.

on this measure, they categorized about 24% of their respondents as tight-wads and 15% as spendthrifts. The remaining 60% were unconflicted, i.e., neither tightwads nor spendthrifts.

**Pain of Paying and Consumer Behavior**: Several scholars have studied how the pain of paying affects consumers' reactions to prices. For example, Prelec and Loewenstein (1998) suggested that consumers might be able to better enjoy their purchases when they pay off the bill in one sitting rather than in monthly installments because the regular payments would trigger their pain of paying. Stated differently, experiences are enjoyed more when the positive experience is decoupled from the pain of paying.

One of the most widely studied antecedents to the pain of paying is the mode of payment. A growing stream of literature has demonstrated that concrete, vivid modes of payment such as bills and coins evoke stronger pain of paying than abstract modes of payment such as debit and credit cards (Chatterjee and Rose 2012; Feinberg 1986; Hirschman 1979; Park *et al.* 2020; Prelec and Simester 2001; Raghubir and Srivastava 2008; Soman 2001, 2003; Srivastava and Raghubir 2002; Thomas *et al.* 2011). Results from several studies suggest that people spend more when they pay with credit or debit cards compared to when they pay with cash. Consumers who pay by check rather than credit card are less willing to incur a given expense (Soman 2001); people bid a significantly smaller amount for a pair of tickets to a sporting event when they have to pay in cash than when they have to pay by credit card (Prelec and Simester 2001); and people spend less when they pay in cash compared to when they pay using equivalent scrips (Raghubir and Srivastava 2008).

Recent studies have identified another important side-effect of paying by cards — card payments can weaken impulse control and increase the purchase of hedonic food items. Soman (2003) was the first researcher to identify this. He analyzed the shopping baskets of shoppers and found that when shoppers paid in cash, their shopping baskets had a smaller proportion of treats such as chocolate, gum, and snacks, relative to when they paid using cards. Thomas *et al.* (2011) and Park *et al.* (2020) observed similar results by analyzing retail store scanner panel data. Shoppers had fewer vice products in their baskets when they paid using cash relative to when they paid using a credit card. Thus, using cash as a mode of payment may act as a safeguard against overspending, especially for products considered frivolous and whose purchase is therefore not easily justifiable. These findings explain the positive correlation between the increasing obesity and the use of cashless payments in the past three decades (Humphrey 2004; Ogden *et al.* 2006). It also raises the inevitable question of how the proliferation of online shopping and the concomitant practice of cashless payments might be changing consumption patterns in society.

**Paradoxical Effects of Pain of Paying**: Although pain of paying usually reduces impulsive purchases, sometimes it can have paradoxical reverse effects on purchase decisions. Bagchi and Block (2011) demonstrated that pain of paying can sometimes increase indulgent purchases. They examined how mode of payment affected consumption behaviors in a frozen yogurt retail store. They observed that those who paid with cash ordered more indulgent, higher calorie frozen yogurt compared to those who paid by card. The authors argue that when people pay in cash, they try to compensate for the pain of paying by consuming more indulgent items. Thus, sometimes pain of paying can trigger compensatory behavior. If a shopper is in a café, bakery, or a dessert store having already decided to buy an indulgent product, then greater pain of paying can cause compensatory behaviors, prompting them to buy more indulgent versions of that product.

In a similar vein, Shah *et al.* (2016) suggested that more painful payment modes can increase post-transaction emotional attachment to products and services purchased. They used an archival data set of alumni donations to test whether higher pain of paying is associated with an increased probability of donating. Consistent with their hypothesis, they found that alumni who donated using checks were more likely to be loyal donors (relative to those who donated using cards) to the alma mater. Replicating this finding in experimental settings, they show that people who purchased a mug by paying in cash were more deeply attached to the mug relative to those who paid by card. Shah and colleagues suggest that higher pain of payment can increase the need to justify the purchase, which in turn can lead to higher emotional attachment to products. This proposal is consistent with Olivola and Shafir's (2013) demonstration of a "martyrdom effect," wherein participants who imagined suffering for a cause (e.g., running a marathon) donate more than those who simply imagined attending a picnic for the same charity.

Having discussed consumers' affective reaction to prices, we now turn to another type of affective response that plays an important role in consumers' price evaluations, metacognitive experience.

# Metacognitive Experience

Can the ease or difficulty of computing the difference between two prices influence consumers' price evaluations? When consumers try to do temporal price comparisons — for example, judging whether this week's price for their favorite brand of yogurt is lower or higher than last week's price — will they be more accurate when they try to consciously recall the past price or when they don't try to do so? The concept of metacognitive experience can help us answer such questions.

Metacognitive experience is the subjective experience elicited by cognition. Metacognitive experiences are a byproduct of the executive monitoring and control function of the brain. When one part of the brain is engaged in a complex analysis, another part of the brain is monitoring the ease or difficulty of the analysis. This cognitive monitoring of the cognitions — a second-order metacognitive evaluation — is important for executive control of attention and effort. When the cognitive processing feels easy, the mind is reassured that it is dealing with familiar and tractable information. However, when the cognitive processing feels difficult, it signals that the information is new, complex, or less tractable. It signals that such information might require more resources — attention might have to be diverted away from less important stimuli to the difficult stimuli, or the heuristic strategy employed to analyze the information might have to be suitably altered. Thus, metacognitive experiences are inevitable, ubiquitous, and vital for effective judgment and decision-making.

There are several types of metacognitive experiences, such as perceptual fluency, conceptual fluency, ease of retrieval, and the feeling of knowing (Alter and Oppenheimer 2009). Psychologists have identified that metacognitive experience plays an important role in many subtle emotions that we frequently experience. The feelings of unfamiliarity or expectation violation, and conversely the feelings of familiarity and expectation confirmation, are said to be caused by metacognitive experiences (Whittlesea 1993; Whittlesea and Williams 2000). Metacognitive experiences also play a crucial role in the feelings of knowing and intuitive confidence (Koriat 1993). Even social judgments such as how assertive one is or how much one likes a stimulus can be influenced by metacognitive experiences (Schwarz 2004). These findings show that although from a functional perspective metacognitive experiences are monitored for the purpose of cognitive control, sometimes metacognitive experience itself becomes an input to make a judgment. For example, when a person tries to recall eight reasons to decide whether she likes a particular brand of car, the feeling of ease or difficulty of recall not only tells her that the cognitive task is challenging, it can also influence how much she likes the car. Thus, somewhat paradoxically, a person who easily recalls four reasons for liking the car might like the car more than the person who recalls eight reasons, but with some difficulty, for liking the car (see Schwarz 2004 for a review).

**The Ease-of-Recall Effect**: Consistent with these findings, Ofir *et al.* (2008) demonstrated that the ease or difficulty with which shoppers can recall the number of low-priced products in a store can influence whether they consider the store a cheap store or an expensive store. Shoppers who were asked to recall two low-priced products were more likely to consider the store as a cheap store, relative to those who were asked to recall five low-priced products. Although shoppers who were asked to recall five low-priced products actually recalled more low-priced products than those who were asked to recall only two, those in the former category also experienced more difficulty in recalling the five products. This difficulty of recalling influenced their store price perception ("Since I cannot recall five low-priced products easily, it must not be a cheap store"). Conversely, those who were asked to recall only two low-priced products reckoned that since they could easily recall the two low-priced products, it must indeed be a cheap store.

Intriguingly, Ofir *et al.* also found that not all shoppers relied on ease of price recall to make inferences about the store price policy. Only the less knowledgeable shoppers relied on ease of recall. The more knowledgeable shoppers relied more on the number of prices recalled. The more low-priced products they could recall, the more likely they were to rate the store as a cheap store regardless of the ease or difficulty of recall.

**The Ease-of-Computation Effect**: Thomas and Morwitz (2009) demonstrated that metacognitive experiences can influence price evaluations. They studied the role of metacognitive experiences in the context of price difference judgments. Consider the following discounted prices of two store brands of corn flakes at two separate retail stores, Walmart and Whole Foods. The two store brands differ in their regular prices and both of them are offered at discounted prices. At which store is the *magnitude of the discount* (i.e. the difference between the regular and sale price) *higher*?

|              | Walmart | Whole Foods |
|--------------|---------|-------------|
| Regular Price | $4.50  | $4.64       |
| Sale Price    | $2.50  | $2.56       |

At first blush, it would seem that the difference between the regular and sale price is higher at Walmart than at Whole Foods. The reader can instantaneously make out that the smaller pack at Walmart is $2 cheaper than the larger pack. Most readers will find the price difference at Whole Foods a bit more difficult to compute. Furthermore, for most readers the price difference will intuitively seem smaller at Whole Foods. However, a more careful scrutiny reveals this initial judgment is misplaced. While the discount is $2 at Walmart, it is $2.08 at Whole Foods. That is, Whole Foods is offering a larger discount on possibly a better-quality cereal.

Thomas and Morwitz (2009) presented participants with several such pairs of prices and asked them to judge the magnitude of the difference between the two prices in each pair on an analog scale. They also measured participants' response times as they made these judgments. Unsurprisingly, participants took more time for difficult-to-compute pairs relative to easy-to-compute pairs. More intriguingly, participants' response time was a significant predictor of the perceived magnitude of price difference. Holding constant the actual difference between the two prices, participants' judgments of numerical difference was smaller for the difficult-to-compute price pair than for the easy-to-compute price pair. This result accords with the notion that metacognitive experiences can serve as a source of information over and above the underlying cognitive information. Thomas and Morwitz (2009) labeled this as the ease-of-computation effect.

The ease-of-computation effect offers insights into the complex mental processes that underlie evaluations of price difference magnitudes. A series of rather sophisticated mechanisms underlie this simple cognitive task that most people take for granted. First, the ease-of-computation effect demonstrates that the monitoring of metacognitive experiences is a pervasive never-ceasing process. When consumers estimate the difference between two prices, there are at least two distinct mental processes that occur in their brains. One part of their brain starts performing mental arithmetic, subtracting the smaller number from the larger number. This task can become somewhat challenging if the numbers involved have multiple digits and entail carryover operations. Another part of the brain monitors the ease or difficulty of processing. When the brain encounters such computational difficulty, the experience of difficulty itself can serve as a cue of the magnitude of the difference between two numbers. This is because the brain has learned to interpret subjective experiences of cognitive ease and difficulty in various contexts.

Thus, the ease-of-computation effect also highlights the role of heuristic interpretation in metacognitive inferences. Right from its early days of infancy, the human brain not only learns to observe metacognitive difficulty and ease, but it also learns to interpret these experiences in various contexts. The heuristic interpretation of cognitive ease or difficulty varies across contexts and over time, and the mind develops a repertoire of likely meaning of cognitive ease and difficulty in various contexts. In the context of magnitude discrimination tasks, cognitive difficulty usually signals greater similarity or lower discriminability. For a phenomenological illustration, consider the two questions.

(A)  *Which of the following two is bigger, an ant or an elephant?*
(B)  *Which of the following two is bigger, an ant or a fly?*

It is easier to answer the former question that the latter one. Even as the reader is perusing the first question, the mental imagery of an ant and that of an elephant spontaneously take shape in her mind and the answer effortlessly drifts into her consciousness. However, the answer to the second question requires more effort. It is not easy to answer the second question based on the imagery of an ant and a fly. One has to think more. And even then, the answer is elusive. This illustrative example highlights a robust ecological association between metacognitive experience and magnitude of size differences. The smaller the size difference between two stimuli being compared, the more difficult is it to discriminate them on size. The larger the size difference between two stimuli being compared, the easier is it to discriminate them on size. Overtime this association, and other such context-specific associations, become etched in people's minds. The robustness of this association can be depicted using a simple forced-choice paradigm using non-numeric stimuli.

*The price difference between X and Y is very small.*
*The price difference between M and N is very large.*

*Which of the two evaluations will be easier and faster for you?*

(A) *Evaluating the price difference between X and Y*
(B) *Evaluating the price difference between M and N*

Note that respondents cannot answer this forced-choice question based on logic and reasoning because we have not specified the numeric values of X and Y. They have to necessarily rely on their intuitive associations. The first author has presented this question to students in several classes. In most cases a vast majority of the respondents, usually between 60% to 70%, choose the second response, suggesting the existence of a heuristic that greater processing difficulty signals that the magnitudes being compared are less discriminable.

The ease-of-computation effect also highlights a third aspect of metacognitive experiences: the misattribution of such experiences. Going back to our original example, the difference between $4.64 and $2.56 is actually larger than the difference between $4.50 and $2.50. That is, the computational difficulty in the former pair is not due to size similarity. The computational difficulty stems from arithmetic complexity. However, the reader's mind is unable to attribute the feeling of difficulty to the correct source. It hastily leaps to the conclusion that "if it is difficult to discriminate the two stimuli, then they must be very similar in size." Thus, the mind misattributes the difficulty to size similarity instead of correctly attributing it to arithmetic complexity.

In summary, the ease-of-computation effect highlights the three steps through which metacognitive experiences influence everyday judgments (see Figure 2). First, the human mind is always and unconsciously monitoring metacognitive experiences. Second, overtime the mind learns to heuristically interpret these metacognitive associations. Finally, because of these heuristic attributions, consumers often misattribute the metacognitive experience to factors made salient by the judgment task rather than to its actual causes.

Several researchers have identified interesting effects of metacognitive experiences in consumer information processing (Bagchi and Davis 2012; Biswas *et al.* 2013; Coulter and Roggeveen 2014; King and Janiszewski 2011; Kwong *et al.* 2011). King and Janiszewski (2011) suggested that numbers that are arithmetically related create more fluent processing, and this metacognitive experience can spillover to price evaluations. For example, consumers evaluate the promotional offer "4 small pizzas, up to 6 toppings for $24" more favorably than the offer "4 small pizzas, unlimited toppings for $24" even though the latter is objectively superior. Researchers have also shown that ease of computation can influence how consumers integrate different types of numerical information in consumption contexts such that computational difficulty can dissuade consumers from integrating different pieces of numerical information, anchoring their evaluations on the most salient numeric information (Bagchi and Davis 2012).

**The Feeling-of-Not-Knowing Effect**: Another important class of meta-cognitive experiences that influences people's judgments and decisions is the FOK and its corollary the FONK. When people try to recall past information or generate new information, these cognitive processes are often accompanied by subjective experience of ease or difficulty of generation. This experience can inform the person whether the knowledge that the mind generated is veridical or reliable.

Kyung and Thomas (2016) proposed that FOK and FONK play important roles in consumers' temporal price comparisons. Shoppers often evaluate prices by comparing the offer price to a memory-based reference price. For example, they might evaluate the price of their favorite cereal by comparing this week's price to the price they paid the last time they purchased it. They can make such memory-based comparisons based on either explicit memory or implicit memory. That is, they can try to explicitly recall the price they paid for the cereal the last time and compare it to the current offer price. Alternatively, they might evaluate the new price relative to the old price without trying to explicitly recall the old price. These two types of memory judgments are referred to as explicit memory judgments (e.g., "the cereal was $5.50 the last time") or as implicit memory judgments (e.g., "the price this week seems lower than last week's price"). Kyung and Thomas (2016) argued that implicit memory judgments rely on FOK. Even though people cannot recall the past price, they have an intuitive feeling that the offer price is lower or higher than the past price.

In delineating the role of FOK in temporal price comparisons, Kyung and Thomas (2016) solved an old conundrum in the grocery pricing literature. Econometric analyses of actual consumer behavior in grocery stores have established that consumers are very sensitive to small temporal changes in prices. Even small deviations from past prices, commonly called reference prices, of grocery products can influence consumers' actual purchase behavior (Briesch *et al.* 1997; Winer 1986; Kalyanaram and Winer 1995). That is, when a shopper is considering whether to buy her favorite cereal, even if she is not able to recall the price that she paid the last time, she will be less likely to buy the cereal if the current week's price is higher than the last price she paid for the product. However, these results are inconsistent with the results observed from surveys on consumers' price memory. Price recall surveys have shown that a majority of consumers are unable to correctly articulate the past prices of products, even seconds after selecting them (Dickson and Sawyer 1990; Le Boutillier *et al.* 1994; Monroe and Lee 1999). For example, Krishna *et al.* (1991) found that more than 40% of consumers were unable to provide a response when asked for the regular prices of products they frequently buy, and only 34% were correct within 20 cents of the actual price. These conflicting results provoke the question: How can consumers know that the current price of a grocery product is higher or lower than the past price when they cannot recall the past price?

Building on Monroe and Lee's (1999) suggestion, Kyung and Thomas argued that FOK and FONK play important roles in temporal or weekly price comparisons. Even when they are unable to accurately recall past prices, consumers have an implicit memory for prices. Because of this implicit memory, when they see a new price they can intuitively feel whether the new price is lower or higher than the past price. This intuitive feeling of knowing (FOK) is what allows them to make temporal price comparisons of scores of grocery products.

To delineate the role of FOK and FONK in temporal price comparisons, Kyung and Thomas designed a two-stage experiment with an encoding phase and a memory-based price comparison phase. The encoding phase was a shopping task wherein participants evaluated and indicated their purchase intentions for 20 grocery products. After the shopping task, without any prior notice, they were presented the same 20 products and were asked to respond to a memory-based price comparison task. In the latter task, the prices of the 20 products were altered such that they were either $1 higher or lower than the original prices in the shopping task. In this task, half the participants were asked to simply judge whether the new price is lower or higher (compare-only condition) whereas the other half were asked to first recall the past price and then judge whether the new price is lower or higher (recall-and-compare condition).

The researchers found that, paradoxically, trying to recall the past price reduced the accuracy of price comparison judgments. For example, in their first study, those who made the comparison judgments without recalling the past price made correct judgments in 57% cases. But the proportion of correct judgments reduced to 52% for the participants who tried to recall the reference price before making the comparisons. In

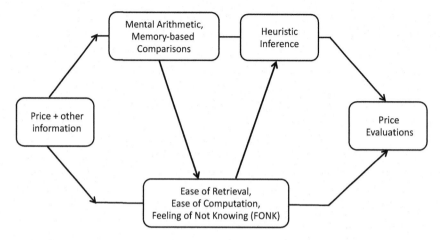

**Figure 2.**   The interplay of cognitive processes and metacognitive experiences in price evaluations

subsequent studies, the authors measured participants' FONK by asking them to predict how many of their 20 answers were incorrect. This subjective estimate of the number of incorrect responses served as the measure of FONK and mediated the effect of explicit recall attempts on judgment accuracy. Further studies demonstrated that the effect of explicit recall was mitigated when their attention was drawn away from the FONK experience. Summarizing all of these findings, Figure 2 presents a schematic summary of how cognitive processes and metacognitive experiences interactively shape consumers' price comparisons.

## Hedonic Price Evaluations

Thus far we restricted our attention to affective responses elicited by prices. However, in many situations affective responses elicited by the product, the decision-making context, or consumers' dispositional state can also alter how prices are evaluated. We now turn our attention to how such affective responses influence price evaluations.

Our conceptualization of the role of price evaluations draws extensively on Hsee and colleagues' work on valuation by feeling and the General Evaluability Theory. Hsee and Rottenstreich (2004) characterized two processes through which consumers form evaluative judgments of products: valuation by feelings and valuation by calculation. Hsee and his colleagues argue that valuation by feelings increases sensitivity to the nature of the product and at the same time decreases sensitivity to quantity magnitude. In a much-cited experiment, Hsee and Rottenstreich (2004) primed half of the participants to be in a valuation-by-calculation mindset, while they primed the other half to be in a valuation-by-feeling mindset. Those assigned to the calculation mindset were asked to respond to arithmetic questions such as "if an object travels at five feet per minute, then by your calculations how many feet will it travel in 360 seconds?" Those assigned to the valuation-by-feeling condition responded to affective questions, such as "When you hear the name 'George W. Bush,' what do you feel?" Thereafter, participants were told to indicate the amount they were willing to pay for a bundle of 5 CDs of Madonna and a bundle of 10 CDs. Two important results emerged. First, priming participants to be in valuation-by-calculation mindset increased their scope sensitivity; the amount they were willing to pay for the 10 CD-bundle was much higher than what they were willing to pay for the 5 CD-bundle. Those primed to rely on their feelings were less scope sensitive. Second, priming participants to rely on their feelings increased their willingness to pay for the smaller set of 5-CDs.

This finding has substantial real-world implications. It suggests that individuals who rely on their affective evaluations are likely to be as satisfied with a 5-oz serving of ice cream as they would be with a 10-oz serving of the same ice cream. But those who rely on calculations might be less happy with the 5-oz serving of the ice cream (Hsee *et al.* 2005).

Monnier and Thomas (2022) identified an interesting manifestation of this insight in the context of price-quantity evaluations. Consider the following question.

> *Lay's regular pack of chips has 8 oz. and it costs $2.19. Lay's is launching a multipack of chips that has 12 snack bags with 1 oz. of chips in each snack bag.*
> *How much would you be willing to pay for the multipack with 12 oz.?*

Monnier and Thomas found that consumers' willingness to pay can be influenced considerably by very subtle changes in the framing of the quantity description. The description can be framed to direct their attention to the standardized unit (*How much would you be willing to pay for the multipack with 12 oz.?*) or to the visual unit (*How much would you be willing to pay for the multipack with 12 snack bags?*). Participants were willing to pay considerably more when the visual unit (snack bags) was made more salient relative to the standardized unit (oz). Monnier and Thomas observed that increasing the salience of visual units (12 snack bags) prompts participants to rely on experiential processing, whereas making the standardized units (12 oz.) salient prompts them to rely more on analytical processing. Importantly, this effect emerges even when full information is provided to participants. Merely changing which unit comes first can alter the nature of the processing of quantity information, and in turn, influence willingness to pay.

In a similar vein, Gao *et al.* (2020) recently demonstrated how marketers can prime shoppers to rely on affective evaluations or on analytical evaluations. Building on an experimental procedure developed by Klein and Melnyk (2016), Gao et al. subtly manipulated participants' evaluation criteria by exposing them to two different advertisements for a new pair of shoes. To induce a more affective evaluation, one advertisement emphasized "comfort, sophistication, and style." To induce a more analytical evaluation, the other advertisement emphasized "quality, stability, and durability." Gao and colleagues found that inducing participants to adopt affective evaluations made them less price sensitive, as indicated by their increased purchase intentions for more expensive products.

However, the hedonic mindset is quite fragile and can easily be disrupted by prompts to compare products or justify expenses. When consumers step out of their hedonic mindsets, they might be hard-pressed to justify their initial willingness to spend money on hedonic items. As philosophers and writers have pointed out since time immemorial, the heart often sways the mind. Although many a times the mind passively follows the heart conjuring up post hoc rationalizations for the emotional responses, when it is prompted to use the language of logic and reasoning, the mind struggles to justify the heart's predilections. Thus, while hedonic mindsets can reduce price sensitivity, hedonic attributes can be difficult to justify in a deliberative mindset. Because of this, products that manage to command the highest price premiums in the market are typically those that appeal to the heart and at the same time offer a good justification for the mind to follow the heart.

In summary, in this review we tried to characterize the role of affective processes in price evaluations. We delineated three types of affective responses, affect elicited by the act of parting with money or even the mental imagery of doing so (the pain of paying), affect elicited by metacognitive monitoring during price cognition (processing fluency, FOK, and FONK), and affect elicited by the products and shopping environment (hedonic experiences) that influence shoppers' price evaluations. We believe that a better understanding of such affective processes can help researchers come up with richer descriptive models of how customers actually evaluate prices in the marketplace.

# References

Alter, A. L. and D. M. Oppenheimer (2009), Uniting the tribes of fluency to form a metacognitive nation, *Personality and Social Psychology Review*, 13(3), 219–235.

Bagchi, R. and L. G. Block (2011), Chocolate cake please! Why do consumers indulge more when it feels more expensive? *Journal of Public Policy & Marketing*, 30(2), 294–306.

Bagchi, R. and D. F. Davis (2012), $29 for 70 items or 70 items for $29? How presentation order affects package perceptions, *Journal of Consumer Research*, 39(1), 62–73.

Biswas, A., S. Bhowmick, A. Guha, and D. Grewal (2013), Consumer evaluations of sale prices: Role of the subtraction principle, *Journal of Marketing*, 77(4), 49–66.

Briesch, R. A., L. Krishnamurthi, T. Mazumdar, and S. P. Raj (1997), A comparative analysis of reference price models, *Journal of Consumer Research*, 24(2), 202–214.

Chatterjee, P. and R. L. Rose (2012), Do payment mechanisms change the way consumers perceive products? *Journal of Consumer Research*, 38(6), 1129–1139.

Coulter, K. S. and A. L. Roggeveen (2014), Price number relationships and deal processing fluency: The effects of approximation sequences and number multiples, *Journal of Marketing Research*, 51(1), 69–82.

Damasio, A. R. (1994), *Descartes' Error: Emotion, Reason, and the Human Brain,* New York: G.P. Putnam.

Dickson, P. R. and Sawyer, A. G. (1990), The price knowledge and search of supermarket shoppers, *Journal of Marketing*, 54(3), 42–53.

Epstein, S. (1994), Integration of the cognitive and the psychodynamic unconscious, *American Psychologist*, 49(8), 709.

Feinberg, R. A. (1986), Credit cards as spending facilitating stimuli: A conditioning interpretation, *Journal of Consumer Research*, 13(3), 348–356.

Gao, H., V. Mittal, and Y. Zhang (2020), The differential effect of local–global identity among males and females: The case of price sensitivity, *Journal of Marketing Research*, 57(1), 173–191.

Haidt, J. (2012), *The Righteous Mind: Why Good People are Divided by Politics and Religion*, New York: Pantheon Books.

Hirschman, E. C. (1979), Differences in consumer purchase behavior by credit card payment system, *Journal of Consumer Research*, 6(1), 58–66.

Hsee, C. K. and Y. Rottenstreich (2004), Music, pandas, and muggers: On the affective psychology of value, *Journal of Experimental Psychology: General*, 133(1), 23.

Hsee, C. K., Y. Rottenstreich, and Z. Xiao (2005), When is better? On the relationship between magnitude and subjective value, *Current Directions in Psychological Science*, 14(5), 234–237.

Humphrey, D. B. (2004), Replacement of cash by cards in US consumer payments, *Journal of Economics and Business*, 56(3), 211–225.

Kalyanaram, G. and R. S. Winer (1995), Empirical generalizations from reference price research, *Marketing Science*, 14(3), G161–G169.

King, D. and C. Janiszewski (2011), The sources and consequences of the fluent processing of numbers, *Journal of Marketing Research*, 48(2), 327–341.

Klein, K. and V. Melnyk (2016), Speaking to the mind or the heart: effects of matching hedonic versus utilitarian arguments and products, *Marketing Letters*, 27(1), 131–142.

Knutson, B., S. Rick, G. E. Wimmer, D. Prelec, and G. Loewenstein (2007), Neural predictors of purchases, *Neuron*, 53(1), 147–156.

Koriat, A. (1993), How do we know that we know? The accessibility model of the feeling of knowing, *Psychological Review*, 100(4), 609.

Krishna, A., I. S. Currim, and R. W. Shoemaker (1991), Consumer perceptions of promotional activity, *Journal of Marketing*, 55(2), 4–16.

Kwong, J. Y., D. Soman, and C. K. Ho (2011), The role of computational ease on the decision to spend loyalty program points, *Journal of Consumer Psychology*, 21(2), 146–156.

Kyung, E. J. and M. Thomas (2016), When remembering disrupts knowing: Blocking implicit price memory, *Journal of Marketing Research*, 53(6), 937–953.

Le Boutillier, J., S. S. Le Boutillier, and S. A. Neslin (1994), A replication and extension of the Dickson and Sawyer price-awareness study, *Marketing Letters*, 5(1), 31–42.

Loewenstein, G. (2010), Insufficient emotion: Soul-searching by a former indicter of strong emotions, *Emotion Review*, 2(3), 234–239.

Loewenstein, G. and J. S. Lerner (2003), The role of affect in decision making, In R. J. Davidson, K. R. Scherer, and H. H. Goldsmith (Eds.), *Series in Affective Science. Handbook of Affective Sciences* (pp. 619–642), New York, NY, USA: Oxford University Press.

Monnier, A. and M. Thomas (2022), Experiential and analytical price evaluations: How experiential product description affects prices, *Journal of Consumer Research*, (forthcoming).

Monroe, K. B. (1973), Buyers' subjective perceptions of price, *Journal of Marketing Research*, 10(1), 70–80.

Monroe, K. B. and A. Y. Lee (1999), Remembering versus knowing: Issues in buyers' processing of price information, *Journal of the Academy of Marketing Science*, 27(2), 207.

Ofir, C. (2004), Reexamining latitude of price acceptability and price thresholds: Predicting basic consumer reaction to price, *Journal of Consumer Research*, 30(4), 612–621.

Ofir, C., P. Raghubir, G. Brosh, K. B. Monroe, and A. Heiman (2008), Memory-based Store Price Judgments: The role of knowledge and shopping experience, *Journal of Retailing*, 84(4), 414–423.

Ogden, C. L., M. D. Carroll, L. R. Curtin, M. A. McDowell, C. J. Tabak, and K. M. Flegal (2006), Prevalence of overweight and obesity in the United States, 1999–2004, *Journal of the American Medical Association*, 295(13), 1549–1555.

Olivola, C. Y. and E. Shafir (2013), The martyrdom effect: When pain and effort increase prosocial contributions, *Journal of Behavioral Decision Making*, 26(1), 91–105.

Park, J., C. Lee, and M. Thomas (2020), Why do cashless payments increase unhealthy consumption? The decision-risk inattention hypothesis, *Journal of Association for Consumer Research*. https://doi.org/10.1086/710251.

Pham, M. T. (2007), Emotion and rationality: A critical review and interpretation of empirical evidence, *Review of General Psychology*, 11(2), 155–178.

Prelec, D. and G. Loewenstein (1998), The red and the black: Mental accounting of savings and debt, *Marketing Science*, 17(1), 4–28.

Prelec, D. and D. Simester (2001), Always leave home without it: A further investigation of the credit-card effect on willingness to pay, *Marketing Letters*, 12(1), 5–12.

Raghubir, P. (2006), An information processing review of the subjective value of money and prices, *Journal of Business Research*, 59(10–11), 1053–1062.

Raghubir, P. and J. Srivastava (2008), Monopoly money: the effect of payment coupling and form on spending behavior, *Journal of Experimental Psychology: Applied*, 14(3), 213–25.

Rick, S. I., C. E. Cryder, and G. Loewenstein (2008), Tightwads and spendthrifts, *Journal of Consumer Research*, 34(6), 767–782.

Santana, S., M. Thomas, and V. G. Morwitz (2020), The role of numbers in the customer journey, *Journal of Retailing*, 96(1), 138–154.

Schwarz, N. (2004), Metacognitive experiences in consumer judgment and decision making, *Journal of Consumer Psychology*, 14(4), 332–348.

Shah, A. M., N. Eisenkraft, J. R. Bettman, and T. L. Chartrand (2016), "Paper or plastic?": How I pay influences post-transaction connection, *Journal of Consumer Research*, 42(5), 688–708.

Slovic, P., M. Finucane, E. Peters, and D. MacGregor (2002), The affect heuristic, In T. Gilovich, D. Griffin, and D. Kahneman (Eds.), *Heuristics of Intuitive*

*Judgment: Extensions and Applications,* New York: Cambridge University Press.

Soman, D. (2001), Effects of payment mechanism on spending behavior: The role of rehearsal and immediacy of payments, *Journal of Consumer Research,* 27(4), 460–474.

Soman, D. (2003), The effect of payment transparency on consumption: Quasi-experiments from the field, *Marketing Letters,* 14(3), 173–183.

Srivastava, J. and P. Raghubir (2002), Debiasing using decomposition: The case of memory-based credit card expense estimates, *Journal of Consumer Psychology,* 12(3), 253–264.

Thomas, M. (2013), Commentary on behavioral price research: The role of subjective experiences in price cognition, *AMS Review,* 3(3), 141–145.

Thomas, M., K. K. Desai, and S. Seenivasan (2011), How credit card payments increase unhealthy food purchases: Visceral regulation of vices, *Journal of Consumer Research,* 38(1), 126–139.

Thomas, M. and V. G. Morwitz (2009), The ease-of-computation effect: The interplay of metacognitive experiences and naive theories in judgments of price differences, *Journal of Marketing Research,* 46(1), 81–91.

Whittlesea, B. W. (1993), Illusions of familiarity, *Journal of Experimental Psychology: Learning, Memory, and Cognition,* 19(6), 1235.

Whittlesea, B. W. and L. D. Williams (2000), The source of feelings of familiarity: The discrepancy-attribution hypothesis, *Journal of Experimental Psychology: Learning, Memory, and Cognition,* 26(3), 547.

Winer, R. S. (1986), A reference price model of brand choice for frequently purchased products, *Journal of Consumer Research,* 13(2), 250–256.

Zajonc, R. B. (2001), Mere exposure: A gateway to the subliminal, *Current Directions in Psychological Science,* 10(6), 224–228.

Zellermayer, O. (1996), The pain of paying, Doctoral dissertation, Department of Social and Decision Sciences, Carnegie Mellon University, Pittsburgh, PA.

https://doi.org/10.1142/9789811292231_0003

# Chapter 3

# Behavioral Pricing and Price Fairness*

Lisa E. Bolton and Haipeng (Allan) Chen

Pricing is a fundamental aspect of the marketplace, and traditional economic models typically assume that firms set prices to maximize their profit. However, consumer reactions to pricing are driven by psychological, as well as economic, considerations. Research has demonstrated, for example, that consumers may not react to small price differences, leading to "kinks" in the classic demand curves (e.g., Monroe 1971). As another example, the manner in which economically equivalent prices are presented affects consumer reactions, yielding some of the well-known framing effects (e.g., Thaler 1985). Additionally, prices involve numerical information and many consumers make errors in calculating prices, which could further bias price information processing (e.g., Chen and Sun 2018).

---

*In *New Directions in Behavioral Pricing*, Chezy Ofir Ed., 2024, World Scientific Publishing Company.

Lisa E. Bolton, Professor of Marketing, Anchel Professor of Business Administration, The Pennsylvania State University, PA 16801, United States (boltonle@psu.edu); Haipeng (Allan) Chen, Professor, Gatton Endowed Chair in Marketing, University Research Professor at the University of Kentucky, Lexington, KY 40506, USA (allanchen@uky.edu).

For assistance with data collection, we thank Sharon Ng (study 1) and Julianne Morgan (study 2A).

The voluminous work that aims at developing descriptive (versus prescriptive) models of consumer behaviors has germinated into the field of behavioral pricing that focuses on examinations of how consumers deal with price information in the marketplace.

A cornerstone of the behavioral pricing literature introduces fairness as a constraint on firm profit seeking and proposes that consumer reactions to pricing are guided by the principle of dual entitlement (Kahneman *et al.* 1986a, 1986b). This pioneering work on price fairness has inspired much additional research, including on its consequences for consumers and firms (e.g., Campbell 1999; Oliver and Swan 1989; Sinha and Batra 1999; for a review, see Xia *et al.* 2004). Our objective in this chapter is to discuss what is currently known about price fairness, showcase some empirical evidence, and identify important research questions that remain unexplored in this area.

## Dual Entitlement

According to the principle of dual entitlement (DE), buyers are entitled to a reference price and sellers are entitled to a reference profit. These terms are established by a relevant precedent or reference transaction, such as current market situations (e.g., list prices, competitors' prices, labor prices) or historical prices and profits (Kahneman *et al.* 1986a, 1986b; Bolton *et al.* 2003; Haws and Bearden 2006). To test DE, Kahneman *et al.* (1986a, 1986b) examined how consumers react to two pricing actions: increasing prices when costs increase and maintaining prices when costs decrease. A series of studies demonstrate that consumers deem it fair for a seller to (1) increase its price when its costs increase (in order to protect the seller's entitlement to a reference profit), and (2) maintain its price when its costs decrease (because doing so does not violate the buyer's entitlement to a reference price). For example, respondents in their studies judged it fair for a retailer to increase its price when its wholesale price increased and judged it fair for a manufacturer to maintain its price when its cost decreased (Kahneman *et al.* 1986a).

While DE provides a rationale for why firms can engage in asymmetric price responses to cost changes (i.e., "asymmetric pricing"), other firm pricing actions are constrained. For example, respondents judged it unfair for a firm to raise prices to exploit product shortages (e.g., of Red Delicious apples) or a lack of competition (e.g., a sole retailer in a geographic location). Using price to ration scarce goods is also judged unfair, but such concerns are alleviated if the firm does not benefit from doing so (e.g., auctioning off a rare sought-after toy for charity rather than firm profit). As Kahneman *et al.* (1986a, 1986b, p. 738) point out, "many actions that are both profitable in the short run and not obviously dishonest are likely to be perceived as unfair exploitation of market power", and therefore "the actions of firms that wish to avoid a reputation for unfairness will depart in significant ways from the standard model of economic behavior."

Dual entitlement was proposed as a principle that "governs community standards of fairness" between firms and consumers (Kahenman *et al.* 1986a, p. 729) and has been empirically verified to be robust by follow-up research (e.g., Kahneman *et al.* 1986b; Urbany *et al.* 1989; Gorman and Kehr 1992). A notable exception, however, emerges when consumers simultaneously consider pricing in response to cost increases and cost decreases, where more support is found for cost-plus pricing (i.e., complete pass-through) and buffering (i.e., zero pass-through) than DE (i.e., asymmetric pass-through; Kalapurakal *et al.* 1991; Dickson and Kalapurakal 1994).

## Expanding DE from a transactional perspective

Building upon Kahneman *et al.*'s pioneering work, subsequent research has expanded DE in multiple ways. One stream of research has focused on identifying and investigating antecedents of the reference transaction, which is the key determinant of entitlement and fairness. The reference prices that consumers feel entitled to and the reference profit that a firm can fairly protect depend on past prices, competitor prices, and costs. By broadening the consideration of reference transactions to these factors, Bolton *et al.* (2003) find that consumers systematically underestimate price fairness. For example, consumers underestimate inflationary effects when assessing fairness vis-à-vis past prices, leading to perceptions that firms are gouging. Consumers also attribute differences in competitor prices to profits rather than costs, tend to underestimate firm costs, and are more accepting of costs related to quality (e.g., material costs), leading to perceptions of high profits and price unfairness. Even after controlling for profit levels, consumers are sensitive to how profits are made, with some marketing strategies (e.g., margin versus volume strategies) judged less fair even when they are beyond the firm's control. Together, these findings suggest a conundrum for firms — many legitimate costs of doing business are judged unfair, and prices will also tend to be judged unfair when assessed against costs, competitors, and past prices.

Follow-up work has provided a closer examination of the role of costs in pricing of goods and services. Bolton and Alba (2006) find that consumers judge a price increase more fair when it is 'aligned' with the cost increase (e.g., labor for a service, material costs for a good). For nonalignable costs that do not obviously relate to a specific offering (e.g., overhead such as rent), consumers judge it less fair to raise the price of a good than a service because goods prices are 'stickier' due to the salience of material costs. Pallas *et al.* (2017) focus specifically on the proliferation of surcharges in service pricing and find that consumers are especially sensitive to internal (versus external) surcharges, which (regardless of surcharge benefit and temporal stability) drive blame attributions and in turn unfairness perceptions. Together, these findings suggest that improved consumer understanding of firm costs will not necessarily improve price fairness perceptions.

Further expanding our view of reference transactions, Haws and Bearden (2006) find that consumers are especially sensitive to comparisons to the price paid by another consumer. A higher price was deemed least fair when compared to a lower price paid by another customer (versus a lower price from another seller or time). In contrast, however, price differences in auctions were judged relatively fair because consumers attribute the auction outcomes to themselves rather than the seller. This research has important implications for dynamic pricing as well as new and emerging forms of price-setting that involve buyer participation (e.g., bidding and negotiation mechanisms).

## *Moving beyond a transactional perspective*

In addition to research that has investigated antecedents of reference transactions, another stream of research has expanded the investigation of price fairness to incorporate individual and contextual factors. We illustrate this research by briefly reviewing selected work on firm (e.g., reputation) and consumer (e.g., cultural) characteristics.

**Firm Motive and Reputation**: Consumers infer a negative motive when firms make an excessive profit (e.g., by auctioning off a rare toy), generating price unfairness perceptions — unless the firm explicitly communicates otherwise (e.g., by donating the excess profit to charity). However, the negative effect of motive inference on price fairness is mitigated for firms with good reputation (Campbell 1999). The inference of motive can also be muffled by low intentionality, such as when a price increase is implemented by a machine (versus an employee, Campbell 2007). Therefore, the same prices can be judged as differentially fair depending on how a price increase is implemented and what firms do with the ensuing profit.

**Culture**: Cross-cultural research on price fairness is scant, with a few exceptions. Building on the findings of Haws and Bearden (2006) regarding sensitivity to cross-consumer comparisons, Bolton *et al.* (2010) examined the effects of such comparisons as a function of culture. A set of studies demonstrated that collectivist (e.g., Chinese) consumers were more sensitive to in-group than out-group differences than were individualist (e.g., American) consumers, driven by collectivists' face concerns that evoke shame when paying a higher price than another in-group consumer. More recently, Chen *et al.* (2018) find that collectivist consumers perceive asymmetric pricing as less fair than do individualist consumers. This cultural variation in the endorsement of DE arises because asymmetric pricing is consistent with the exchange norms of individualist consumers but violates the communal norms of collectivist consumers that mandate firm benevolence. (Such norms may also vary within culture: for example, consumers hold more communal-related expectations of medical doctors than financial advisors and are therefore less accepting of asymmetric pricing by the former than the latter.) Norm-based cultural differences in fairness perceptions can be mitigated when firms that practice asymmetric pricing show community concern (e.g., through their CSR efforts), which is consistent with communal norms mandating firm benevolence (i.e., concern for others' welfare without consideration of benefits to oneself). Together, this work casts doubt on the notion of a "community standard of fairness" (Kahneman *et al.* 1986a, 1986b); rather, community standards seem rooted in cultural and relational norms and, as a result, contextually nuanced.

**Power**: Given increasing interest in power in consumer behavior, researchers have asked: how does power affect price fairness perceptions? On the one hand, Jin *et al.* (2014) examine how *consumer power* states affect price fairness perceptions, arguing that other- (self-) comparisons pose a greater threat to the self-importance of high- (low-) power consumers. As a result, their work demonstrates that consumers with high power are more sensitive to paying more than other consumers whereas consumers low in power are more sensitive to paying more than they did in the past. On the other hand, Lu *et al.* (2018) examine how *firm power* affects consumer fairness perceptions for a price increase. When prices increase due to costs, consumers judge it less fair when a higher versus lower power firm raises prices — driven by perceptions of greater controllability and exploitation (cf. Vaidyanathan and Aggarwal 2003). (When prices increase due to demand, consumers judge it equally unfair regardless of firm power because such actions are inherently exploitative.) These findings demonstrate an important boundary condition on DE: the firm's entitlement to a reference profit (which makes it fair for them to raise prices in response to cost increases) holds more for lower than higher power firms. In addition, disclosing costs is not necessarily beneficial unless costs are perceived as uncontrollable, which constrains the previously identified benefits of cost transparency to firms (Carter and Curry 2010, Mohan *et al.* 2020).

## Empirical Demonstrations

As this short review attests, there are many aspects of price fairness that remain unexplored. Figure 1 is intended as a helpful (and deliberately

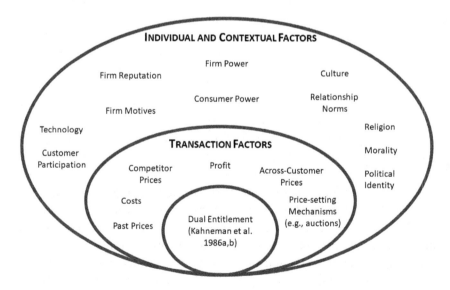

**Figure 1.** Exploring price fairness beyond dual entitlement.

loose) framework for considering gaps in current research, as well as future research directions. The figure encompasses factors arising from the transaction and its immediate context, such as salient price and cost information as well as price-setting mechanisms. The figure also encompasses broader individual and situational factors, including cultural and social norms and firm and marketplace characteristics. We will discuss some of these factors in terms of research we have conducted, as well as potentially interesting future research questions.

To illustrate the usefulness of adopting a broader framework when investigating price perceptions, we begin by reporting two demonstration studies designed to showcase interesting findings pertaining to what we know — and, as importantly, what we do not know — regarding DE and price fairness. Study 1 examines cross-cultural differences, and study 2 examines industry differences in fairness response to asymmetric pricing, united by an underlying explanation based on relationship norms.

# Study 1: Culture and Perspective-Taking

Prior research argues that collectivist consumers are guided by communal norms whereas individualist consumers are guided by exchange norms (Chen *et al.* 2018). The key distinction between communal and exchange relationships lies in the rules or norms that govern the giving and receiving of benefits in the relationship. A communal relationship is characterized by benevolence (or care and concern for others); an exchange relationship is characterized by each party looking after its own self-interest (Aggarwal 2004; Clark and Mills 1979, 1993; Mills and Clark 1982).

According to the principle of dual entitlement, asymmetric pricing is fair: it is fair for a firm to raise its prices when costs increase (because doing so protects the seller's entitlement to a reference profit) and maintain its prices when costs decrease (because doing so does not violate the buyer's entitlement to a reference price). Indeed, according to dual entitlement, each party in a transaction is entitled to its reference terms — but, importantly, the firm has the right to "protect its profits at transactors' expense" (Kahneman *et al.* 1986a, p. 730). From a culture-based norm perspective, dual entitlement therefore seems to align more with exchange norms endorsing the pursuit of self-interest and to violate communal norms mandating concern for others (i.e., firm benevolence).

Hence, collectivist consumers are expected to perceive asymmetric pricing as less fair than do individualist consumers, as demonstrated in Chen *et al.* (2018).

However, if the communal norm and associated focus on firm benevolence drive the cultural differences, shifting consumers' focus away from that concern should dampen the perception that asymmetric pricing violates communal norms, thus enhancing the fairness perceptions among collectivist consumers. In contrast, individualist consumers are guided by exchange norms that do not emphasize concern for others (Clark *et al.* 1998) and should therefore be relatively less affected by judgment focus. Following this logic, we predict that:

> H1: Price fairness perceptions for asymmetric pricing will be lower among collectivist versus individualist consumers when consumer focus is spontaneously or explicitly directed toward the firm's (lack of) concern for others — but should be mitigated when consumer focus is shifted away from this concern.

We test H1 by priming culture and by manipulating the focus of consumers when making price fairness judgments. Doing so not only provides evidence of the underlying psychological process (i.e., the violation of communal norm of concern for others) but also demonstrates how unfairness perceptions due to asymmetric pricing can be mitigated.

**Method**: The study adopted a 2 (Culture: collectivist, individualist) by 3 (Judgment focus: spontaneous, first-person, third-person) between-subjects design. A total of 204 undergraduate business students at a major university in Singapore participated in this study for a cash reward of Sing$5. (Two participants were removed from the data set who took less than five minutes to complete the study, when the average was seventeen minutes.) Culture was primed via picture collages of American or Chinese cultural symbols (e.g., Statue of Liberty versus Great Wall), an established procedure for manipulating individualist/collectivist culture (Hong *et al.* 2000; Chen *et al.* 2005, 2018).

Then in an ostensibly unrelated study, consumer judgment focus was manipulated using a procedure adapted from Galinsky *et al.* (2008). Specifically, participants were shown a picture of an individual making a presentation in front of an audience (see Figure 2). Participants in the spontaneous condition were simply told to focus on thoughts that came to

**Figure 2.** Picture used in manipulation of judgment focus (Study 1).

their mind when they were looking at the picture. In the first-person condition, participants were instead told to "try to imagine what you would feel and think if you were that person." In the third-person condition, participants were instead told to "try to imagine how the person is feeling and what the person is thinking." Prior research shows that asking participants to view the picture as a first-person (third-person) would influence the extent to which the self is more (less) salient (Galinksy *et al.* 2008). In the context of this research, we argue that when the self is salient, participants would focus on how the firm's action affects them and whether the firm shows concern for them. However, when the self is less salient, they would focus less on how the firm's action affects them or whether the firm shows concern for them.

Then in another ostensibly unrelated study, participants were asked to read a newspaper article describing asymmetric pricing in a coffee shop context (see Figure 3).

After reading the article, participants indicated whether they felt the pricing policy was fair on three seven-point scales (anchored by "very unfair/very fair", "not at all just/just" and "unreasonable/reasonable"; Bolton *et al.* 2010). Then, as a measure of the underlying process (i.e., perceived violation of communal norms), participants were asked to indicate the extent to which they felt that the firm's pricing showed a lack of concern for consumers and the extent to which they felt the firm was benefiting at the expense of consumers (each on a seven-point scale with 1 = strongly disagree and 7 = strongly agree). Finally, as a manipulation

## THE
# STRAITS TIMES.

Coffee Shops' Pricing Policy

Singapore - The price of a cup of coffee has risen in Singapore. What used to be $1.20 for a cup of coffee is now priced at $1.40. This price increase happened 6 months ago. Interviews with coffee shop owners at that time revealed that the price increase was in response to an increase in the cost of sugar and coffee beans.

Mr. Lim Teong Lean, 38, who manages the beverage stalls in all the Kopi-Oh outlets said he had to increase prices due to the rising cost.

However, recently, when the prices of coffee beans and sugar decreased, we did not see a parallel adjustment of the price downwards.

Our data show that when the price of coffee beans and sugar increased by 10%, the chain increased its prices by 10%. However, when the price of the ingredients decreased by 10%, the firm still charged the same price for the item.

So the new price is here to stay.

**Figure 3.**   Asymmetric pricing stimuli (Study 1).

check of judgment focus, participants were asked the extent to which they agree with the following statements: "When I was looking at the picture, I thought of how I would feel if I were the one making the presentation" and "When I was looking at the picture, I thought of how the presenter feels", each on seven-point scales with 1 = strongly disagree and 7 = strongly agree). The latter was subtracted from the former to create a measure of relative focus.

## *Results*

**Manipulation check**: Analysis of variance (ANOVA) on the two-item manipulation check measure ($r = -.49$, $p < .001$) revealed a significant effect of judgment focus ($F (2, 196) = 14.10$, $p < .001$); no other effects were significant ($p > .10$). Planned contrasts indicated that the degree to which participants thought about themselves was similarly high in the spontaneous and first-person conditions ($M_{\text{spontaneous}} = 1.03$, $M_{\text{first-person}} = .59$, $p = .39$), but was lower in the third-person condition ($M_{\text{spontaneous}} = 1.03$

versus $M_{\text{third-person}} = -.70$, $p < .001$; $M_{\text{first-person}} = .60$ versus $M_{\text{third-person}} = -.70$, $p < .001$). Therefore, the judgment focus manipulation was successful.

**Fairness**: Our analyses focus on two key interaction contrasts on fairness (coefficient $\alpha = .94$): First, we compared reactions in the spontaneous condition to that of the first-person condition. As expected, the interaction contrast was non-significant ($F < 1$), indicating that consumers spontaneously adopt a first-person focus when forming price fairness perceptions. Second, we compared reactions in the third-person condition against the combined spontaneous and first-person conditions. As expected, ANOVA reveals a significant effect of culture ($M_{\text{Collectivist}} = 3.82$ versus $M_{\text{Individualist}} = 4.32$, $F(1, 196) = 6.62$, $p < .01$), qualified by a marginally significant interaction contrast with third-person (versus first-person and spontaneous focus) conditions ($F(1, 196) = 3.49$, $p = .06$). To understand the nature of this interaction contrast, we conducted simple effects follow-up tests. In the first-person conditions (either spontaneous or manipulated), asymmetric pricing actions were perceived as less fair by collectivist versus individualist consumers ($M_{\text{Collectivist\_First}} = 3.67$ versus $M_{\text{Individualist\_First}} = 4.36$, $F(1, 196) = 8.80$, $p < .01$). In contrast, in the third-person focus condition, this difference was mitigated ($M_{\text{Collectivist\_Third}} = 4.35$ versus $M_{\text{Individualist\_Third}} = 4.25$, $F < 1$). Looked at another way, shifting away from a first-person focus enhanced fairness perceptions of asymmetric pricing among collectivist consumers ($M_{\text{Collectivist\_First}} = 3.67$ versus $M_{\text{Collectivist\_Third}} = 4.35$, $F(1, 196) = 4.38$, $p < .01$), but not among individualist consumers ($M_{\text{Individualist\_First}} = 4.36$ versus $M_{\text{Individualist\_Third}} = 4.25$, $F(1, 196) = .16$, $p > .10$). This pattern of results, illustrated in Figure 4, supports H1.

**Underlying Psychological Process**: ANOVA of the two-item measure of the firm's lack of concern for consumers ($r = .81$, $p < .01$) revealed a similar pattern of results: a significant effect of culture ($M_{\text{Collectivist}} = 4.93$ versus $M_{\text{Individualist}} = 4.36$, $F(1, 196) = 6.37$, $p < .01$), qualified by an interaction contrast (of third-person versus first-person and spontaneous conditions) ($F(1, 196) = 5.21$, $p < .05$), with a non-significant interaction contrast of culture and first-person versus spontaneous conditions ($F < 1$). Turning to the focal interaction, planned contrasts revealed that, in the first-person conditions (either spontaneous or manipulated), collectivist participants judged the firm to be more lacking in concern for consumers than did individualist participants ($M_{\text{Collectivist\_First}} = 5.08$ versus $M_{\text{Individualist\_First}} = 4.24$, $F(1, 196) = 10.04$, $p < .01$). However, in the third-person condition, this difference was mitigated ($M_{\text{Collectivist\_Third}} = 4.43$ versus $M_{\text{Individualist\_Third}} = 4.70$, $F(1, 196) = .43$, $p > .10$).

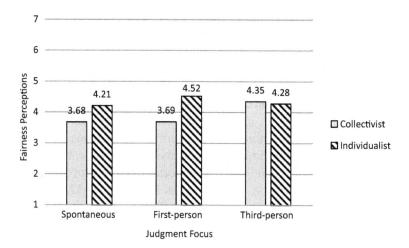

**Figure 4.**    Fairness of asymmetric pricing as a function of culture and judgment focus.

To test for mediation, we used the bootstrapping method (Hayes 2012, model 8) and treated culture as the independent variable, fairness as the dependent variable, the perception of firm's lack of concern for consumers as the mediator, and third-person focus as the moderator. The analysis revealed that the conditional indirect effect through the mediator was significant under first-person focus ($a*b = -.22$, 95% CI $= -.38 \sim -.09$) but not under third-person focus ($a*b = .04$, 95% CI $= -.17 \sim .25$). Therefore, collectivist (versus individualist) consumers are more likely to perceive a lack of firm's concern for consumers under first-person focus (either spontaneous or manipulated), which in turn dampens their fairness perceptions of asymmetric pricing.

**Discussion**: The findings support H1. Collectivist consumers judge asymmetric pricing in accordance with dual entitlement as less fair than do individualist consumers, replicating Chen *et al.* (2018). We additionally find, however, that this difference only arises when consumers adopt a first-person focus (either spontaneously or through priming), which highlights the firm's lack of concern for consumers under the communal norm of collectivists (but not under the exchange norms of individualists). When consumer focus shifts away from the firm's concern for them, collectivists' (but not individualists') fairness perceptions are enhanced, thus mitigating the cultural difference.

These findings provide support for (i) cultural differences in fairness perceptions and endorsement of DE; and (ii) the underlying psychological process based on communal norms mandating concern for others. More broadly, these findings also demonstrate (iii) the egocentric nature of price fairness perceptions (which spontaneously favor the self over others); and (iv) the general malleability of fairness perceptions, in this case influenced by salient cultural norms and perspective-taking. Given these findings, future research might fruitfully expand upon it by further investigating the impact of cultural variables and social norms on consumer price fairness perceptions, as well as the underlying egocentrism of fairness perceptions and its malleability to perspective-taking in various pricing contexts.

# Study 2: Industry Differences Arising from Relationship Norms

Whereas study 1 demonstrates fairness differences in asymmetric pricing that vary by culture, the objective of study 2 is to explore price fairness differences that can arise at the industrial rather than cultural level. That is, we exploit natural variation across industry in communal versus exchange norms to test our theorizing.

First, we build upon H1 by proposing that buyer–seller relationship norms can vary by industry and reflect either communal norms mandating care and concern for others or exchange norms reflecting the pursuit of self-interest. Importantly, industry norms are expected to override broader cultural or community norms because they are more specific to the situation at hand (Landesman 1995; Raz 1975). In turn, we expect fairness perceptions for asymmetric pricing to vary by industry in accordance with such industry-specific relationship norms. Specifically, we predict that the consumer will perceive asymmetric pricing to be less fair in buyer–seller relationships guided by communal versus exchange norms, driven by consumer perceptions that the firm lacks concern for others.

Second, we seek to provide further evidence for the role of concern for others by manipulating the underlying process (Spencer *et al.* 2005). Specifically, we assess whether justifications of asymmetric pricing that are consumer-oriented mitigate unfairness perceptions. Our theorizing argues that consumers perceive asymmetric pricing as less fair under communal norms because consumers perceive that the firm lacks concern for others. If so, then providing a justification for asymmetric pricing that is consumer-oriented should mitigate unfairness perceptions driven by this concern. Formally:

> H2: Price fairness perceptions for asymmetric pricing will be lower in buyer–seller relationships guided by communal versus exchange norms, driven by perceptions of the firm's (lack of) concern for others — but should be mitigated when a consumer-oriented justification for asymmetric pricing is salient.

## *Pilot*

To assess H2, we first conducted a pilot study to assess the extent to which buyer–seller relationship norms vary by industry. Specifically, we conducted a pretest with 55 undergraduate business students enrolled in introductory marketing classes at a major U.S. university. First, we explained the two types of relationships to them, as follows:

> Communal relationships refer to relationships in which parties provide benefits to each other because they are concerned for the welfare of each other, even when they do not receive a commensurate return. Exchange relationships refer to relationships in which parties provide benefits on a quid pro quo basis, such as the exchange of money for goods/services.

Participants were then asked "Which of the two types of relationships would be more appropriate to guide the behaviors of the following service/product providers?" and provided ratings for ten different organizations on seven-point scales (1: Communal is more appropriate; 4: Both are equally appropriate; 7: Exchange is more appropriate). The ten organizations were: software company (5.78), retailer (5.75), utility company (5.31), financial advisor (4.57), lawyer (4.38), realtor (4.26), insurance agent (4.20), pharmaceutical company (3.96), medical doctor (3.37), and university (3.27), which appeared in a random order for evaluation (In parentheses are the average rating for each organization). The ratings for lawyer ($p = .075$), realtor ($p = .29$), insurance agent ($p = .43$), and pharmaceutical company ($p = .89$) did not differ from the midpoint of the scale, while the other ratings did ($p < .05$ or better). In addition, participants were given a description of asymmetric pricing and asked whether it showed that a company was concerned for its bottom line rather than its customers (1 = its bottom line; 4 = Both; 7 = its customers). We obtained evidence consistent with our basic premise that asymmetric pricing reflects the seller's pursuit of self-interest ($1.98 < 4$, $p < .001$).

A week later, these participants were asked to judge the fairness of asymmetry pricing for two organizations that lie on opposing ends of the exchange–communal continuum based on the pretest, i.e., computer software companies and medical doctors. Asymmetric pricing was described as follows: "One pricing strategy that firms sometimes use is to raise prices when costs increase but maintain prices when costs decrease. For example, when costs of a company increase, the company passes on the cost increase to its customers by increasing the prices of its products or services. But when costs decrease, the company maintains the prices of its products or services." Analysis of the fairness results indicate that asymmetric pricing was perceived to be fairer when it was practiced by a computer software company than when it was practiced by a medical doctor ($4.00 > 2.87$, $p < .001$, where 1 = very unfair; 4 = neither unfair nor fair; 7 = very fair), and communal norms were perceived as being more appropriate for a medical doctor than for a computer software company ($2.69 < 5.96$, $p < .0001$, where 1 = communal is more appropriate; 4 = both are equally appropriate; 7 = exchange is more appropriate). In addition, the norm measure predicted fairness perceptions ($p < .005$), consistent with H2.

Given that industry-specific operationalizations may differ in other ways beyond relationship norms, our main studies provide converging evidence by (i) incorporating an interaction with consumer-oriented justification to help rule out competing explanations (study 2A); and (ii) utilizing a direct manipulation of relationship norms while holding industry constant (study 2B).

## Study 2A method

**Participants and Design**: Participants were drawn from a convenience sample of Chinese consumers in a large city in the People's Republic of China who volunteered to participate. Participants skewed young (91% between the ages of 18 and 34) and female (73%) and had desirable heterogeneity in education (high-school or less 31%, some university or university graduate 56%, and some or graduate-level university 13%). The design was a 2 (relationship norm: communal versus exchange) × 2 (justification: none versus consumer-oriented) between-subjects design. A total of 103 participants completed the study.

Medical doctor versus financial advisor were the industry-specific operationalizations of communal versus exchange norms in buyer–seller relationships, respectively. Participants were given a description of asymmetric pricing as follows:

> Imagine the following situation. You have moved to a new location and found a [medical doctor for personal healthcare/financial advisor for personal financial matters.] The [medical doctor/financial advisor] has an independent practice. You are pleased with the [doctor's/advisor's] care. As you visit the [doctor/advisor] one day, you discover how the [medical doctor/financial advisor] sets his prices. When costs (e.g., rent, overhead) increase, the [medical doctor/financial advisor] raises his prices. When costs decrease, prices remain the same. For example, the price of a consulting fee for seeing the [medical doctor/financial advisor] would rise by 10% when costs increase 10%. However, if costs declined by 10%, the consulting fee would remain the same.

In the consumer-oriented justification condition, participants were told "The [doctor/financial advisor] uses this money to offset fees and help indigent [patients/clients]." Other participants were not provided with a justification.

Participants were then asked "How fair do you think the [medical doctor's/financial advisor's] pricing policy is?" and responded on three seven-point scales (with endpoints "very unfair/very fair", "not at all just/just", and "unreasonable/reasonable"). Participants also indicated their likelihood to "go to this financial advisor/medical doctor" and "to recommend this financial advisor/medical doctor to others" on a 0–100% scale (with endpoints "very unlikely/very likely").

To assess the firm's concern for others, participants also indicated their agreement that "the financial doctor/medical advisor… is simply following the rules of business" and "… shows a lack of concern for clients/patients" on two seven-point scales (with endpoints "strongly disagree/strongly agree"). A difference score was calculated by subtracting the first item from the second item; higher scores reflect greater concern for others. Participants also rated net profit margin on a seven-point scale (with endpoints "very low/very high").

As a manipulation check of communal/exchange norms, participants were also asked to "Consider in general the relationship between a medical doctor/financial advisor and his patients/clients. To what extent do you feel that a medical doctor/financial advisor should... put your needs/ interests first", "... care about you", "... give service to get business", and "... act out of self-interest" on four five-point scales (with endpoints "not at all/a great deal"). The first two items reflect communal norms, the latter two items reflect exchange norms; the difference was calculated and used as an index representing communal (relative to exchange) relationship norms. Finally, participants responded to various background questions, including gender, age, and education.

## Results

**Manipulation checks**: ANOVA of the communal/exchange index indicates that medical doctors are perceived as more communal than financial advisors ($M_{\text{medical doctor}} = 1.11$ (1.12) versus $M_{\text{financial advisor}} = 0.67$ (0.95); $F(1, 98) = 4.20$, $p < .05$), supporting the intended manipulation of communal versus exchange norms.

**Fairness Perceptions**: ANOVA of the fairness index (coefficient alpha = 0.89) as a function of norm and justification reveals a significant interaction ($F(1, 98) = 7.23$, $p < .01$); the main effects are not significant ($F$'s < 1). Planned contrasts reveal that fairness perceptions were lower under communal versus exchange norms (i.e., medical doctor versus financial advisor) when no justification was given ($M_{\text{Communal\_No Justification}} = 4.01$ versus $M_{\text{Exchange\_No Justification}} = 4.58$; $F(1, 97) = 3.12$, $p = .08$) but were higher for communal versus exchange norms when a consumer-oriented justification was given ($M_{\text{Communal\_Justification}} = 4.73$ versus $M_{\text{Exchange\_Justification}} = 3.73$; $F(1, 97) = 7.67$, $p < .01$). Looked at another way, a consumer-oriented justification increased fairness perceptions for asymmetric pricing under communal relationship norms ($M_{\text{Communal\_No justification}} = 4.01$ versus $M_{\text{Communal\_Justification}} = 4.73$; $F(1, 97) = 5.02$, $p < .05$) but decreased fairness perceptions under exchange relationship norms ($M_{\text{Exchange\_No justification}} = 4.58$ versus $M_{\text{Exchange\_Justification}} = 3.73$; $F(1, 97) = 5.25$, $p < .05$) (because it violates the exchange norm mandating pursuit of self-interest). The pattern of means, illustrated in Figure 5, supports H2.

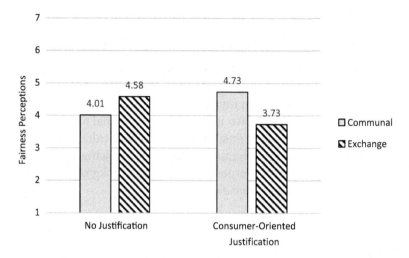

**Figure 5.**  Fairness of asymmetric pricing as a function of norm and justification (Study 2A).

**Table 1.**    Fairness, behavioral intentions, and consumer concern (Study 2A).

| Relationship norm | Justification | $n$ | Fairness perceptions | Behavioral intentions | Consumer concern |
|---|---|---|---|---|---|
| Exchange | None | 23 | 4.58 (1.36) | 47.6 (22.4) | 0.48 (1.26) |
| Exchange | Consumer-oriented | 22 | 3.73 (1.66) | 40.5 (15.8) | 0.20 (1.24) |
| Communal | None | 27 | 4.01 (1.46) | 48.5 (22.5) | 0.46 (1.12) |
| Communal | Consumer-oriented | 30 | 4.73 (1.40) | 53.5 (25.3) | 0.98 (0.99) |

**Behavioral Intentions**: A similar ANOVA of the likelihood index ($\lambda = .68$, $p < .01$) also reveals a two-way interaction ($F$ (1, 97) = 3.10, $p < .10$), after controlling for profit perceptions ($F$ (1, 97) = 4.03, $p < .05$). Under a consumer-oriented justification, intentions were higher for communal versus exchange relationships ($F$ (1, 97) = 5.54, $p = .02$) but otherwise did not differ ($F < 1$). See Table 1 for descriptive statistics.

**Underlying Psychological Process**: ANOVA of the two-item measure of the firm's lack of concern for consumers revealed a similar two-way interaction of communal/exchange relationship and justification ($F$ (1, 97) = 3.14, $p$ = .08). Under communal relationship norms, providing a justification enhanced perceptions of the firm's concern for consumers (i.e., medical doctor; $M_{\text{no justification}}$ = 0.46 versus $M_{\text{justification}}$ = 0.98; $F$ (1, 97) = 3.05, $p$ = .08); under exchange relationship norms, providing a justification had no effect (i.e., financial advisor; $M_{\text{no justification}}$ = 0.48 versus $M_{\text{justification}}$ = 0.20; $F$ < 1).

To test for mediation, we used the bootstrapping method (Hayes 2012, model 8) and treated justification as the independent variable (i.e., medical doctor versus financial advisor), fairness as the dependent variable, perceptions of the firm's concern for consumers as the mediator, and relationship norm as the moderator. The analysis revealed that the conditional indirect effect through the mediator was significant for a communal relationship (i.e. medical doctor; $a^*b$ = 4.31, 95% CI = .515 ~ 10.29) but not an exchange relationship (i.e., financial advisor; $a^*b$ = − 702, 95% CI = −6.73 ~ 3.93). That is, a consumer-oriented justification mitigates unfairness driven by perceptions that in a communal (but not exchange) relationship a firm lacks concern for consumers.

Together, these results support H2. To strengthen causality and provide evidence of robustness, we conducted a follow-up study that directly manipulated specific norms governing the buyer–seller relationship while holding industry constant.

## Study 2B method

**Participants and Design**: Participants were college students at a major U.S. university who voluntarily participated for extra credit in a business class. The design was a 2 (relationship norm: communal versus exchange) × 2 (justification: consumer-versus business-oriented) between-subjects design. A total of 181 participants completed the study.

Participants were asked to read a short scenario describing a pharmaceutical company (which did not favor either communal or exchange norms based on the aforementioned pilot) and its pricing practices. To manipulate relationship norms, participants in the exchange condition read: "You believe pharmaceutical companies are like any other business and their primary goal should be to provide good value for money to customers". Participants in the communal condition read: "You believe pharmaceutical companies are *not* like other businesses and their primary goal should be to look out for the welfare of their customers". All participants then read a description of asymmetric pricing as follows:

The pharmaceutical company is determining the prices for its products and services. When costs (e.g., rent, overhead) increase, the pharmaceutical company passes on those costs to customers by increasing its prices. When costs decrease, the pharmaceutical company maintains prices.

Participants then read either a consumer-oriented or business-oriented justification for the practice of asymmetric pricing. In the consumer-oriented condition, participants read that: "The company invests that money in research and development of new drugs that benefit its customers". In the business-oriented condition, participants read that "The company invests that money in streamlining its operations to improve efficiency". (The business-oriented justification helps rule out the possibility that any justification enhances fairness perceptions.)

Participants were then asked "How fair do you think the pharmaceutical company's pricing policy is?" and responded on three seven-point scales (with endpoints "very unfair/very fair", "not at all just/just", and "unreasonable/reasonable"). As a manipulation check for relationship norms, participants were asked to characterize the kind of relationship that they expected the company to have with its customers on two seven-point scales (with end points "Close/Distant" and "Like a friend/Like a business partner"). As a manipulation check for justification, participants responded to two items on seven-point scales, "This company is _____ in investing the additional profits it makes" (with endpoints "customer oriented/business oriented") and "This company has its own business interests in mind when investing the additional profits it makes" (with endpoints "strongly disagree/strongly agree").

## *Results*

**Manipulation checks**: ANOVA of the index for relationship norms ($r = .68$, $p < .001$) revealed greater endorsement of an exchange relationship in the exchange versus communal conditions ($M_{exchange} = 3.93$ (1.42) versus $M_{communal} = 3.51$ (1.45), $F$ (1, 170) = 4.07, $p < .05$). ANOVA of the justification index ($r = .52$, $p < .001$) revealed greater endorsement of a business-(versus consumer-oriented) justification in the business- versus consumer-oriented conditions ($M_{\text{business-oriented}}$ = 5.03 (1.00) versus $M_{\text{consumer-oriented}}$ = 4.33 (1.45); $F$ (1, 170) = 13.03, $p < .01$). No other effects were significant ($p$'s > .10). These results indicate that the manipulations succeeded as intended.

**Fairness Perceptions**: As expected, ANOVA of the fairness index (coefficient $\alpha$ = .94) revealed a two-way interaction of relationship norms and justification ($F$ (1, 173) = 4.56, $p < .05$). No other effects were significant ($p$'s > .10). Follow-up planned contrasts revealed that a consumer- (versus business-) oriented justification enhanced fairness perceptions of asymmetric pricing under communal norms ($M_{\text{communal\_consumer}}$ = 4.81 (1.35) versus $M_{\text{communal\_business}}$ = 4.17 (1.54), $F$ (1, 173) = 4.49, $p < .05$) but not under exchange norms ($M_{\text{exchange\_consumer}}$ = 4.53 (1.47) versus $M_{\text{exchange\_business}}$ = 4.77 (1.12), $F$ (1, 173) = .74, $p > .10$) (Figure 6). Looked at another way, asymmetric pricing was perceived as less fair under communal versus exchange norms when a business-oriented justification was provided ($M_{\text{communal\_business}}$ = 4.17 versus $M_{\text{exchange\_business}}$ = 4.77, $F$ (1, 173) = 4.08, $p < .05$) — consistent with concerns for consumer welfare under communal norms, but the difference disappeared when a consumer-oriented justification was provided ($M_{\text{communal\_consumer}}$ = 4.81 versus $M_{\text{exchange\_consumer}}$ = 4.53, $p > .10$).

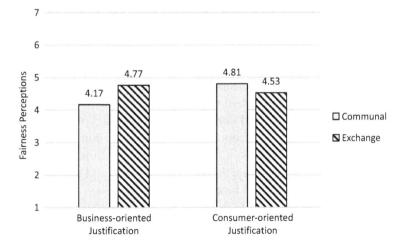

**Figure 6.** Fairness of asymmetric pricing as a function of norm and justification (Study 2B).

**Discussion**: The findings support H2. Relationship norms vary across industry but can also be manipulated within the same industry. Differences in relationship norms in turn predict consumer response to asymmetric pricing in buyer–seller relationships, driven by perceptions of the firm's lack of concern for consumers under the communal norm. Moreover, a consumer-oriented justification for asymmetric pricing mitigates the norm-based difference and enhances fairness perceptions of asymmetric pricing.

These findings provide support for (i) norm-based differences in fairness perceptions and endorsement of DE; and (ii) the underlying psychological process based on communal norms mandating concern for others. More broadly, these findings also demonstrate (iii) the general malleability of fairness perceptions, in this case influenced by salient industry relationship norms or consumers' top-of-mind norm expectations and justifications for pricing practice; and (iv) pragmatic implications for marketers inasmuch as when communal relationship norms are violated, fairness perceptions for asymmetric pricing suffer — but marketers can mitigate unfairness perceptions by providing a justification based on concern for customers. Given these findings, future research might fruitfully expand upon it by further investigating the impact of various industry norms on consumer price fairness perceptions, including how such norms develop within an industry and change across consumers and over time, and the degree to which fairness perceptions are malleable to the benefit or detriment of the firm in various pricing contexts.

## Future Research

As the empirical work demonstrates, price fairness perceptions are not monolithic and vary in important ways based on transactional (e.g., cost), individual (e.g., culture), and contextual (e.g., industry norm, justification) factors. Research is encouraged to build upon our current understanding of price fairness to shed light on important pricing phenomena — and we illustrate this by discussing several areas where we believe future research would be especially fruitful.

**Cultural/Social:** We remain particularly interested in cross-cultural research on price fairness, given the view of dual entitlement as "community standards of fairness" (Kahenman *et al.* 1986a, p. 729). Prior research has investigated cultural differences in individual/collectivism and their implications for dynamic pricing (Bolton *et al.* 2010) and asymmetric pricing (Chen *et al.* 2018) — and there is ample opportunity for future research, expanding the consideration of pricing contexts as well as important cultural/social factors. For example, power distance belief, i.e., the tendency to accept and expect inequalities in society (Hofstede 1984, 2001), might be expected to influence how consumers respond to asymmetric pricing, dynamic pricing, pay-what-you-will pricing, and other firm price behaviors that differentially affect consumers. Likewise, does long-term orientation affect how consumers respond to price changes over time, such as the tendency to under-estimate inflation and therefore under-save for future expenditures (Bolton *et al.* 2003)?

**Religion and Morality**: From a cultural standpoint moving beyond Hofstede's dimensions, religion may also be a useful lens with which to consider price fairness perceptions. Religion is influential in the marketplace (e.g., via consumer religiosity, firm positioning on religious values, and religious holidays) and, indeed, religious beliefs proscribe certain pricing practices (e.g., Islam and usury). How might religion's emphasis on pro-social values (e.g., Schumann *et al.* 2014; Hyodo and Bolton 2021) alter fairness perceptions for (non-proscribed) pricing practices, for example, via waste aversion (Bolton and Alba 2006) or the religious devaluation of money (Watson *et al.* 2004)? Likewise, research on price fairness might also benefit from considering the foundations of moral reasoning (Haidt and Graham 2007). These foundations — including, for example, care/harm, fairness, and loyalty/betrayal — may vary across consumers (e.g., by culture, political ideology) and alter fairness perceptions of pricing phenomena (e.g., group buying, most-favored-nation pricing).

**The Role of Profit**: Research on price fairness would be helped by an improved understanding of consumers' beliefs and attitudes toward profit. For example, price fairness might be usefully investigated within the context of the ultimatum game, arguably the most widely used game in the economics literature (Guth *et al.* 1982). In a nutshell, the game has a similar structure as the interaction between a retailer and consumers: The retailer as the proposer posts a price that in effect splits the "pie" into its profit and consumer surplus, and consumers as the responder decide whether to take the price or not. Although past research has argued for the role of fairness in the ultimatum game

(Nowak *et al.* 2000), variations across countries (Osterbeek *et al.* 2004) have not been successfully explained. However, as the research in the current paper attests, relationship norms and acceptance of social hierarchy vary across culture, alter fairness perceptions, and could, in turn, explain cross-country differences in allocation outcomes in the ultimatum game.

More broadly, the question of consumer anti-profit beliefs (Bhattacharjee *et al.* 2017) would also be useful to investigate given the relationship between profit and price fairness and its implications for the marketplace. For example, Lee *et al.* (2017) find that consumer perceptions of greed undermine acceptance of for-profit social ventures (i.e., organizations that seek to advance a social purpose while making a profit) — and extending this work to new and emerging non-traditional business models would be interesting.

**Innovation**: Pricing strategies and tactics continue to innovate in the marketplace and raise questions about consumer fairness perceptions for these practices. For example, how do fairness considerations affect pay-what-you-will pricing, which gives consumers control over prices? Interestingly, Lee *et al.* (2018) find that consumers take advantage of pricing opportunities by paying less than the suggested price — but concerns for fairness to the seller and prestige sensitivity with respect to other consumers will lead to higher prices.

Also of growing interest to marketing is the role of consumer participation in design and production of products as a source of innovation for firms. Whereas prior research finds higher willingness-to-pay for participation-based products (e.g., the IKEA effect; Mochon *et al.* 2012; Norton *et al.* 2012), recent work suggests that fairness constrains such pricing due to consumer consideration of participation costs like time and effort (Stadler Blank and Bolton 2019). Other innovations in pricing (e.g., digital price tags, group-buying, crowd-funded pricing) also raise interesting research questions related to pricing and fairness that merit investigation as the marketplace continues to innovate and evolve.

**Technology**: Beyond pricing innovation, the broader role of technology in the marketplace also raises interesting research questions related to fairness. To illustrate: The development of high-technology has increasingly instilled (perceived) intentionality into what were traditionally considered non-human entities. While anthropomorphism has been studied in the marketing context (e.g., Aggarwal and McGill 2012) and with respect to fairness (Kwak *et al.* 2015), how fairness varies as a function of the degree of intentionality affiliated with technologies such as artificial intelligence and adaptation of social norms is another interesting avenue for future research. For example, does a price change implemented by a computer algorithm with or without a human interface alter motive inferences and, in turn, price fairness? How does reciprocity and benevolence operate in human–AI interactions and affect fairness perceptions?

In closing, we suggest that adopting a fairness lens can shed light on "marketplace metacognition" (i.e., how consumers think the marketplace does and should work; Wright 2002), with important implications for consumers, firms, and society. We are excited to learn more about consumers' fundamental understanding of the marketplace through asking, and investigating, research questions pertaining to price fairness.

# References

Aggarwal, P. (2004), Do the ones we love sometimes hurt us the most: The role of relationship norms on consumers' perception of fairness and brand evaluations, *Advances in Consumer Research*, 31(1), 430.

Aggarwal, P. and A. L. McGill (2012), When brands seem human, do humans act like brands? Automatic behavioral priming effects of brand anthropomorphism, *Journal of Consumer Research*, 39(2), 307–323.

Bhattacharjee, A., J. Dana, and J. Baron (2017), Anti-profit beliefs: How people neglect the societal benefits of profit, *Journal of Personality and Social Psychology*, 113(5), 671–696.

Bolton, L., H. T. Keh, and J. Alba (2010), How do price fairness perceptions differ across culture? *Journal of Marketing Research*, 47(3), 564–576.

Bolton, L., L. Warlop, and J. W. Alba (2003), Consumer perceptions of price (Un) fairness, *Journal of Consumer Research*, 29(4), 474–491.

Campbell, M. (1999), Perceptions of price unfairness: Antecedents and consequences, *Journal of Marketing Research*, 36(2), 187–199.

Campbell, M. (2007), Says who?! How the source of price information and affect influence perceived price (Un)fairness, *Journal of Marketing Research*, 44(2), 261–271.

Carter, R. E. and D. J. Curry (2010), Transparent pricing: Theory, tests, and implications for marketing practice, *Journal of the Academy of Marketing Science*, 38(6), 759–774.

Chen, H. (Allan) and H. Sun (2018), Mental accounting for percentages revisited: The interplay of a computational error and constituent outcome categorization, *Journal of Marketing Behavior*, (forthcoming).

Chen, H., L. E. Bolton, S. Ng, D. Lee, and D. Wang (2018), Culture, relationship norms, and dual entitlement, *Journal of Consumer Research*, 45(June), 1–20.

Clark, M. and J. Mills (1979), Interpersonal attraction in exchange and communal relationships, *Journal of Personality and Social Psychology*, 37, 12–24.

Clark, M. and J. Mills (1993), The difference between communal and exchange relationships: What it is and is not, *Personality and Social Psychology Bulletin*, 19(December), 684–691.

Clark, M., P. Dubash, and J. Mills (1998), Interest in another's consideration of one's needs in communal and exchange relationships, *Journal of Experimental Social Psychology*, 34, 246–64.

Dickson, P. D. and R. Kalapurakal (1994), The use and perceived price fairness of price-setting rules in the bulk electricity market, *Journal of Economic Psychology*, 15, 427–448.

Galinksy, A. D., C. S. Wang and G. Ku (2008), Perspective-takers behave more stereotypically, *Journal of Personality and Social Psychology*, 95(2), 404–419.

Gorman, R. and J. Kehr (1992), Fairness as a constraint on profit seeking: Comment, *American Economic Review*, 82(1), 355–358.

Guth, W., R. Schmittberger, and B. Schwarze (1982), An experimental analysis of ultimatum bargaining, *Journal of Economic Behavior & Organization*, 3(4), 367–388.

Haidt, J. and J. Graham (2007), When morality opposes justice: Conservatives have moral intuitions that liberals may not recognize, *Social Justice Research*, 20(1), 98–116.

Haws, K. and W. Bearden (2006), Dynamic pricing and consumer fairness perceptions, *Journal of Consumer Research*, 33(Dec), 304–311.

Hayes, A. (2012), PROCESS: A versatile computational tool for observed variable mediation, moderation, and conditional process modeling, http://www.afhayes.com/public/process2012.pdf.

Hong, Y.-Y., M. Morris, C.-Y. Chiu, and V. Benet-Martinez (2000), Multicultural minds: A dynamic constructivist approach to culture and cognition, *American Psychologist*, 55(7), 709–720.

Hyodo, J. and Bolton, L. E. (2021), How does religion affect consumer response to failure and recovery by firms?, *Journal of Consumer Research*, 47(5), 807–828.

Jin, L., Y. He, and Y. Zhang (2014), How power states influence consumers' perceptions of price unfairness, *Journal of Consumer Research*, 40(February), 818–833.

Kahneman, D., J. L. Knetsch, and R. Thaler (1986a), Fairness as a constraint on profit seeking: Entitlements in the market, *American Economic Review*, 76(4), 728–741.

Kahneman, D., J. L. Knetsch, and R. Thaler (1986b), Fairness and the assumptions of economics, *Journal of Business*, 59(4), S285–S300.

Kalapurakal, R., P. Dickson and J. Urbany (1991), Perceived price fairness and dual entitlement, *Advances in Consumer Research*, 18(1), 788–793.

Kwak, H., M. Puzakova, and J. F. Rocereto (2015), Better not smile at the price: The differential role of brand anthropomorphization on perceived price fairness, *Journal of Marketing*, 79(4), 56–76.

Landesman, C. (1995), Voluntary provision of public goods, Ph.D. Dissertation, Princeton University, Princeton, NJ.

Lee, S., H. Baumgartner, and R. Pieters (2018), Why don't you pay as little as possible? Constraints on consumers' self-interest seeking in participative pricing, Working paper.

Lee, S., L. E. Bolton, and K. P. Winterich (2017), To profit or not to profit? The role of greed perceptions in consumer support for social ventures, *Journal of Consumer Research*, 44(Dec), 853–876.

Lu, Z., H. (Allan) Chen, L. E. Bolton, and S. Ng (2018), The price of power: How does firm power affect consumer response to price increases? Working paper.

Mills, J. and M. Clark (1982), Exchange and communal relationships, in *Review of Personality and Social Psychology*, Vol. 3, L. Wheeler, ed., Beverly Hills, CA: Sage, 121–44.

Mochon, D., M. I. Norton, and D. Ariely (2012), Bolstering and restoring feelings of competence via the IKEA effect, *International Journal of Research in Marketing*, 29(4), 363–369.

Mohan, B., Buell, R. W., and John, L. K. (2020), Lifting the veil: The benefits of cost transparency, *Marketing Science*, 39(6), 1105–1121.

Monroe, K. B. (1971), Measuring price thresholds by psychophysics and latitudes of acceptance, *Journal of Marketing Research*, 8 (November), 460–464.

Norton, M. I., D. Mochon, and D. Ariely (2012), The IKEA effect: When labor leads to love, *Journal of Consumer Psychology*, 22(3), 453–460.

Nowak, M., K. Page, and K. Sigmund (2000), Fairness versus reason in the ultimatum game, *Science*, 289 (5485), 1773–1775.

Oliver, R. L. and J. E. Swan (1989), Equity and disconfirmation perceptions as influences on merchant and product satisfaction, *Journal of Consumer Research*, 372–383.

Osterbeek, H., R. Sloof, and G. van de Kuilen (2004), Cultural differences in ultimatum game experiments: Evidence from a meta-analysis, *Experimental Economics*, 7(2), 171–188.

Pallas, F., L. E. Bolton, and L. Lobschat (2018), Shifting the blame: How surcharge pricing influences blame attributions for a service price increase, *Journal of Service Research*, 21(3), 302–318.

Raz, J. (1975), Reasons for action, decisions and norms, *Mind*, 84(336), 481–499.

Schumann, K., I. McGregor, K. A. Nash, and M. Ross (2014), Religious magnanimity: Reminding people of their religious belief system reduces hostility after threat, *Journal of Personality and Social Psychology*, 107(3), 432–453.

Sinha, I. and R. Batra (1999), The effect of consumer price consciousness on private label purchase, *International Journal of Research in Marketing*, 16(3), 237–251.

Spencer, S., M. Zanna, and G. Fong (2005), Establishing a causal chain: Why experiments are often more effective than mediational analyses in examining psychological processes, *Journal of Personality and Social Psychology*, 89(6), 845–851.

Stadler Blank, A. and L. E. Bolton (2019), Putting a price on user innovation: How consumer participation can decrease perceived price fairness, *Journal of the Association for Consumer Research*, 4(3), 256–268.

Thaler, R. (1985), Mental accounting and consumer choice, *Marketing Science*, 4(3), 199–214.

Urbany, J., T. Madden and P. Dickson (1989), All's not fair in pricing: An initial look at the dual entitlement principle, *Marketing Letters*, 1(1), 17–25.

Vaidyanathan, R. and P. Aggarwal (2003), Who is the fairest of them all? An attributional approach to price fairness perceptions, *Journal of Business Research*, 56(6), 453–463.

Watson, P. J., N. D. Jones, and R. J. Morris (2004), Religious orientation and attitudes toward money: Relationships with narcissism and the influence of gender, *Mental Health, Religion & Culture*, 7(4), 277–288.

Wright, P. (2002), Marketplace metacognition and social intelligence, *Journal of Consumer Research*, 28(March), 677–682.

Xia, L., K. Monroe, and J. Cox (2004), The price is unfair! A conceptual framework of price fairness perceptions, *Journal of Marketing*, 68(4), 1–15.

# Chapter 4

# Communicating Price Changes and Price Differences*

### Kent B. Monroe

Price change messages are an important aspect of marketing, whether announcing a price increase or communicating a price discount. Major forms of price promotions include money-off or percentage-off deals, buy X and receive Y free or at a reduced price (i.e., buy one, get one free (BOGO)), bonus packs, free samples, coupons, refunds, and rebates. Price promotions are an important marketing tactic because they are an acceptable method of reducing prices. Price promotions are designed to achieve specific objectives in a limited period of time in a target market directed at customers, consumers, or the trade.

One objective of a price promotion is to enhance unit sales of a product or, if used to increase store traffic, to enhance total sales of a store. From a pricing manager's perspective, the tradeoff between lower unit margin and additional sales volume determines whether a promotion will have a positive impact on revenues. However, if sufficient buyers do not perceive there is a "deal" or an increase in value for them, the promotion might not have the desired effect on a seller's revenues.

---

*In *New Directions in Behavioral Pricing*, Chezy Ofir Ed., 2024, World Scientific Publishing Company.

Kent B. Monroe, John M. Jones Distinguished Professor of Marketing Emeritus, Gies College of Business, University of Illinois, Urbana-Champaign; Visiting Distinguished Scholar in Marketing at the Robins School of Business at the University of Richmond in Richmond, Virginia (kentmonroe2021@gmail.com).

The objective of this chapter is to integrate concepts from behavioral price research on buyer responses to price changes and differences with relevant results from price perception and numerical cognition research. Based on this synthesis managerially relevant prescriptions for more effectively communicating price changes or price differences are presented.

# Behavioral Price Concepts

## Internal reference price[1]

A goal of behavioral price research is to help us understand how individuals perceive price information, form value judgments, and make purchase decisions. Such explanations help us learn why people may be more sensitive to a perceived price increase than a perceived price decrease, or how they respond to price promotions and other price messages. An underlying premise for these behavioral responses is people judge prices comparatively, that is, an *internal reference price* ($P_{ref}$) anchors their judgments (Monroe 1973). An internal reference price is unique to each individual and situation. It may be a price a person remembers from a previous purchase or marketing message, an expected price, a belief about what would be a fair price for the item, or perhaps a vague notion of what the product might be worth. People may not be consciously aware a reference price is in their mind and influencing their price judgment.

Because of the variability in reference prices influencing people's judgments for similar purchases, sellers often provide a "regular" or "original" price through their communications. This seller-provided *external anchor price* typically is higher than the seller's current price ($P_{selling}$). Sellers use this tactic, expecting people are more likely to buy an item if they perceive a selling price is lower than its "original" price.

## Gain–loss asymmetry

In 1738, Bernoulli (1954) proposed a basic model of perceived value. Based on that conceptualization, we assume the following:

---

[1] See Cheng and Monroe (2013a) for a more complete description of the internal reference price and other key behavioral price concepts.

1. People have a value function defined over *perceived* gains and losses relative to a reference point, their current position. This assumption is based on the psychophysical principle that people respond to perceived differences in stimuli rather than absolute levels.
2. This value function exhibits *decreasing* marginal increments in value for perceived gains but *increasing* marginal decrements in value for perceived losses, relative to the reference point.[2]

A purchase or transaction occurs when a person acquires (gains) a product or receives a service but gives up (loses) what is paid to obtain it. Whether people expect a transaction to be satisfactory or not depends in part on their perceptions of the offer in addition to the acquisition itself. Paying a price perceived to be less than an individual's internal reference price for such an acquisition, (i.e., $P_{ref} > P_{selling}$) normally would be judged positively (i.e., gain), inducing a favorable evaluation.

Buyers may be dissatisfied when they perceive a selling price is more than their reference price for that acquisition (i.e., $P_{ref} < P_{selling}$). If so, the extra amount they would pay relative to their reference price would be perceived negatively (i.e., loss). *For the same amount of absolute price difference between an individual's reference price for a product and its promoted selling price, a perceived negative difference or loss ($P_{ref} < P_{selling}$) will be larger than a perceived positive difference or gain ($P_{ref} > P_{selling}$)* (Cheng and Monroe 2013a). This conclusion has been labeled the gain–loss asymmetry.

When $P_{ref} < P_{selling}$ (a perceived loss due to a price increase or price higher than expected) perceived value decreases at an increasing rate as perceived losses increase. For a perceived price difference of $\Delta p$, ($\Delta p = P_{ref} - P_{selling}$), from a reference price reflecting a price increase (loss) the decline in perceived value will be perceptually larger than if the $\Delta p$

---

[2]In 1738 Bernouilli (1954) formulated a value function with these particular characteristics. Moreover, a change in wealth of a given magnitude from a specific level of wealth (reference point) would be more noticeable if it was a decrement (i.e., loss) than an increment (i.e., gain). Later Weber (1834) formulated the concept of differential thresholds that conceptually we apply to price perception. "[T]he first question of whether a person perceives a price difference is an issue of whether a *differential price perceptual threshold* has been reached. Once a price difference has been noticed, whether a person changes his/her buying behavior is an issue of *differential price response threshold*" (Cheng and Monroe 2013a, p. 109).

reflects a price reduction or increase in perceived value. This asymmetry between perceived gains and losses from the same reference point needs additional study across many different situations such as price promotions, deal retractions, and quality-price positioning and competition (Wathieu *et al.* 2004).

## Price thresholds

There are two relevant price threshold concepts: *absolute* acceptable price thresholds and *differential* price thresholds. These two threshold concepts refer to different phenomena. Every human sensory system has an upper and lower limit or threshold of responsiveness to the intensity of a stimulus. Accordingly, at points in time for a considered purchase there will be an upper and a lower acceptable price limit (Monroe and Venkatesan 1969; Monroe 1971a, 1971b). A low absolute price threshold implies there are prices greater than zero that would be unacceptable to pay.[3] A person may be suspicious of a product's quality below that low price. There is also a high absolute price threshold above which a person would be unwilling or unable to pay for the item. Prices between a person's highest and lowest acceptable prices form an *acceptable price range* for that product and occasion. Our current concern is with perceived differences between prices and we will expand on the concept of differential price thresholds.

In the region around a reference price, small differences in selling price from a person's reference price (whether positive or negative) would induce slight (if any) perceptions of price differences (*latitude of price indifference*) (Cheng and Monroe 2013a). Although a person may notice a reference and a selling price differ numerically, the two prices may not be perceived to differ relative to degree of expensiveness. If so, the perceived price difference would be insufficient to influence purchase behavior. As suggested by Weber's law, ($\Delta P/P_{ref} = k$), the magnitude of an actual price difference, $\Delta P = (P_{ref} - P_{selling})$, necessary to produce a perceived price difference increases as the reference price level increases (Grewal and Marmorstein 1994; Lambert 1978; Uhl and Brown 1971). Estimates of the magnitude of latitude of price indifference in specific situations have ranged from ±2% to ±10% of the reference price or more.

---

[3] One study did find a small percentage of low-income respondents did not exhibit an unwillingness to buy at very low prices (Ofir 2004).

Once a price difference has been perceived, a *differential price perceptual threshold* has been reached. Whether people change purchase behavior is an issue of the *differential price response threshold*.[4] As a buyer's reference price level increases, larger actual price differences will be necessary (increases or decreases) to induce changes in perceived price differences. Price discounts of 15–20% (Della Bitta *et al.* 1981; Kalyanaram and Little 1987, 1994; Gupta and Cooper 1992), or more (Xia and Monroe 2009; Raghubir *et al.* 2004) may be necessary to induce an increase in willingness to buy.[5]

# Relevant Numerical Cognition Concepts

"Numbers can influence decisions" (King and Janiszewski 2011, p. 337). Evidence from studies in marketing and numerical cognition indicates there are multiple influences affecting the effectiveness of a price communication. But how can numbers *per se*, whether in monetary and/or percentage form, influence how people process a price message? The answer revolves around using numbers, individually and in combination in a message, that are more easily processed by people.

## *Processing price information*

Knowledge of how people process numerical information indicates it is more complex than previously assumed. Number processing involves an ability to mentally manipulate sequences of words or symbols according to specific rules. These manipulations occur when people calculate or estimate the numerical difference between two prices, add the additional amounts for shipping, handling, and tax, or tip to determine the total cost of a purchase, calculate the effect of an advertised percentage discount, or determine the unit price of an offering. A price indicates the amount of money (or other asset) a

---

[4]A differential price response threshold is a different concept than an absolute price threshold.

[5]This expectation is consistent with numerical cognition research. However, there is little research documenting this expectation across a range of actual price levels. Judging by the proclivity of current advertised discounts of 50% and up to 80% or more suggests that sellers have found that buyers' need for increasingly larger discounts makes it necessary to use ever larger discounts to stimulate buyer purchase behavior.

buyer gives up to acquire a product or service. Processing price information begins with exposure to price information, followed by price encoding (bringing the numerical information to attention), representing and storing price information in memory, processing the information, and responding (or not) to this information (Cheng and Monroe 2013b). Numerical information is abstract in nature even though we often think of numbers as "objective."

The way price information is presented to people influences their psychological, physiological, and emotional reactions inducing sensations. Our sensory systems receive and process a large amount of information and our brain almost instantly relates this information to what we already know. The brain makes inferences (best guesses) about these inputs and decides where to send the sensory signals. The cortical region where the sensory information is sent determines what we perceive. Because our senses are inferential, we obtain a lot of information from our environment quickly and in rich detail.

*Attention* is necessary for perception to occur. When we focus attention on something, we necessarily focus attention away from other things. Even so there is still some processing outside of our intentional focus. That is, there is some mental processing for all incoming sensory information, particularly if the stimulus is meaningful to us. Attention allows us to allocate our finite mental resources.

Our perceptual systems learn as we gain experience. If we spend a sufficient amount of time perceiving a set of objects, we slowly become perceptual experts in that area. *Perceptual learning* is driven primarily by a process called differentiation, allowing us to segment a set of items into separate categories along a particular attribute. For example, we are able to differentiate, or group, a set of similar products into different price categories such as low-, medium-, and high-priced products. Perceptual learning occurs non-consciously and is a complex information processing activity.

Central to the issue of price information processing is understanding how people attend to, encode, and represent price and price-related information in their minds. Previous price memory research has led to some mistaken conclusions about whether people can or do remember prices of items they have purchased (Monroe and Lee 1999). If buyers do not recall the actual symbols accurately, it has been inferred they did not attend to nor process the price information when purchasing. Such inferences may not be warranted because buyers may encode and *represent* price information in memory as approximations (e.g., "less than $100") or as evaluations (e.g., "not expensive").

Approximation is the process of first converting Arabic or verbal numerals into an internal magnitude representation in our minds. The input mode, e.g., dollars, ounces, is then ignored and the numerical quantities are represented and processed similarly as other physical magnitudes such as size, weight, or distance (Crollen *et al.* 2013; Dastjerdi *et al.* 2014; Kadosh *et al.* 2005). The encoding is automatic, fast, and independent of the actual number. Individuals' judgments of quality, sacrifice, and value do not differ regardless of whether the numerical stimuli is presented in units of money or weight (Adaval and Monroe 2002).

Since these different physical magnitudes are processed in the same brain area, the right intraparietal sulcus (IPS), our brain may misinterpret a perceived spatial distance between prices in a message as a numerical difference between the prices. This misinterpretation has been called an *interference effect*.

When numbers are used to denote amounts, such as prices, age, weight, and duration of time, the magnitude of the number becomes meaningful. Either the exact or an approximation of the number is encoded and represented in memory. For example, "24" may be represented as "young" (as in age), or light (as in weight), cold (as in temperature), or cheap (as in prices). For price information to influence purchase decisions, normally people must encode the price information as a magnitude representation rather than a nominal representation.

Research on how people make numerical comparative judgments indicates that numerical quantities are not compared at a symbolic level, but initially are recoded and compared as quantities. Numerical quantity refers to the question "how many?" The intraparietal sulcus area of the prefrontal cortex consistently is activated whenever human adults compare or calculate with Arabic numerals. The intraparietal region can be activated also by spelled-out or spoken number words across countries and cultures (Nieder and Dehaene 2009; Piazza *et al.* 2007). When prices are processed as magnitudes or as relative quantities, even if people are actively evaluating different alternatives in their choice set and are consciously processing the price information, the actual prices in symbols may not be encoded or stored in memory.

## Processing effects

The *distance effect* indicates the time required to compare two numbers is an inverse function of the numerical distance between them. It takes people longer to decide that 8 is larger than 6 than to decide that 8 is larger than 2 (Algom, Dekel, and Pansky 1996). The distance effect suggests digits are not compared as numbers per se, but are initially compared as quantities.

The digit 5 has a special status in our numbering system. Initially, the digits 1, 2, 3, and 4 are encoded as "small," while 6, 7, 8, and 9 are encoded as "large." That is, the mental representation of digits below 10 is divided into numbers above and below 5. For equal numerical distance, the *magnitude effect* indicates it is easier to differentiate between small numbers (e.g., 1 compared to 2) than large numbers (e.g., 8 compared to 9) (Dehaene and Akhavein 1995; Dehaene 1989). When comparing or discriminating between two prices, people automatically encode each price independently and non-consciously classify the prices as "small" or "large" (Tzelgov, Meyer, and Henik 1992).

When judging which number in a pair of numbers is *larger*, people find the task is easier when both numbers are "large" than when both are "small" (again 5 serves as the neutral point between "small" and "large"). The opposite is true when people have to decide which number is smaller. This effect is called the *semantic congruency effect* since it was initially observed in various semantic comparison tasks. The *size congruity effect* occurs when people are judging which of two numbers is larger. It is an easier task if the larger of the compared numbers is also displayed in larger font size. Similar results occur when people are judging which of two numbers is smaller, for example, searching for a lower price, and the lower number is displayed in smaller font size.

People may not only perceive and encode the numerical values of the prices (actual or magnitude representations), they may also make comparisons or discriminations, for example, an item is priced higher than another item, and they may make evaluative judgments, such as it is expensive, or it must be of better quality. Price comparisons involve an internal reference price and may result in people encoding a representation such as more or less than brand X, or more than previously.

Number processing research indicates some processing of price information may be more automatic than others. Also, price comparisons in the lower-price range (i.e., smaller numbers involving fewer digits), that are typical for most supermarket purchases, may be more likely to be processed automatically. Moreover, identifying whether a specific price is more than another price will be processed faster when that price is higher than the individual's reference price.

People may process and retrieve price information either consciously or non-consciously. When people process price information consciously, they pay attention to the price, make perceptual inferences regarding the value of the product using information retrieved from memory and from the external environment before making a purchase decision. A magnitude representation of the price, and an evaluative judgment such as good or bad, favorable or unfavorable, expensive or inexpensive may be transferred from working memory into long-term memory (Adaval and Monroe 2002).

Alternatively, only their comparative or evaluative judgments, but not the actual price information, might be transferred into long-term memory. Even so, these people may be able to indicate that the product is "too expensive", "a bargain", or "priced reasonably." This scenario is consistent with the idea that an overall evaluation of a product may be more easily remembered than attribute information when the evaluation is formed at the time of exposure.[6]

Conversely, when price information is processed non-consciously, a person may not focus attention on the prices. Nonetheless, a perceptual inference regarding the value of the product and a purchase decision may have occurred. When such non-conscious processing of price information occurs, the individual may demonstrate "price unawareness," and not be able to recall the price of the product at a later time. However, this same person who cannot recall the exact price may still be able to indicate that the product is "too expensive", "a bargain", or "reasonably priced," indicating the price information had been processed and evaluated.

# Framing Price Changes and Price Differences

Framing is establishing a mental context for evaluating options prior to choosing an alternative. A "frame" is a person's perception of the behaviors, outcomes, and contingencies associated with a message. People's perceptions and experiences with a product, service, or business are influenced by a combination of focus, contextual, and organism cues. These cues activate associated representations in memory, making them more

---

[6]This observation is also consistent with research results relative to construal effects on the influence of price on perceptions of quality (Bornemann and Homburg 2011).

accessible and this activation can spread to related constructs in one's mind.

Table 1 lists 11 combinations of four pieces of information that may be presented in a price message. Some messages provide only the selling price accompanied by a semantic cue such as "Regular," "Original," "Sale," or "Special". Most other price messages fit into one of the other formats listed. Formats 2–7 and 9–11 require customers to make some calculations or estimations when assessing the attractiveness of an offer. People often make errors when performing such calculations (Chen and Rao 2007; Suri *et al.* 2013; Thomas and Morwitz 2009). Some price promotions may also include specific numerical information about the monetary or percentage amount customers would "save" if they take advantage of the price offer. Although the actual monetary gain or loss people may incur due to a specific price change may not vary, their perceptions and responses could differ depending on how the price and related information is presented. The way a price change or difference is presented stimulates peoples' sensations, brain inferences, and perceptions influencing their processing of the information in the message, and judgment of the price change or difference.[7]

**Table 1.**   Price promotion formats

| | |
|---|---|
| 1. | Sale price only |
| 2. | Regular or original price and sale price |
| 3. | Regular or original price and percentage off |
| 4. | Regular or original price and monetary amount off |
| 5. | Regular or original price, sale price and monetary amount off |
| 6. | Regular or original price, sale price and percentage off |
| 7. | Regular or original price, percentage off and monetary amount off |
| 8. | Regular or original price, sale price, percentage off, and monetary amount off |
| 9. | Sale price and percentage off |
| 10. | Sale price and monetary amount off |
| 11. | Sale price, percentage off and monetary amount off |

[7]See Bertini and Wathieu (2008), Ramanathan and Dhar (2010), Choi *et al.* (2012), Dolansky and Vandenbosch (2013), Suri *et al.* (2013), Barone *et al.* (2016).

Four variables influence a person's perception of and response to a price change message: (1) a perceived price difference ($P_{former} - P_{selling}$) serves as a stimulus; (2) the individual, (3) the numbers in the price message, and (4) the relationships between these numbers (Coulter and Roggeveen 2014; King and Janiszewski 2011; Monroe 1971a; Suri *et al.* 2012; Thomas and Morwitz 2009). When an individual perceives a price difference, a response may be to purchase one or more units, to reduce purchases by one or more units, or to not change purchase behavior. A perceived price reduction might induce an inference quality has been reduced, and no purchase is made. A perceived price increase may induce a judgment the benefits received from the item are now less than what the person must give up to acquire it and no purchase is made.

Peoples' responses to a price change message depend on their perceptions of the numbers used, their perceived price difference, and their interpretation of the words (semantic cues) in the message. Their motivation to process and the relative ease of processing the numerical and verbal information (i.e., numerical and verbal fluency) are determinants of these perceptions and interpretations. Processing fluency will have a positive effect on their perceived attractiveness of the message and purchase intentions.

Communications comparing a regular, previous, or competitors' price with a lower current selling price provide customers with a price frame of reference. Emphasizing a lower amount to be paid may enhance perceptions of value for customers interested in the offer. Comparative price promotions suggesting a "deal" may induce some people to infer a gain or positive outcome is possible if they take advantage of an offer. Other people may consider the same message as an opportunity to reduce a sacrifice or loss.

Individuals' value perceptions are a function of their perceptions of quality or benefits augmented by comparing their reference price to the promoted selling price (Grewal *et al.* 1998). People need to feel confident they can determine quality prior to purchase, or infer the quality correctly because the seller's signals are bonafide indicators of quality (Urbany *et al.* 1997). Previous behavioral price promotion research implicitly has assumed quality is either known or invariant across purchase occasions. Also, a positive perceived price difference (i.e., $P_{ref} > P_{selling}$) might induce a reduction in perceived monetary sacrifice, further enhancing perceptions of a gain.

Perceptions of gains or losses are context dependent. Using data from two different consumer panels, for quantity decisions loyal buyers responded more strongly to (1) perceived gains when purchasing *after* running out of their preferred brand, or (2) perceived losses when purchasing *before* a stock-out. Conversely, switchers responded more to perceived gains than losses in choice decisions (Krishnamurthi *et al.* 1992).[8]

## Buyers' purchase goals

Goals play a fundamental role in influencing how information in a price message will be processed. Some people may seek to save money and minimize losses whereas others may seek to acquire things and gain value. Different message framing may lead to different customer information processes. "Pay less" may induce people to process the sacrifice aspect of a purchase while "save more" or "save now" may induce them to focus attention on a gain from the price message. Messages framed as gains prime people to make positive inferences (e.g., "$x off"; "save"). Messages framed to minimize perceived losses prime people to reduce negative inferences (e.g., "pay less now") (Ramanathan and Dhar 2010).

People planning to purchase a specific product are more responsive to promotions for that product framed as reduction of a loss while customers without a pre-purchase goal are more responsive to messages framed as additional gains (Xia and Monroe 2009). Price communications featuring selling prices just below round prices (e.g., $29.99) may lead to a gain inference thereby inducing a promotion focus (Choi *et al.* 2012). These priming effects emerge without intentional learning, occur non-consciously, and may transfer to other products in the buying situation unrelated to a specific message.

## Motivation to process price information

The processing of price information depends both on individuals' motivation to process the information and whether they have the mental resources to do this processing. If they do not have sufficient motivation to process the information in a price message, they may process the information heuristically. At relatively low price levels, they might infer a product to

---

[8]Like other researchers who did not model the differential price threshold effect, they did not measure a region of indifference around a reference price.

be of low quality. Because of the differential emphasis placed on this quality assessment, the product would be perceived to provide low value. Or, at relatively high prices, when using a price-perceived quality heuristic, they would place more emphasis on the quality inference and perceive the product as providing relatively high value. But, when people do process the information, they will place relatively more emphasis on a price's sacrifice dimension and higher-priced products will be perceived to offer less value (Suri and Monroe 2003).

When buyers are motivated to process available information, but are constrained by either mental resources or time available to make a decision, they are more likely to process information heuristically. To evaluate a price offer message, people have to encode the product and price information, and perhaps perform calculations to determine the net price they would pay if they accept the offer. Such calculations require the use of working memory, a limited-capacity system for temporary storage, and manipulation of relevant information in the prefrontal cortex of the brain. The various mathematical procedures required during these calculations place demand on working memory. Moreover, the stress or anxiety many people experience when performing these calculations will have a draining effect on working memory resources.

Combining the required numerical magnitude assessments when judging a price offer with a concurrent task of processing relevant product information strains people's cognitive resources. These demands on cognitive resources impede their ability to process the information in a price message thoroughly. Consequently, if there is low motivation to process, or if the ability to process information is constrained, people may rely on choices requiring less processing effort and cognitive capacity (Suri *et al.* 2012).

### Round versus sharp (*Odd*) prices

"[C]ertain numerals, called 'round numbers' can refer to an approximate quantity, while all other numerals necessarily have a sharp and precise meaning" (Dehaene 2011, p. 95). Round numbers, such as 10 and 25 are used more frequently, are better liked, and when used to express approximate quantities, facilitate numerical processing. Round prices induce evaluation by feelings whereas non-rounded prices induce evaluation by cognition (the *rounded price effect*) (Wadhwa and Zhang 2015).

People process round numbers more easily and are more likely to reproduce them when asked. "[T]he roundness of a number is determined by whether it is divisible by (1) a base number (e.g., 10), (2) half of a base number (e.g., 5), and/or (3) a quarter of a base number (e.g., 2.5)" (Coulter and Roggeveen 2014, p. 70). Round numbers are more likely to come to mind when one attempts to estimate or remember a specific price (e.g., "I paid about $60"). Non-round prices are perceived to be precise and derived from calculations, the *price precision effect* (Thomas, Simon, and Kadiyali 2010). Round numbers serve as reference points and may become performance goals (Pope and Simonsohn 2011).

Even digits are processed faster and more accurately than odd digits. When judging multiple-digit numbers, people are slower when judging even numbers from 10 through 19 than when judging numbers from 0 through 9. The odd–even status of the tens digits interferes with judging the ones digit slowing down processing (Hines 1990; Dehaene, Bossini, and Giraux 1993).

There is a general preference for round numbers in a variety of contexts. However, non-round (odd) numbers are much more common in prices. There is evidence people prefer round (even) prices (Diller and Brielmaier 1995; Guido and Peluso 2004). An examination of the distribution of prices over time in pay-what-you-want outlets indicates a majority of prices paid were round (Lynn *et al.* 2012; Riener and Traxler 2012). Over 80% of tips left in a restaurant for more than 9,000 receipts were either a round, whole-dollar amount or rounded to a half-dollar amount. Also, 56% of 1301 self-pumped gasoline purchases from one outlet were a round whole-dollar amount (Lynn *et al.* 2012).

Most previous research related to round or non-round prices has concentrated on the sales effect of 9-ending or 5-ending odd prices compared to 0-ending even prices. Traditional pricing practices relying on such odd prices have not been consistently supported by such research (Balan 2013). One study in England provided evidence about preferences for round prices (Bray and Harris 2006). In a study of automobile parts and accessories stores, six stores continued using 9-ending prices for 10 products while six other stores increased the prices by a penny to be 0-ending. Over a 12-week period, sales of nine products increased significantly in the 0-ending price stores compared to the 9-ending price stores. Similarly, a German study of drug store prices highlighted a revenue loss when reducing prices to a 9-ending (Diller and Brielmaier 1995).

## *Price promotion information processing*

As Table 2 indicates, price promotion messages typically contain a combination of different pieces of numerical information (regular price, sale price, absolute (monetary) discount, relative (percentage) discount). Usually, various semantic cues accompany the numerical information (e.g., save, sale, now only) to influence people's processing and interpretation of the message. The way this information is presented (i.e., framed) influences information processing and message effectiveness.

Table 2. Price promotion examples

| 50% OFF | SAVE | SALE 119.99 |
|---|---|---|
| DESIGNER COATS | $801 | Save $120. Reg. 239.99 |
| Reg./Orig. $400 | SECTIONAL SOFA | Single serve blender |
| Sale $200 | Now only | With preprogrammed |
| | $1599 | Settings. |
| Wool blend or | originally | |
| down styles | $2400 | |
| | SAVE | |
| | $801 | |
| a | b | c |
| **$15.99** | **SALE** | **60%**OFF |
| Pajama sets for misses. | **$42⁹⁹** | Reg. 36.00–40.00 |
| Select styles | Complete bed set | Sweaters for misses. |
| Orig. $40 | • comforter | Women's sizes and |
| | • sheet set | Petites also available. |
| | • sham | Multiple styles |
| | • bedskirt | |
| | Reg. 59.99 | |
| d | e | f |
| **50%**OFF | **$250 OFF** | SAVE |
| | 349⁹⁸ MOUNTAIN | **37%** |
| **$219⁹⁷** | BIKE | SAVE $300 |
| **11-drawer ball-bearing** | Reg. 599.99 | **$499** |
| **tool chest** | | Home Theater Power |
| **3-pc set** | | Chair |
| g | h | i |

People's processing of price information involves conscious and non-conscious processes operating simultaneously (Monroe and Lee 1999; Barden 2013). Much of the information contained in a price message is processed non-consciously but still influences responses to the message. Color, font and font size, spatial location of the pre-change and post-change prices (e.g., "regular" price and "sale" price), numerical differences between the pre- and post-change prices, and overall layout influence buyers' perceptions of a message (Bogomolova *et al.* 2018).

In a price message, relationships between the numbers can influence the relative ease with which people perceive (perceptual fluency), assign meaning (conceptual fluency), remember, and later retrieve (retrieval fluency) the numerical information. Such processing fluency induces positive feelings, enhancing message effectiveness. A managerial objective is to choose and place numbers in a price message that: (1) are easier to process, (2) minimize customers' need to make calculations, and (3) reduce their anxieties about numbers and calculations. The goal is to foster customers' comfortableness with the information in the message and enhance their purchase intentions.

*Choosing the numbers.* A price message may contain one price or a combination of two, three, or multiple numerical prices along with other relevant textual and numerical information (see Tables 1 and 2). When the individual numbers, in combination, are perceived by people to belong together such as being multiples of two, five, or ten, they are processed faster, more easily, and are better liked, enhancing purchase intentions (Coulter and Roggeveen 2014).

For example, if a regular or original price is discounted 10%, will customers perceive this reduction as a "small", "medium", or "large" discount? If a 10% reduction is perceived small, but the message presents this small potential savings in a font size larger than the original price, people may have difficulty processing this price information due to the semantic congruency effect. If a "small" discount is presented in a "large" font size the perceptual incongruent information interferes with the information processing. Complicating this situation would be the fact that the discount is also numerically smaller but in larger font size than the original price. Such magnitude inconsistency within the message interferes with information processing, making it more difficult. Complicating this processing is the fact that people may have only a few seconds to attend to, process, and interpret such incongruent information.

Table 2 portrays the verbal and price information for some actual price promotions.[9] Promotion 2a promotes 50% off on designer coats originally priced at $400 and on sale for $200. The message uses round numbers and the sale price, being one half the original price, is consistent with the headline. The price information is presented in a high to low sequential order as the higher original price, $400, precedes and lies above the lower $200 sale price. The combination of numbers 400, 200, and 50 are multiples of 50. If 50% off is perceived to be large, the larger font size used is perceptually congruent.

The order of the numerical sequence in promotion 2b is low to high: 801, 1599, 2400, and 801 repeated. Increasing the promotion price by one dollar to 1600 and rearranging the sequence of numbers would have been a more easily processed high to low order and combination: 2400, 1600, 800. Also, the smallest number in the message, 801, is in a larger font size than the original larger price, 2400, complicating the information processing due to this incongruence.

Revising promotion 2c to present a sequence of regular price of 240, a discount of 120, and a sale price of 120 would be an easier combination of numbers for people to process. The numbers are round; and 120 is one half (50%) of 240. Promotion 2d could be revised to present a sequence of regular price of 40, a discount of 24, and a sale price of 16. Each of these numbers in the combination is a multiple of 8, an even number. Revising promotion 2e to present a sequence of regular price of 60, discount of 18, with a sale price of 42, multiples of 6, would be preferable. Likewise, promotion 2g could be revised to present a sequence of original price 440, discount of 220, with a sale price of 220, which is one half of the original price. Promotion 2h could be presented with a regular price of 600, discount of 240, and a sale price of 360, using multiples of 6. Promotion 2i could be presented with a regular price of 800, discount of 320, a sale price of 480, using multiples of 8 and a 40% savings. Each of these suggested revisions minimally changes the economics of an offer, but would be more easily processed and more attractive to people.

Promotion 2f is an example of a *tensile price claim* in that the regular prices for the sweaters were between 40 and 36. Using a discount of 60% would create sale prices between 16 and 14.40 if applied exactly. A tensile

---

[9]Each block presents the non-pictorial information from a promotional message. The messages were either in black or black and red color and the relative font sizes are presented as near to actual sizes as possible.

price claim uses vague wording that increases ambiguity and reduces the concreteness of the information in a message. When a price reduction range is used (e.g., 30–50% off), people will tend to anchor on the minimum value (30%) and adjust upwards to estimate the amount of savings they might obtain. For promotions indicating only a potential maximum amount (e.g., save up to 50%) people will anchor on the maximum amount and adjust downwards to estimate the expected savings they might receive. Because of the uncertainty induced by the ambiguity of the magnitude of the price reduction, buyers' expected savings might be greater than they obtain. Such promotions could be considered deceptive or unfair.

Reducing the perceptual processing effort for people when presenting price information has the beneficial effect of increasing liking and purchase intentions. The key to effectively communicating price information to others is to understand how our brains are able to represent the corresponding quantities the symbols or words indicate. Given the limited amount of processing resources people have relative to the vast amount of "deals" they encounter in the marketplace, marketing and pricing managers need to present price information in ways that reduce processing efforts.

*Location of price information*: Given that people judge a price of an offering relative to a reference price, i.e., $(P_{ref} — P_{actual})$, a managerial issue is where to place price information in a message such that customers perceive the offer as intended. Comparative price messages may present both a "regular" (original) price and a "sale" price. These prices may be presented in vertical (Table 2a) or horizontal order (Table 2c), close together, or some distance apart (Table 2d, 2e). As in Table 2a, the higher (original or regular) price may occur before the lower (sale) price, for example, on the upper left side of a printed message. Often the reverse order occurs and the lower (sale) price is presented before the higher original price (Table 2b, c, d, e, h). Sometimes the higher price is in a larger font size than the lower price; however, more often the lower price is in a larger font size (Table 2b, c, d, e, h). Generally, the intent of the seller is to promote an item that will be sold at a lower price than previously (or sometimes lower than competition).

Spacial separation of price information in a message influences perceptions of the magnitude of the difference between pre- and post-change prices. The greater the physical horizontal distance between two prices the greater the perceived numerical difference between them, e.g., the amount of a discount. A perceived discount was underestimated when the regular and sale prices were 1.5 inches apart, but over estimated when these prices were 5 inches apart (Coulter and Norberg 2009). If prices are placed physically close horizontally, then perception of a *narrow* physical distance interferes with the perception of the discount magnitude leading to an underestimation of the discount. When prices are further apart horizontally, however, perception of a *wide* physical distance exaggerates the perception of the amount of the discount and overestimation of the discount occurs.

When the lower selling price is presented in font size larger than the higher former price, a perceptual incongruity occurs creating interference in the processing of the magnitudes in the message. This interference increases the difficulty of estimating accurately the actual magnitude of a price reduction offer (Choi and Coulter 2012).[10]

If the two prices are presented physically close, vertically, and in the same metric, it is easier for people to process the price information (DelVecchio *et al.* 2009). Presenting a price change or difference as a percentage (e.g., Table 2a, f, g, i) involves multiple metrics (percentage and monetary) increasing processing difficulty (Estelami 1999; Suri *et al.* 2013). Prices shown on the right side of a message may be perceived to be higher than when shown on the left (Cai *et al.* 2012). This result may be due to a general left to right orientation of people's logarithmic mental number line (Dehaene 1997, 2003).

**Ease of computing price differences**: When the left intraparietal sulcus (IPS) area of the brain is involved in comparison tasks, physical distance, perceived differences between prices, and in font sizes are processed as magnitudes (Kadosh *et al.* 2005).[11] When there are incongruities between forms of magnitude of the different stimuli in a comparative price message, they interfere with the *non-conscious* processing

---

[10] See Monroe and Lee (1999) for a more extensive summary of these types of incongruities and their effect on processing numerical and price information.

[11] Studies have shown that electrical activity in a group of nerve cells in the intraparietal sulcus spiked when, and only when, volunteers were performing calculations. Outside the experimental settings when a person mentioned a number — or even a quantitative reference, such as "some more," "many" or "bigger than the other one" — there was a spike of electrical activity in the same nerve-cell population of the intraparietal sulcus. (Dastierdi *et al.* 2014).

of the different magnitude information leading to anomalies in people's perceptions and judgments of price differences as identified here.

Presenting the two prices vertically (versus horizontally) makes it comparatively less difficult mentally to compute or estimate the numerical difference between them (Barone *et al.* 2016). This effect is more likely to occur if the higher (original) price is presented above the lower (sale) price (Table 2a). School children learn to subtract by proceeding right to left when computing the difference between two multi-digit numbers. (Alternatively, presenting the lower "sale" price vertically above (or before) the regular price (Table 2b, c, d, e, h) increases the computational difficulty.) Easier to compute numerical price differences were perceived to be larger than actual while more difficult to compute price differences of similar magnitude were perceived to be smaller than actual for price discounts and price differences between brands (Thomas and Morwitz 2009).

Not only is it relatively common for price messages to place the lower sale price above (before) the higher regular price but often in a larger font size as well. Such presentations induce a perceptual incongruity in that the *lower* price is in a *larger* font size. The size incongruity effect occurs when people are comparing two numbers. It is an easier processing task if the larger of the two numbers is displayed in larger font size and above the lower sale price. A perceptual incongruity in magnitude between font size and the numbers increases the difficulty in processing the message.

**Size of right digit endings**: In our numbering system, people nonconsciously tend to semantically encode the digits 1, 2, 3, 4 in their minds as small, whereas 6, 7, 8, 9 are encoded as large. The mental representation of digits less than 10 is divided into numbers above and below 5. People encode the prices separately, automatically and non-consciously categorizing prices as "small" or "large" (Monroe 2003).

Price promotions often are presented with a reduced selling price just under a round number, e.g., in Table 2: 1599, 119.99, 15.99, 42.99, 219.97, 349.98; the "right digit" or "odd price" effect. Sale prices presented with "small" right digit endings (e.g., xx.22) were perceived to have larger percentage discounts than sale prices presented with "large" right digit endings (e.g., xx.99) even though the former prices had smaller actual percentage discounts. The sale prices with the small right digit endings and larger perceived discounts were judged to offer more value (Coulter and Coulter 2007). The perceived "small" right digits of the sale price led to an inference the sale price was *less* than when the perceived "large" right digits were used to present the sale price. This is another example of the interference that may occur non-consciously when multiple magnitude judgments are made in the same area of the brain. The perceived magnitude of the price discount was larger when "small" right digits were used relative to the price promotion using "large" right digits. Comparative price promotions may influence people's perceptions in ways unintended by the seller.

### *Absolute versus relative price differences*

Price perceptions are influenced by context and are relativistic (Monroe 1977). Buyers would perceive a $40 reduction on either a $200 jacket or an $800 television similarly if they process the $40 savings absolutely. If people process the offers relatively, a 20% savings on the jacket would be perceived more favorably than a 5% savings on the television (Heath *et al.* 1995; Chen *et al.* 1998; Gendall *et al.* 2006).

For a given amount of monetary savings, the attractiveness of a price decrease is inversely related to an item's price (Grewal and Marmorstein 1994). A $50 reduction on a $100 product is relatively more attractive than on a product listed at $500. As Weber's Law suggests, the attractiveness (or not) of a price difference depends not only on the amount of the monetary difference, but also on the magnitude of the comparative (reference) price (DelVecchio 2005; Weathers *et al.* 2012; González *et al.* 2015).

Both monetary and percentage forms of price changes or differences require calculations to determine or estimate the price to pay. However, people may not calculate correctly or they may not calculate and instead rely on a heuristic (Chen and Rao 2007; Suri *et al.* 2013; Thomas and Morwitz 2009). The percentage of a price change or difference is a relative indicator of the magnitude of the difference and is bounded by 0% and 100%. When evaluating a price change or difference, people may non-consciously encode a percentage difference as relatively small, moderate (average), or large, depending on its perceived place on the percentage scale. Similarly, a monetary price change or difference might also be judged as a small, moderate (average), or large change or difference depending on its position on an individual's subjective number line.

## *Communicating price differences*

Some price promotions provide information about the magnitude of a price difference in either (or both) percentage or monetary amounts. Previous research suggests percentage-off price promotions are perceived more favorably for low-price products while money-off promotions are perceived more favorably for high-price products.[12] A percentage surcharge on an item priced less than (more than) 100 was evaluated less (more) favorably than if presented as a monetary amount (Weathers *et al.* 2012). Is there a numerical price delineating when people are more likely to perceive a percentage price difference to be more or less attractive than an equivalent monetary price difference? Does this price differ according to whether the price difference is due to a price decrease (promotion) or a price increase (surcharge)?

People automatically represent number stimuli in their minds in an analogue magnitude code. This code is a perception of quantity, size, or distance, and magnitude is represented semantically on a mental number line (e.g., small, medium, large). These codes occur from nonverbal, automatic, and associative processing (i.e., non-consciously) (Dehaene 1997; Cheng and Monroe 2013a; Thomas and Morwitz 2005).[13] When a monetary reference (or external anchor) price is less (more) than 100, the amount of a percentage difference is always larger (smaller) than the equivalent monetary difference (González *et al.* 2015).[14] If a reference price is 80, a 50% change is

---

[12]Bonini and Rumiati, experiment 3, (2002), Chen *et al.* (1998), Darke and Freedman (1993), Darke *et al.* (1995), González *et al.* (2015), Heath *et al.* (1995), McKechnie *et al.* (2012), Weisstein *et al.* (2013).

[13]"Each time we are confronted with an Arabic numeral, our brain … treat[s] it as an analogical quantity and represents it mentally with decreasing precision…" (Dehaene 1997, p. 73).

[14]This observation is relevant only for monetary systems in which items can be priced above or below 100.

*numerically* larger than a $40 (euro) change. If a reference price is 120, a 50% change is *numerically* smaller than a $60 (euro) change. More formally:

1. When a reference price is *less* than 100:
   a. A price decrease presented as a percentage difference will be perceived *more* favorably than an equivalent reduction presented as a monetary difference.
   b. A price increase (or surcharge) presented as a percentage difference will be perceived *less* favorably (i.e., more unfavorably) than an equivalent increase (or surcharge) presented as a monetary difference.
2. When a reference price is *more* than 100:
   a. A price decrease presented as a percentage difference will be perceived *less* favorably than an equivalent reduction presented as a monetary difference.
   b. A price increase (or surcharge) presented as a percentage difference will be perceived *more* favorably (i.e., less unfavorably) than an equivalent increase (or surcharge) presented as a monetary difference.

## Price differences and information processing

Besides presenting price changes monetarily (e.g., $s, €s) or relatively (%s), sellers may offer gifts, bonus packs, cash gift cards for future purchases, or offer a discount for a product when full price is paid for another product (Weisstein *et al.* 2013). A bonus pack could be "Crest toothpaste, 50% more free, 7.8 oz. at the 5.2 oz. price" (Hardesty and Bearden 2003). These alternative price presentation formats create an information integration problem for people because different metrics (monetary and nonmonetary) are used (Gupta *et al.* 2007; Suri *et al.* 2013). People may be unable to estimate a price promotion's benefit for them and they may make incorrect inferences about an offer. Free gifts might enhance perceptions of quality and value (Darke and Chung 2005) but only when given by a high-priced brand (Raghubir 2004).

There is an inverted U-shape relationship between arousal, information processing, and judgments (Pham 1996; Suri and Monroe 2003).

When "moderate" discount amounts are offered, people being uncertain about an offer might process price information more completely. A perceived "low" discount would not stimulate much information processing and a perceived "high" discount needs little processing as the magnitude of savings is less uncertain. Using a dress shirt and three discount levels (low: $29.99/$24.99; moderate: $34.99/$24.99; and high: $49.99/$24.99) this prediction was supported (Grewal *et al.* 1996).[15]

Similarly, Wathieu and Bertini (2007) argued that prices either "slightly" or "highly" *above* buyers' willingness to pay would not stimulate thinking about a product's additional benefits due to a perceived higher price. Using lettuce and coffee in an online survey, price differentials based on prices "intermediately" above average market prices were more acceptable than price differentials based on prices either slightly or highly above average market prices.

When might people prefer monetary discounts relative to bonus packs, or promotions framed in dollars versus percentages? Discounts for toothpaste were presented separately as either "SAVE $.26, $.65, or $1.29".[16] The bonus pack promotion offered a percentage increase in quantity with "x % MORE FREE, y.y oz. [5.7, 6.5, or 7.8] at the 5.2 oz. price." The SAVE $1.29 offer was preferred over the bonus pack (50% free) at the "high" level, but participants were indifferent between price discounts or bonus packs at the "low" and "moderate" promotional levels (Hardesty and Bearden 2003).

Adults chose four low-priced household products in either the above "moderate" or "high" promotion level conditions. Comparing a bonus pack with a price discount, participants chose a 50% more quantity offer over an economically equivalent price reduction, but were indifferent between choosing 25% more quantity versus an economically equivalent monetary discount. Participants using different numerical judgment scales may have encoded the 50% more as relatively "large" but the money discounts as "small" because of the relatively small cumulative price discount for the four items ($2.49). The results imply they preferred a perceived "large" percentage discount to a perceived "small" monetary discount.

---

[15]While the discount manipulations were presented as given, comparatively, the discounts were $5 or 16.7%; $10 or 28.6%; and $25 or 50%. Designating a price change as low, moderate, or high in these studies has been a researcher's prerogative. Whether participants perceive and encode the price changes they encounter as low, moderate (or intermediate) needs to be verified by research.

[16]These discount levels were 10%, 25%, or 50%.

Initially, a field study over a 16-week period was conducted in a store using hand lotion regularly priced at $13.50 per bottle. On alternate weeks customers were offered either a 35% off price discount or a 50% more free bonus pack. The store sold significantly more bottles using the 50% more bonus pack promotions compared to the 35% price discount, receiving a significant positive effect on revenue for the product (Chen *et al.* 2012). Then a mall intercept survey using toothpaste and mouthwash revealed a preference for a bonus pack offering 50% more quantity free over an offer of 35% off the price of $3.89. *The deal condition with the larger number 50 was preferred over the economically equivalent condition with the smaller number 35.*

Four additional studies using coffee beans at $11.59 per lb. compared preferences for a bonus pack versus a percentage discount promotion. First, considering both price increases and decreases, participants responded to two variations (Chen *et al.* 2012, p. 69):

Now due to the price decrease (increase), you will get 50% more (33.33% less) of Brand A for the same price. In the meantime, the price of Brand B has decreased by 33.33% (increased by 50%) per lb.

In the price *decrease* condition participants preferred receiving 50% *more* coffee to paying 33.33% less money (50% more is preferable). However, in the price *increase* condition they preferred receiving 33.33% *less* coffee to paying 50% more money (33.33% less is preferable).

Second, using a similar scenario, individuals responded to three different conditions: (1) receiving 50% more coffee versus paying 33% less; (2) receiving 100% more coffee versus paying 50% less; or (3) receiving 11% more coffee versus paying 10% less. Participants preferred receiving 50% more coffee in the first condition but were indifferent between the bonus pack or price discount in the other two conditions.

Third, using either a $11.59 per lb. price (high level) or a $.69 per oz. price (low level) individuals responded to either (1) 50% more coffee versus 33% price discount; or (2) 33% more coffee versus 33% price discount. People preferred receiving 50% more coffee to paying 33% less at either price level. They were indifferent between the bonus pack or the price reduction at $.69 per oz., but preferred a 33% price discount over 33% more coffee at $11.59 per lb. Consistent with the earlier result, people preferred receiving 50% more coffee over paying a 33% lower price for either brand at $.69 per oz. People were indifferent between receiving 33%

more coffee to paying 33% less for a familiar brand, but preferred paying 33% less to receiving 33% more coffee for an unfamiliar brand.

## *Mixed leader bundling*

Mixed leader bundling is a form of promotion pricing when the price of one product is reduced if another product is purchased at regular price (Monroe 2003). The economic rationale for bundling assumes the way a bundle offer is presented will not influence people's judgments and choices. However, people may not perceive a bundle offer similarly even if the amount of savings from the individual prices is equivalent. A retailer with two stores about 20 minutes apart offers a pair of downhill skis for $300 and a portable CD player for $150 when purchased separately (Bonini and Rumiati 2002). A person buying both products is told at checkout in one store that the other store sells the CD player for $120 when the skis are purchased for $300. Or, assume the person wishes to buy the downhill skis for $300 and a pair of cross-country skis for $150 and is told the other store will sell the cross-country skis at $120 when the $300 downhill skis are also purchased. Respondents were more willing to go to the second store for the skis and CD player bundle than when the bundle consisted of the two types of skis.

The researchers concluded people in the first scenario perceived the $30 saving to be for the CD player (20%) and judged the offer to be attractive. However, in the skis bundle because the products were related conceptually, the $30 saving was perceived to be relative to the $450 (6.7%) and the offer was not perceived as attractive. A $30 saving on a $150 product was more attractive than a $30 saving on a $450 purchase. When two products are related conceptually, people may judge a mixed leader bundle promotion relative to the bundle's total price, but if the products are perceived to be unrelated, they may evaluate a discount relative to the price of the specific product that is reduced.[17]

---

[17] It is possible that buyers of downhill skis are not interested in buying cross-country skis, as they would not do both types of skiing. The pretesting of the skis manipulation indicated that respondents perceived the two types of skis to be related while the downhill skis and CD player were not. Monroe (2003) suggests that mixed joint bundling promotions would be effective if the discounted product complemented the focal product, for example using ski poles rather than a CD player or a functionally substitute product (cross-country skis).

An alternative explanation for this result comes from research showing that framing a promotion as savings on a hedonic item will be more effective than an equivalent discount framed as savings on a utilitarian item. "In bundles containing both hedonic and utilitarian items ... framing a discount as savings on the hedonic component will make it easier [for a buyer] to justify the purchase of the bundle" (Khan and Dhar 2010, p. 1091).

People may not automatically perceive a promotion for a bundle in a way that helps them justify purchasing the bundle. Presenting a discount as savings on either the total purchase (e.g., on the $450) or on a utilitarian item (e.g., second set of skis) will be less effective in spurring bundle purchases than framing an equivalent discount on an item that may be more guilt inducing. A key point here is to intentionally present a bundle offer by framing the savings in a way most likely to motivate buyers. Otherwise, people may frame an offer in ways a seller has not intended.

## Effects on quality inferences and internal reference prices

When a price promotion reduces a previous price, if a buyer's internal reference price does not change, perceived value would increase when the reduced selling price is compared to that reference price. Some assumptions are necessary to support this conclusion. Assuming the lower price does not negatively affect perceived quality implies the buyer knows quality has not been reduced. This situation would occur if a buyer knows the brand, has purchased from the seller before, and can judge quality has not been reduced. Otherwise, a buyer might infer the item's quality is inconsistent with its advertised regular price (Darke and Chung 2005; Rao and Monroe 1996). Inferring quality has been reduced along with the price could decrease perceived value.

Similarly, focusing on the reduced selling price could lower an individual's internal reference price for the item thereby reducing perceived value (Compeau and Grewal 1998; DelVecchio *et al.* 2007). When quality is unknown or difficult to judge, discounted prices could induce negative quality inferences and undermine a potential increase in perceived value due to the price promotion (Raghubir and Corfman 1999).

Whether buyers perceive an advertised external anchor price as plausible is also an issue (Urbany *et al.* 1988). If a promotion indicates an item is usually sold at a higher price and people believe it represents market price, they may use that price to infer quality. Judging the plausibility of an external anchor price depends on a buyer's price knowledge (i.e., internal reference price) (Blair *et al.* 2002). Buyers may wonder whether the lower selling price represents a bonafide savings. While the believability of the advertised external price and the size of the discount are important, it is a buyer's perception of the reduced selling price that influences responses to a promotion (Della Bitta *et al.* 1981; Lichtenstein *et al.* 1991).

## Effects on post-promotion price expectations

When a price promotion ends, do buyers expect prices to revert to previous levels? Has their internal reference price become lower than before the price promotion? What will be the effect on post-promotion purchases? In general, has the price promotion affected buyers' price expectations? Will the post-promotion effects differ depending on the amount of the price discount or whether the promotion was framed as a percentage or money discount?

A buyer's internal reference price could become lower than prior to the promotion (Kalwani and Yim 1992). In one study using low-price products (shampoo and tomato sauce) people in a $1.07 off promotion had lower post-promotion price expectations than people in a 40% off condition (DelVecchio *et al.* 2007). There were no differences across frames in a 15% off condition. The researchers surmised the cognitive cost to calculate the discount magnitude in the percentage-off promotion led to less downward adjustment of post-promotion price expectation (internal reference price). Participants could easily add the approximate $1.00 off in the money-off promotion to estimate the post-promotion price. This conclusion needs to be documented for other difficult comparisons involving monetary discounts.

## Perceived fairness of price promotions

Perceptions of price promotion fairness involve comparisons not only between an internal reference price and reduced selling prices but also between prices paid relative to what others pay (Feinberg *et al.* 2002; Xia *et al.* 2004). A price promotion might induce people to engage in inter-buyer price comparisons and to wonder whether they are being treated equitably. When prices paid by buyers who qualify for price promotions are lower than prices for others who are not qualified, there are questions about the fairness of such promotions. If some buyers perceive a price promotion is unfair, their perceptions of sacrifice might increase, reducing their perceptions of value of the promoted product. Such a result reduces the potential of the price promotion to enhance perceived value.

## Conclusions

Drawing on a relatively recent history of behavioral price and numerical cognition research, we have updated evidence on how people perceive price information, form value judgments, and make decisions when they have imperfect information about alternative choices. An important contribution stemming from behavioral price research is the recognition that peoples' perceptions effect how they respond to price information. These explanations help us understand why people may be more sensitive to price increases than to price decreases, or how they respond to comparative price advertisements, coupons, rebates, and other price promotions.

An important underlying premise for these responses is people judge prices comparatively; a *reference price* anchors their judgments. A reference price is a dynamic, internal price to which an individual compares another price. It may be an internal price the individual remembers from a previous purchase, accurate or not, an expected price, a belief about what would be a fair price for the product in the same market area, or even a vague notion of what the product might be worth. Moreover, a reference price is manifested as a level and people may not know consciously a reference price is actually in their mind as their judgments are made.

Unlike this behavioral approach, an economic approach does not invoke an uninformed consumer making "irrational" or sub-optimal decisions. Rather, there is an underlying assumption of a utility-maximizing buyer dealing with a profit-maximizing seller.[18] Unfortunately, people seldom are good information processors and they often take shortcuts consciously and non-consciously. "A heuristic is a strategy that ignores part of the information, with the goal of making decisions more quickly,

---

[18] Stiglitz (2012).

frugally, and/or accurately than more complex methods."[19] Such a shortcut, while facilitating the choice process, actually may be more likely to maximize value than a deliberate scrutiny of all alternatives. It can be conscious as well as non-conscious, can be defined as a rule, and could be more accurate than so-called optimizing strategies.

Evaluations of products and services may depend on different types of information or knowledge: (a) declarative information (i.e., features, facts, and benefits) and (b) experiential information (emotions and experiences evoked by the product or service). Judgments formed with the information or knowledge utilize both conscious feelings toward the product/service as well as non-conscious affective influences.[20] Feelings are an essential source of information.

Knowledge is the dynamic accumulation of personal assimilation and interpretation of data and contextual information received through the senses from experiences. It is a basis for evaluating and incorporating new experiences and information. All knowledge is personal and that is why the fundamental concepts discussed in this chapter have been presented at the individual person level. Through learning and experience, the prices of these products and services become "marked" by associations that are expressed through emotions and feelings.[21]

Behavioral researchers from multiple perspectives agree that the initial response to any environment is affective (positive and negative), and that the images marked by these feelings guide subsequent customer judgments and decisions within that environment. Yes, most people can judge that one number (offer price) is more or less than another number (internal reference price), but this judgment does not preclude an affective response. Individuals may become upset if the offer price exceeds their reference price, or if other buyers pay less than they do. Conversely, people may become elated if the offer price is less than their reference price. Also, we should not presume that people always prefer lower prices.

The way price information is initially presented to buyers will influence their psychological, physiological, and emotional reactions inducing sensations. It is these sensations that individuals must interpret leading to their perceptions of the information. We are reminded that our reactions

---

[19] Gigerenzer and Gaissmaier (2011, p. 454).
[20] Slovic, Finucane *et al.* (2007).
[21] Bechara and Damasio (2005).

are always subject to our interpretation of the environment within a "system of beliefs" we assimilate through personal experiences.

Central to studying price information processing is understanding how people encode and represent price and price-related information in their minds. Previous price memory research has assumed that the Arabic numerals would be encoded and represented in buyers' minds exactly in symbolic form. When people do not recall the actual symbols accurately, it has been inferred that they have not attended to the price information when making their choices. However, such inferences perhaps are not warranted because people may encode and *represent* the price information in memory as approximations (e.g. less than $100) or as evaluations (e.g., not expensive). Also, working memory capacity in humans is limited and information decays within 2–3 seconds unless it is rehearsed. Simply, recall is an inadequate indicator of how fluent recently encountered price information may be in a person's memory.

People compare prices, make calculations and estimates when evaluating options, and then making choices. They may not always handle these tasks effortlessly or accurately. Moreover, people have difficulty making calculations relative to everyday living and they often avoid doing so, at times choosing a heuristic to simplify their task.

# References

Adaval, R. and K. B. Monroe (2002), Automatic construction and use of contextual information for product and price evaluations, *Journal of Consumer Research*, 28, 572–588.

Algom, D., A. Dekel, and A. Pansky (1996), The perception of number from the separability of the stimulus: The stroop effect revisited, *Memory & Cognition*, 24, 557–572.

Balan, C. (2013), Research on odd prices, in *Innovation in Pricing*, A. Hinterhuber and S. Liozu, eds., New York: Routledge, 376–392.

Barden, P. (2013), *Decoded: The Science Behind Why We Buy*, Chichester, UK: John Wiley & Sons.

Barone, M. J., K. B. Lyle, and K. P. Winterich (2016), When deal depth doesn't matter: How handedness consistency influences consumer response to horizontal versus vertical price comparisons, *Marketing Letters*, 26, 213–223.

Bertini, M. and L. Wathieu (2008), Attention, arousal through price partitioning, *Marketing Science*, 27, 236–246.

Bogomolova, S., H. Oppewal, J. Cohen, and J. Yao (2018), How the layout of a unit price label affects eye-movements and product choice: An eye-tracking investigation, *Journal of Business Research*, 111, 102–116.

Bonini, N. and R. Rumiati (2002), Acceptance of a price discount: The role of the semantic relatedness between purchases and the comparative price format, *Journal of Behavioral Decision Making*, 15, 203–220.

Bornemann, T. and C. Homburg (2011), Psychological distance and the dual role of price, *Journal of Consumer Research*, 38, 490–504.

Bray, J. P. and C. Harris (2006), The effect of 9-ending prices on retail sales: A quantitative UK based field study, *Journal of Marketing Management*, 22, 601–617.

Cai, F., H. Shen, and M. Hui (2012), The effect of location on price estimation: Understanding number-location and number-order associations, *Journal of Marketing Research*, 49, 718–724.

Chen, H. and A. R. Rao (2007), When two plus two is not equal to four: Errors in processing multiple percentage changes, *Journal of Consumer Research*, 34, 327–340.

Chen, H., H. Marmorstein M. Tsiros, and A. R. Rao (2012), When more is less: The impact of base value neglect on consumer preferences for bonus packs over price discounts, *Journal of Marketing*, 76(4), 44–63.

Chen, S-F. S., K. B. Monroe, and Y-C. Lou (1998), The effects of framing price promotion messages on consumers' perceptions and purchase intentions, *Journal of Retailing*, 74, 353–372.

Cheng, L. L. and K. B. Monroe (2013a), An appraisal of behavioral price research (part 1): Price as a physical stimulus, *AMS Review*, 3(3), 103–129.

Cheng, L. L. and K. B. Monroe (2013b), Some reflections on an appraisal of behavioral price research (part 1), *AMS Review*, 3(3), 155–159.

Choi, J., K. Lee, and Y.-Y. Ji (2012), What type of framing message is more appropriate with nine-ending pricing? *Marketing Letters*, 23, 603–614.

Choi, P. and K. S. Coulter (2012), It's not all relative: The effects of mental and physical positioning of comparative prices on absolute versus relative discount assessment, *Journal of Retailing*, 88, 512–527.

Compeau, L. D. and D. Grewal (1998), Comparative price advertising: An integrative review, *Journal of Public Policy & Marketing*, 17, 257–273.

Coulter, K. S. and R. A. Coulter (2007), Distortion of price discount perceptions: The right digit effect, *Journal of Consumer Research*, 34, 162–173.

Coulter, K. S. and P. A. Norberg (2009), The effects of physical distance between regular and sale prices on numerical difference perceptions, *Journal of Consumer Psychology*, 19, 144–157.

Coulter, K. S. and A. L. Roggeveen (2014), Price number relationships and deal processing fluency: The effects of approximation sequences and number multiples, *Journal of Marketing Research*, 51, 69–82.

Crollen, V., S. Grade, M. Pesenti, and V. Dormal (2013), A common metric magnitude system for the perception and production of numerosity, length, and duration, *Frontiers in Psychology*, 4, 1–11.

Darke, P. R. and J. L. Freedman (1993), Deciding whether to seek a bargain: Effects of both amount and percentage off, *Journal of Applied Psychology*, 78, 960–965.

Darke, P. R., J. L. Freedman, and S. Chaiken (1995), Percentage discounts, initial price, and bargain hunting: A heuristic-systematic approach to price search behavior, *Journal of Applied Psychology*, 80, 580–586.

Darke, P. R. and C. M. Y. Chung (2005), Effects of pricing and promotion on consumer perceptions: It depends on how you frame it, *Journal of Retailing*, 81, 35–47.

Dastjerdi, M., M. Ozker, B. L. Foster, V. Rangarajan, and J. Parvizi (2014), Numerical processing in the human parietal cortex during experimental and natural conditions, *Nature Communications*, 4 (October 15), accessed November 24, 2014, doi: 10.1038/ncomms3528.

Dehaene, S. (1989), The psychophysics of numerical comparison: A re-examination of apparently incompatible data, *Perception and Psychophysics*, 45, 557–566.

Dehaene, S. (1992), Varieties of numerical abilities, in *Numerical Cognition*, S. Dehaene, ed., Cambridge, MA: Blackwell, 1–42.

Dehaene, S. (1997), *The Number Sense: How the Mind Creates Mathematics*, New York: Oxford University Press.

Dehaene, S. (2011), *The Number Sense: How the Mind Creates Mathematics* (Revised edition), New York: Oxford University Press.

Dehaene, S. (2003), The neural basis of the Weber-Fechner law: A logarithmic mental number line, *TRENDS in Cognitive Science*, 7, 145–147.

Dehaene, S. and R. Akhavein (1995), Attention, automaticity, and levels of representation in number processing, *Journal of Experimental Psychology*, 21, 314–326.

Dehaene, S., S. Bossini, and P. Giraux (1993), The mental representation of parity and number magnitude, *Journal of Experimental Psychology: General*, 122, 371–396.

Della Bitta, A. J., K. B. Monroe, and J. M. McGinnis (1981), Consumer perceptions of comparative price advertisements, *Journal of Marketing Research*, 18, 416–427.

DelVecchio, D. (2005), Deal-prone consumers' response to promotion: The effects of relative and absolute promotion value, *Psychology & Marketing*, 22, 373–391.

DelVecchio, D., H. S. Krishnan, and D. C. Smith (2007), Cents or percent? The effects of promotion framing on price expectations and choice, *Journal of Marketing*, 71 (July), 158–170.

DelVecchio, D., A. Lakshmanan, and H. S. Krishnan (2009), The effects of discount location and frame on consumers' price estimates, *Journal of Retailing*, 85(3), 336–346.

Diller, H. and A. Brielmaier (1995), The impact of rounding up odd prices: Results of a field experiment in German drugstores, *Pricing Strategy & Tactics*, 3, 4–13.

Dolansky, E. and M. Vandenbosch (2013), Price sequences, perceived variability, and choice. *Journal of Product & Brand Management*, 22, 314–321.

Estelami, H. (1999), The computational effect of price endings in multi-dimensional price advertising, *Journal of Product & Brand Management*, 8, 244–256.

Feinberg, F. M., A. Krishna, and Z. J. Zhang (2002), Do we care what others get? A behaviorist approach to targeted promotions, *Journal of Marketing Research*, 39, 277–291.

Gendall, P., J. Hoek, T. Pope, and K. Young (2006), Message framing effects on price discounting, *Journal of Product & Brand Management*, 15(7), 458–465.

González, E. M., E. Esteva, A. L. Roggeveen, and D. Grewal (2015), Amount off versus percentage off — when does it matter? *Journal of Business Research*, http://dx.doi.org/10.1016/j.jbusres.2015.08.014.

Grewal, D. and H. Marmorstein (1994), Market price variation, perceived price variation, and consumers' price search decisions for durable goods, *Journal of Consumer Research*, 21, 453–460.

Grewal, D., H. Marmorstein, and A. Sharma (1996), Communicating price information through semantic cues: The moderating effects of situation and discount size, *Journal of Consumer Research*, 23, 148–155.

Grewal, D., K. B. Monroe, and R. Krishnan (1998), The effects of price-comparison advertising on buyers' perceptions of acquisition value, transaction value, and behavioral intentions, *Journal of Marketing*, 62, 46–59.

Guido, G. and A. Peluso (2004), Consumers' perception of odd-ending prices with the introduction of the Euro, *Journal of Product & Brand Management*, 16, 200–205.

Gupta, O., S. Tandon, S. Debnath, and A. Rominger (2007), Package downsizing: Is it ethical? *AI & Society*, 21(3), 239–250.

Gupta, S. and L. G. Cooper (1992), The discounting of discounts and promotion thresholds, *Journal of Consumer Research*, 19, 401–411.

Hardesty, D. M. and W. O. Bearden (2003), Consumer evaluations of different promotion types and price presentation: The moderating role of promotional benefit level, *Journal of Retailing*, 79, 17–25.

Heath, T. B., S. Chatterjee, and K. R. France (1995), Mental accounting and change in price: The frame dependence of preference dependence, *Journal of Consumer Research*, 22, 90–97.

Hines, T. M. (1990), An odd effect: Lengthened reaction times for judgments about odd digits, *Memory & Cognition*, 18, 40–46.

Homburg, C., N. Koschate, and D. Totzek (2010), How price increases affect future purchases: The role of mental budgeting, income, and framing, *Psychology & Marketing*, 27(1), 36–53.

Kadosh, R. C., A. Henik, O. Rubinstein, H. Mohr, H. Dori, and V. van de Ven (2005), Are numbers special? The comparison systems of the human brain investigated by fMRI, *Neuropsychologia*, 43, 1238–1248.

Kalwani, M. U. and C. K. Yim (1992), Consumer price and promotion expectations: An experimental study, *Journal of Marketing Research*, 29, 90–100.

Kalyanaram, G. and J. D. C. Little (1994), An empirical analysis of latitude of price acceptance in consumer package goods, *Journal of Consumer Research*, 21, 408–418.

Khan, U. and R. Dhar (2010), Price-framing effects on the purchase of hedonic and utilitarian bundles, *Journal of Marketing Research*, 47, 1090–1099.

King, D. and C. Janiszewski (2011), The sources and consequences of the fluent processing of numbers, *Journal of Marketing Research*, 48, 327–341.

Krishnamurthi, L., T. Mazumdar, and S. P. Raj (1992), Asymmetric response to price in consumer brand choice and purchase quantity decisions, *Journal of Consumer Research*, 19, 387–400.

Lambert, Z. V. (1978), Differential thresholds in consumer perception of retail prices, *The Journal of Psychology*, 100, 139–150.

Lichtenstein, D. R., S. Burton, and E. J. Karson (1991), The effect of semantic cues on consumer perceptions of reference price ads, *Journal of Consumer Research*, 18, 380–390.

Lynn, M., S. M. Flynn, and C. Helion (2013), Do consumers prefer round prices? Evidence from pay-what-you-want decisions and self-pumped gasoline purchases, *Journal of Economic Psychology*, 36, 96–102.

McKechnie, S., J. Devlin, C. Ennew, and A. Smith (2012), Effects of discount framing in comparative price advertising, *European Journal of Marketing*, 46, 1501–1522.

Monroe, K. B. (1971a), The information content of prices: A preliminary model for estimating buyer response, *Management Science*, 17, B-519–532.

Monroe, K. B. (1971b), Measuring price thresholds by psychophysics and latitudes of acceptance, *Journal of Marketing Research*, 8, 460–464.

Monroe, K. B. (1977), Objective and subjective contextual influences on price perceptions, in *Consumer and Industrial Buying Behavior*, A. G. Woodside, J. N. Sheth, and P. D. Bennett, eds., New York: North-Holland, 287–296.

Monroe, K. B. (2003), *Pricing: Making Profitable Decisions* (3rd edn.), New York: McGraw-Hill Book Co.

Monroe, K. B. and A. Y. Lee (1999), Remembering vs. knowing: Issues in buyers' processing of price information, *Journal of the Academy of Marketing Science*, 27, 207–225.

Nieder, A. and S. Dehaene (2009), Representation of number in the brain, *Annual Review of Neuroscience*, 32, 185–208.

Ofir, C. (2004), Reexamining latitude of price acceptability and price thresholds: Predicting basic consumer reaction to price, *Journal of Consumer Research*, 30, 612–621.

Piazza, M., P. Pinel, D. Le Bihan, and S. Dehaene (2007), A magnitude code common to numerosities and number symbols in human intraparietal cortex, *Neuron*, 53, 293–305.

Pham, M. T. (1996), Cue representation and selection effects of arousal on persuasion, *Journal of Consumer Research*, 22, 373–387.

Pope, D. and U. Simonsohn (2011), Round numbers as goals: Evidence from baseball, SAT takers and the lab, *Psychological Science*, 22, 71–79.

Raghubir, P. (2004), Free gift with purchase: Promoting or discounting the brand? *Journal of Consumer Psychology*, 14, 181–186.

Raghubir, P. and K. Corfman (1999), When do price promotions affect pretrial brand evaluations? *Journal of Marketing Research*, 36, 211–222.

Raghubir, P., J. J. Inman, and H. Grande (2004), The three faces of consumer promotions, *California Management Review*, 46, 23–42.

Ramanathan, S. and S. K. Dhar (2010), The effect of sales promotions on the size and composition of the shopping basket: Regulatory compatibility from framing and temporal restrictions, *Journal of Marketing Research*, 47, 542–552.

Rao, A. R. and K. B. Monroe (1996), Causes and consequences of price premiums, *Journal of Business*, 69, 511–535.

Riener, G. and C. Traxler (2012), Norms, moods, and free lunch: Longitudinal evidence on payments from a pay-what-you-want restaurant, *Journal of Socio Economics*, 41, 476–483.

Suri, R. and K. B. Monroe (2003), The effects of time constraints on consumers' judgments of prices and products, *Journal of Consumer Research*, 30, 92–104.

Suri, R., J. Z. Cai, K. B. Monroe, and Thakor, M. V. (2012), Retailers' merchandise organization and price perceptions, *Journal of Retailing*, 88, 168–179.

Suri, R., Monroe, K. B. and U. Koc (2013). Math anxiety and its effects on consumers' preference for price promotion formats, *Journal of the Academy of Marketing Science*, 41, 271–282.

Thomas, M. and V. Morwitz (2005), Penny wise and pound foolish: The left digit effect in price cognition, *Journal of Consumer Research*, 32, 54–65.

Thomas, M. and V. Morwitz (2009), The ease of computation effect: The interplay of metacognitive experiences and naïve theories in judgments of price differences, *Journal of Marketing Research*, 46, 81–91.

Thomas, M., D. H. Simon, and V. Kadiyali (2010), The price precision effect: Evidence from laboratory and market data, *Marketing Science*, 29, 175–190.

Tsiros, M. and D. M. Hardesty (2010), Ending a price promotion: Retracting it in one step or phasing it out gradually, *Journal of Marketing*, 74(1), 49–64.

Tzelgov, J., J. Meyer, and A. Henik (1992), Automatic and intentional processing of numerical information, *Journal of Experimental Psychology: Learning, Memory, and Cognition*, 18, 166–179.

Urbany, J. E., W. O. Bearden, and D. C. Weilbaker (1988), The effect of plausible and exaggerated reference prices on consumer perceptions and price search, *Journal of Consumer Research*, 15, 95–110.

Urbany, J. E., W. O. Bearden, A. Kaicker, and M. Smith-de-Borrero (1997), Transaction utility effects when quality is uncertain, *Journal of the Academy of Marketing Science*, 25, 45–55.

Wadhwa, M. and K. Zhang (2015), This number just feels right: The impact of roundness of price numbers on product evaluations, *Journal of Consumer Research*, 41, 1172–1185.

Wathieu, L. and M. Bertini (2007), Price as a stimulus to think: The case for willful overpricing, *Marketing Science*, 26, 118–129.

Weathers, D., S. D. Swain, and J. P. Carlson (2012), Why consumers respond differently to absolute versus percentage descriptions of quantities, *Marketing Letters*, 23, 943–975.

Weisstein, F. L., K. B. Monroe, and M. Kukar-Kinney (2013), Effects of price framing on consumers' perceptions of online dynamic pricing practices, *Journal of the Academy of Marketing Science*, 41, 501–514.

Xia, L. and K. B. Monroe (2009), The influence of pre-purchase goals on consumer perceptions, *International Journal of Retail & Distribution Management*, 37, 680–694.

Xia, L. K. B. Monroe, and J. L. Cox (2004), The price is unfair! A conceptual framework of price fairness perceptions, *Journal of Marketing*, 68, 1–15.

https://doi.org/10.1142/9789811292231_0005

Chapter 5

# Buyer Behavior in Pay-What-You-Want Pricing*

**Lucas Stich and Martin Spann**

Pay-What-You-Want (PWYW) pricing delegates full control over the price to prospective buyers. Contrary to the rational self-interest prediction that all buyers will take the product and pay nothing, field applications of PWYW show that many buyers do not exploit this control but pay positive prices voluntarily. In this chapter, we discuss three key theoretical accounts that explain buyer behavior in PWYW pricing settings. Based on these theoretical accounts, we discuss implications for the design and effectiveness of PWYW as a pricing mechanism. In addition, we discuss opportunities for future research and practice.

## Introduction

When sellers relinquish control over selling prices completely and leave it to buyers to decide how much to pay for their goods or services, that pricing mechanism is called *Pay-What-You-Want* (*PWYW*). Under PWYW

---

*In *New Directions in Behavioral Pricing*, Chezy Ofir Ed., 2024, World Scientific Publishing Company.

Lucas Stich, Julius-Maximilians-Universität Würzburg, Würzburg, Germany (lucas. stich@uni-wuerzburg.de); Martin Spann, Ludwig-Maximilians-Universität München, Germany (spann@lmu.de).

pricing, buyers can pay the seller any price they deem appropriate. Importantly, this delegated pricing power also includes the freedom of paying nothing at all. Sellers thus naturally expose themselves to the risk of buyers exploiting their pricing power and consuming goods or services without paying anything. However, research shows that buyers rarely pay nothing (e.g., Gneezy *et al.* 2012; Kim *et al.* 2009). Instead, in many cases a substantial fraction of buyers pays positive prices voluntarily. This insight has led to a surge of research on the innovative pricing format.[1] PWYW has also triggered significant attention in practice, with numerous organizations in various domains having gained experience with short and long-term implementations of PWYW.

From a seller's perspective, contemplating the introduction of a pricing mechanism that gives buyers full control over prices requires a thorough understanding of buyer behavior. In this chapter, we therefore review key theoretical explanations of buyer behavior under PWYW pricing and elaborate on their empirical support. We focus on three theoretical accounts that can explain whether people participate in PWYW pricing and, if so, whether and how much they pay to a PWYW seller. More generally, these accounts can explain *why* people behave as they do in PWYW settings. We then use these accounts as an organizing framework to discuss implications for the design and effectiveness of PWYW. Eventually, we outline and debate opportunities for research and practice.

# Classification of Pay-What-You-Want and Prevalence in Practice

The *Pay-What-You-Want* (*PWYW*) pricing mechanism (sometimes also referred to as *Pay-As-You-Wish*) belongs to the class of *participative pricing mechanisms*. The term participative pricing mechanism captures the central notion that buyers participate in the price-setting process and have (some) control over the final transaction price. Spann *et al.* (2018) provide a taxonomy to classify different participative pricing mechanisms.[2] This

---

[1] For other reviews see Natter and Kaufmann (2015) or Gerpott (2016). Related terms are "Pay-As-You-Wish" and "Pay-What-You-Wish".

[2] Bertini and Koenigsberg (2014) and Kim *et al.* (2009) suggested alternative taxonomies and classifications of participative pricing mechanisms.

taxonomy classifies participative pricing mechanisms along two dimensions. The first dimension, the role of the buyers, distinguishes whether the outcome of a transaction depends on competition among (potential) buyers for the same object or not. The second dimension, the interactivity of the mechanism, distinguishes whether the seller takes an active role in the outcome (interactive mechanisms) or not (non-interactive mechanisms). Consequently, PWYW can be classified as a non-interactive (i.e., the seller is passive) participative pricing mechanism where there is no competition between potential buyers. By contrast to interactive mechanisms that involve no competition between potential buyers (e.g., Name-Your-Own-Price, bargaining), transactions in PWYW are unconditional. Buyers can pay any price they deem appropriate (including zero) and the seller must accept it. PWYW sellers thus fully delegate pricing power to their buyers.

Asking people to pay what they want (or can) is common practice. In fact, one of the fundamental problems studied in economics is the design of and the behavior in the voluntary contributions mechanism (VCM). In the VCM, people need to determine what amount to contribute to a public good and the dominant, selfish strategy appears to be contributing nothing at all (Bochet *et al.* 2006; Carpenter 2007; Isaac and Walker 1988; Masclet *et al.* 2003). Unlike the VCM, PWYW commonly refers to products that are intended for consumers' private consumption as well as public consumption, although the public-good connotation is sometimes apparent.

Since 2007, when the British band Radiohead released their album *In Rainbows* exclusively as a digital download and let their fans decide how much to pay for it (Kim *et al.* 2009), PWYW has been used as a pricing mechanism across a wide range of goods and services. We classify example applications of PWYW in Table 1, where we distinguish between (1) goods and services/experiences and (2) for-profit and not-for-profit organizations.

## Theoretical Explanations of Buyer Behavior

In this section, we present three theoretical accounts that can explain buyer behavior under PWYW pricing. In particular, these accounts provide insights into whether people participate in PWYW pricing and, if so,

**Table 1.** Applications of pay-what-you-want pricing.

| | For-Profit Organizations | Not-for-Profit Organizations |
|---|---|---|
| Goods | • Digital content: games, e-books, and software on humblebundle.com, journalism on theguardian.com<br>• Offline game cards: "Cards Against Humanity"<br>• Product samples (men's razor, portrait prints)<br>• Music: musicians like Amanda Palmer and Moby, bands including Radiohead and Nine Inch Nails, the online music store Magnatune | • Digital content: Wikipedia |
| Services/Experiences | • Gastronomy: restaurants Kish in Frankfurt (Germany) and Der Wiener Deewan in Vienna (Austria), wine bar Weinerei in Berlin (Germany)<br>• Hotels: NH hotels in Belgium and Netherlands, Ibis hotel Chennai City Centre<br>• Banking: Aspiration<br>• Agencies: design agency 8k (Poland), travel agency Atrápalo (Spain)<br>• Cinemas/theaters: The New Parkway Theater in Oakland (CA, USA)<br>• Publishers: Thieme Publishers for article processing charges of Open Access publications | • Zoos: Zoos in Augsburg and Münster (both Germany)<br>• Museums: Metropolitan Museum of Art in New York City (NY, USA), Museum König in Bonn (Germany) |

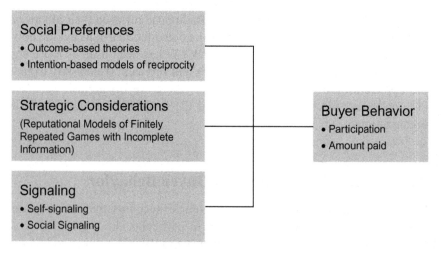

**Figure 1.** Theoretical accounts explaining buyer behavior in PWYW pricing.

whether and how much they pay to a PWYW seller. Eventually, we review selected research on buyer behavior in PWYW pricing that provide evidence for each of the three theoretical accounts. Figure 1 outlines these theoretical explanations of PWYW buyer behavior.

## Social preferences

### Outcome-based theories

Outcome-based theories of social preferences state that many people, in various economic situations (e.g., dictator games, ultimatum games), behave unselfishly and care about the well-being of others. People frequently behave altruistically (Andreoni and Miller 2002) and are influenced by fairness considerations in their behavior (Fehr and Schmidt 1999). Yet, there is also evidence that suggests that fairness motives are less important and that people behave as if they were only interested in their own material payoffs (Fehr and Schmidt 1999). Thus, considerable individual heterogeneity exists and the interaction between altruists and more selfish individuals is crucial to human cooperation (Fehr and Fischbacher 2003).

Fairness can be modeled as inequity aversion, meaning that people prefer to achieve more equitable outcomes and are willing to sacrifice some of their own resources to avoid inequitable outcomes (Fehr and Schmidt 1999). Note that in Fehr and Schmidt's model of inequity aversion there also exist purely selfish individuals. However, in addition, there are some individuals who experience inequity and therefore disutility if they are worse off in material terms than other individuals (i.e., disadvantageous inequality), but they also feel inequity if they are better off (i.e., advantageous inequality).

Outcome-based theories of social preferences predict that fair-minded buyers in PWYW will pay positive prices voluntarily, and they will pay higher prices the greater their surplus from transacting with the seller and the higher the cost of the seller. The reasoning behind this prediction is that buyers are motivated to achieve an equal income distribution in which the PWYW seller is not worse off than they are. If buyers' willingness-to-pay for a product is sufficiently large (i.e., greater than the cost of the seller) and other-regarding preferences are strong enough, they will pay even more than the cost that accrues to the seller. Yet, buyers may shy away from a PWYW seller if they feel obliged to pay positive prices but are uncertain about the appropriate amount or if they cannot afford paying cost-covering prices. In case a posted-price seller is available, they may then prefer to buy from this seller or forego the transaction altogether. In addition, outcome-based models of social preferences predict that people are willing to pay more to a not-for-profit organization or to small and financially weaker firms than to larger and financially more powerful corporations (Schmidt *et al.* 2015).

Fairness motives and altruism have been identified as important factors for explaining buyers' positive payments under PWYW pricing in numerous field studies (e.g., Kim *et al.* 2009; Kunter 2015) across various industries (e.g., gastronomy, entertainment, and culture). Additionally, results from several (field) experiments report fairness considerations as a significant predictor of PWYW payment decisions (e.g., Jang and Chu 2012; Kim *et al.* 2014a). Schmidt *et al.* (2015) provide causal evidence for outcome-based social preferences as a driver of buyers' voluntary payments to PWYW sellers. Consistent with this account, their results from induced-value laboratory experiments show that buyers pay more the greater their valuations and the higher the sellers' cost.

## Intention-based models of reciprocity

Models of intention-based reciprocity (e.g., Dufwenberg and Kirchsteiger 2004; Falk and Fischbacher 2006; Rabin 1993) are based on psychological game theory and argue that the behavior of some people is influenced by their beliefs about the intentions of others (Fehr and Schmidt 2006). A player that cares about the intentions of her opponent will happily reciprocate kind actions if she believes that the opponent intends to be kind to her. Conversely, the player will try to retaliate if she believes that the other person wanted to hurt her. The player will reciprocate kind actions even if she was hurt by her opponent's action as long as she believes that the action was well intended.

What does this imply for buyer behavior in PWYW? Buyers that are motivated by intention-based reciprocity will respond to the actions of the seller regardless of the seller's cost or their own willingness-to-pay. Moreover, changes in seller's cost or buyers' willingness-to-pay will not affect buyer behavior unless these changes are induced by the seller's actions. Following these theories, the only driver of buyer behavior is their belief about the intentions of the seller. When buyers perceive a seller's adoption of PWYW as a kind deed (e.g., because it allows them to save money relative to a posted price or just because it is more entertaining), they will reciprocate and pay higher prices. Buyers may even reciprocate a seller's kind action to employ the PWYW pricing mechanism by refraining from buy from this seller if they cannot pay prices that match this kind behavior (e.g., cost-covering prices). In fact, it is then a kind move of buyers not to purchase from this seller at prices below the seller's cost.

Empirical evidence for concerns of reciprocity and reputation as major drivers of voluntary payments in PWYW settings were documented in the context of a former Google service (Google Answers) and in the domain of online music (Regner 2014; Regner 2015; Regner and Barria 2009). For example, Regner (2015) studied customers of the online music label/store Magnatune who could pay what they wanted for music albums as long as their payment was within a given price range ($5–$18). To explain the finding that customers paid on average significantly more than what they had to, he conducted an online survey with more than 200 Magnatune customers who had made at least 10 purchases in the past. Controlling for both individual response bias and sample selection bias, he finds reciprocity to be the major driver for more generous voluntary payments. Across studies (Regner 2014; Regner 2015; Regner and Barria 2009), the authors consistently report positive and substantial voluntary payments by buyers for different services.

## *Strategic considerations/reputational models of finitely repeated games with incomplete information*

Reputational models of finitely repeated games with incomplete information can explain the frequent observation that people (players) in repeated interactions (games) cooperate and do not choose the single-round dominant strategy (Kreps *et al.* 1982). For example, a frequent outcome of experiments playing a finite number of the prisoners' dilemma is that human players do not always choose the strategy ("finking") that is dominant in a single-round world (Kreps *et al.* 1982). Although finking is the only Nash equilibrium in the finitely repeated game, players regularly cooperate to some degree. Incomplete information about one or both players' options, motivation, or behavior can rationalize why players may strive to establish a reputation (e.g., for being "tough" or "benevolent") in the early rounds of such games (Kreps and Wilson 1982).

What are the implications from these models for buyer behavior in PWYW? Repeated interactions between buyers and sellers gives scope for strategic considerations (Schmidt *et al.* 2015). For instance, buyers may be motivated to purchase from and offer higher prices to a PWYW seller to keep the seller in business or to continue the provision of PWYW in the future. This might be the case, for example, for a shop or restaurant in the neighborhood that the buyer wants to continue operating (using PWYW). If the future provision of PWYW is contingent on whether buyers' payments are sufficient for the seller to achieve financial goals, then buyers' payments are akin to the contributions of individuals in a threshold or step-level public good game (Croson and Marks 2000; Mak *et al.* 2015). Therefore, even purely self-interested buyers may pay positive prices if this behavior entails the seller's future provision of PWYW, under which they are better off than if the seller uses posted prices. This argument also applies to the avoidance of seller's bankruptcy.

Assume a seller who faces demand from purely self-interested as well as fair-minded or reciprocal buyers. However, the seller has incomplete information about buyers' types. Here, purely self-interested buyers will strive in the early rounds of interaction for a reputation of paying positive and cost-covering prices that keep the seller in business and encourage future market entry and provision of PWYW. While fair-minded and reciprocal buyers will pay positive prices in every round, self-interested buyers will randomize between paying and not paying in the last rounds. Hence, we should observe decreasing average prices paid to the seller if there are only a few rounds of interaction left. It is important to note that for the seller to enter the market, it requires at least some buyers with other-regarding preferences to pay positive prices in all rounds. If a posted-price alternative is available, buyers will reduce their payments and efforts to keep the PWYW seller in the market because they are less dependent on this channel.

Besides the support of reputational models to explain voluntary payments in PWYW settings identified in field data (Regner 2014), there is evidence for strategic considerations to explain positive voluntary payments from laboratory experiments. Mak *et al.* (2015), in their theoretical model and experimental analysis, establish that sustained cooperative equilibria among buyers can make the continuous provision of PWYW viable for the seller even if all buyers are purely self-interested. The results of the laboratory experiments by Schmidt *et al.* (2015) provide further support for strategic reasons as a driving force behind voluntary payments to PWYW sellers. They find that a significant fraction of the buyers in their experiments pay for the strategic reason of keeping the seller in business. This result also suggests that a seller (e.g., a store or a restaurant in the neighborhood) that repeatedly interacts with its customers is likely to receive higher payments than a seller that only interacts with most of its customers once (e.g., a snack bar at a train station).

## Signaling

### Self-signaling

Image concerns can play an important role in motivating people to behave prosocially in markets (e.g., Ariely *et al.* 2009; Dubé *et al.* 2017). This can be seen more formally in the model of Bénabou and Tirole (2011). In their model of identity management, individuals derive utility from prosocial behavior as a signaling mechanism (Gneezy *et al.* 2012). The basic idea is that people want to be liked and respected, by others, and by themselves. By behaving prosocially, people send an informative signal to others, but also to themselves (self-signaling), such that they are judged more positively, by others, and by themselves. Conversely, actions that imply character traits such as being unfair or greedy reduce a positive image or even result in a negative image (Ariely *et al.* 2009).

In the context of PWYW, self-image concerns can help to explain whether people buy from a PWYW seller and if so, how much they pay to the seller. For example, Dana *et al.* (2006) show across two lab experiments that about one-third of their participants prefer to avoid a $10 dictator game and take $9 instead. While opting out of the dictator-game option left the potential receiver nothing, it also ensured that the potential receiver never learned that a dictator game was even about to be played. This result can be rationalized by self-image concerns of participants. Apparently, participants preferred giving up $1 to not appear selfish. Taken to PWYW, this result suggests that some people may rather avoid buying from a PWYW seller than paying too little and corrupting their prosocial self-image. The self-signaling model also enables predictions about how much buyers voluntarily pay to a PWYW seller. In the self-signaling model (Bénabou and Tirole 2011), people can at times be uncertain about their preferences and deepest beliefs, for example, regarding their concern for others. By the actions they take, people can influence their beliefs about themselves and infer what kind of individuals they are. If people want to achieve or maintain a self-image of high morals and concern for others under PWYW pricing, then paying a "fair" price to the PWYW seller for a good or service received seems like the right strategy.

A substantial body of experimental research demonstrates evidence for self-signaling as a driving force of buyers' participation in PWYW pricing and the voluntary payment of positive prices (e.g., Gautier and van der Klaauw 2012; Gneezy *et al.* 2012; Jang and Chu 2012). Consider the theme park experiment in Gneezy *et al.* (2012) as an example. This field experiment was carried out in collaboration with a large amusement park. The setup of this experiment was simple. Participants were riders of a rollercoaster attraction who were photographed during their ride and were given the choice to purchase a print of the photo later on. Riders were randomly assigned to one of two conditions. In the first condition, participants could purchase their photo in a regular PWYW setting. In the other condition, participants were informed that half of their payment would be donated to a charitable cause. Consistent with a self-signaling motive, the authors found that significantly more riders opted to make a purchase in the regular PWYW condition but that, conditional on purchase, payments were more than five times higher in the *PWYW* + *charitable cause* condition.

Taken together, the results from this literature (e.g., Gautier and van der Klaauw 2012; Gneezy *et al.* 2012; Jang and Chu 2012) strongly suggest that identity and self-image concerns are important determinants of buyers' prosocial behavior in different market contexts. However, Gautier and van der Klaauw (2012) also point out that there may exist considerable heterogeneity in buyers' prosocial preferences, which may translate into different behaviors.

## Social signaling

Similar to self-signaling motivations, social-image considerations can be an important motivator of people's (prosocial) behavior (e.g., Ariely *et al.* 2009; Bernheim 1994). The basic idea is that people are at least partly motivated in their behavior by how they are perceived by others, i.e. they derive utility from the opinion of others about themselves. As a result, people seeking social approval of their behavior would try to send signals that are considered desirable or "good" by their social environment. Since non-selfish and fair-minded behavior is typically perceived as good, pro-social behavior is a way of signaling one's good traits (e.g., kindness, generosity) to peers. Given that prosocial behavior translates into a positive social image, a desire for social approval would induce people to behave more prosocially in the public rather than in private domains.

People who care about their status (e.g., esteem or popularity) would consider what others might think about them when making payment decisions. Under PWYW pricing, buyers can use their payments to signal to others. For example, buyers can make high payments voluntarily to signal their prosperity or generosity. If such payments are visible to others and buyers are motivated by social-image concerns, then we should expect even higher payments compared to situations in which buyers pay anonymously. Conversely, one would expect buyers who care about their status not to make low payments or pay nothing at all.

Santana and Morwitz (2011) and Kim *et al.* (2014a) offer empirical support for the social-signaling account. In an experiment, manipulating whether payments are made privately or publicly, Santana and Morwitz (2011) show that participants in the public payment condition had a significantly higher willingness-to-pay and were more strongly motivated to impress others when determining their payment amount. Kim *et al.* (2014a) conduct an online experiment and two field experiments to examine varying conditions of PWYW, including social distance (buyer–seller relationship), provision of an external reference price, product value, seller's reputation, and duration of PWYW application. In a similar vein to the findings of Santana and Morwitz (2011), Kim *et al.* (2014a) report a positive correlation between the desire for social approval (buyers who stated that a positive perception by accompanying colleagues or friends was important to them) and buyers' voluntarily paid prices, relative to their willingness-to-pay.

# Implications of Theoretical Explanations of Buyer Behavior for PWYW Design and Effectiveness

Having presented three theoretical accounts that can explain buyer behavior under PWYW pricing, we now use these accounts as an organizing framework to discuss implications for the design and effectiveness of PWYW.

## Social preferences

### Outcome-based theories

Regarding outcome-based theories of social preferences, information cues (e.g., external reference prices, payment norms, and cost information) seem to play an important role in influencing buyers' voluntary payments to a PWYW seller. To illustrate this, let us consider Fehr and Schmidt's (1999) model of inequity aversion. Here, to judge whether outcomes are perceived as fair, a kind of neutral reference outcome is required. In the context of a PWYW transaction, to determine a mutually accepted equitable division of the transaction's surplus, a mutually accepted fair price for that transaction is required (Chen *et al.* 2017). What buyers perceive as their fair share of the transaction's surplus depends on their generosity, but may also be influenced by the PWYW seller's provision of reference prices, payment norms, and cost information.

The effects of (external) reference prices on buyer behavior under PWYW pricing have been extensively studied. Prior research has documented consistently that different types of reference prices (e.g., minimum, maximum, and suggested prices or seller's costs) act as anchors in PWYW settings, influencing buyers' voluntary payments toward the direction of the provided anchor (e.g., Jang and Chu 2012; Johnson and Cui 2013; Kim *et al.* 2014a; Soule and Madrigal 2015). However, experimental results by Soule and Madrigal (2015) and Jang and Chu (2012) point to the fact that the meaning of the provided anchor plays an important role as well. Specifically, an anchor that refers to a descriptive norm (e.g., "what others were paying on average") instead of an injunctive norm (e.g., "what should be paid") appears to be more powerful in influencing buyer behavior (in some cases).

However, information about payment norms in the real world is often more subtle. Feldhaus *et al.* (2019) manipulate implicit-norm relevant information in a PWYW setting. The authors find that buyers' voluntary payments are significantly affected by subtle information cues (i.e., values shown in answer scales), such that cues that signal a high (vs. a low) payment norm increase payments by 27%. More generally, switching from a very low price (e.g., $0.01) to a price of zero (as possible under PWYW) may transform a "market relationship", in which demand is driven by price and market norms, into a "social–moral relationship", in which demand is driven by social and moral norms (Ariely *et al.* 2018).

Relatedly, (online) sellers may provide buyers with a choice set of price options to choose from (including a "custom amount" option) and possibly set a default option (see for example the software seller humblebundle.com). These price options may influence both buyers' willingness-to-pay and their beliefs about what the fair price is. Prior research on auction-type mechanisms has demonstrated substantial effects of predetermined price-option lists on submitted bids (e.g., Spann *et al.* 2012). Specifically, Spann *et al.* (2012) demonstrate that the level of candidate bid amounts has a positive effect on actual bid amounts, whereas it has a negative impact on the likelihood that a consumer will actually submit a bid. Critically, the authors find that the former effect can more than outweigh the latter and even result in an increase in retailer profit. They explain this phenomenon by the candidate bid amounts influencing bidders' valuations of the offered product and shaping bidders' beliefs about what bid amounts will be successful.

If buyer behavior is influenced by prosocial motives (e.g., altruism or inequity aversion), then cost information of sellers can be another cue affecting buyers' payment decisions. Sellers can disclose their cost to provide a reference point to potential buyers. However, in many situations, it is reasonable to assume that buyers already have some information about the magnitude of sellers' marginal cost. For example, it is obvious that the marginal cost of digital products are (close to) zero. For other products, buyers may infer cost from past prices or from prices offered by competing firms. Experimental results by Jang and Chu (2012), Krämer *et al.* (2017), and Schmidt *et al.* (2015) provide evidence that information about higher cost induce buyers to pay higher prices to PWYW sellers voluntarily.

Lastly, structural characteristics (e.g., framing) of the pricing mechanism may also interact with buyers' social preferences. Specifically, sellers may provide buyers with a reference price and then ask them to either "pay what you want" or "reduce as much as you want" (e.g., Schröder *et al.* 2015). In a natural field experiment, Schröder *et al.* (2015) find that more buyers make payments greater than zero and their voluntary payments are significantly higher on average under a PWYW mechanism rather than a mark-off-your-price (MOYOP) mechanism, which asks them to determine a mark-off instead of a price. The authors argue that their results are consistent with a social mode interpretation, such that the framing of the pricing mechanism evokes different social modes. Specifically, the PWYW frame corresponds to a positive frame in which paying positive prices benefits others, whereas the MOYOP frame represents a negative frame, which emphasizes the egoistic benefit by reducing the reference price. However, Spann *et al.* (2017) find in a field experiment with a similar framing manipulation, although in a different context (open access article processing charges), that buyers paid substantially higher prices in the condition where they had to specify a discount. Similarly, Atlas (2015) shows that presenting buyers with the option to rebate what they want from a posted price (rebate frame) instead of asking them to pay what they want (PWYW frame) yields significantly higher voluntary payments, although both frames are identical in terms of buyers' decision space.

## *Intention-based models of reciprocity*

In the context of intention-based models of reciprocity, in particular the idea that the behavior of some people is influenced by their beliefs about the intentions of others, another notable framing manipulation of the PWYW mechanism is Pay It Forward (Jung *et al.* 2014). In Pay It Forward (PIF), the payment is framed differently and buyers are told that someone else has paid for the product on their behalf and their payment in turn will be used to pay for the product of a subsequent consumer. PIF is financially equivalent to PWYW from the viewpoint of the seller, but alters the direction of the payment from the buyer's perspective. In PIF, the payment is directed to another buyer, thus creating a symbolic social exchange between buyers, rather than evoking a reciprocal relationship between the buyer and the seller. Under such a framing, the social influence to comply with norms and pressures of social exchanges might be stronger than motives to reciprocate in PWYW. However, buyers would need to make an estimate about what others perceive to be an appropriate price to pay in order to adhere to this norm. When people believe that others pay more in PIF or have a higher willingness to pay as suggested by existing research (Frederick 2012; Jung *et al.* 2014), the indirect social influence would induce buyers to pay more under PIF than under PWYW. In fact, Jung *et al.* (2014), across four field studies, provide evidence that buyers pay more under PIF (vs. PWYW) in both profit and non-profit settings.

The time at which (potential) consumers are asked to make a voluntary payment can also have an important impact on the amount of their payment. Specifically, whether the voluntary payment takes place before or after the consumption of a product can affect buyer behavior. On the one hand, buyers may voluntarily pay higher prices prior to consumption of a good or service to encourage the supplier of the good or service to deliver a better quality. For example, if payments in a restaurant are made prior to consumption, buyers may use the amount of their payments strategically to induce receiving a better (e.g., faster) service. Conversely, by asking for payments after consumption, sellers may reduce information asymmetries and convince consumers over the quality of their goods and services. Additionally, having already consumed a good or service may give rise to stronger concerns of reciprocity, motivating people to make ultimately higher voluntary payments to a PWYW seller. Indeed, recent research by Viglia *et al.* (2019), from both field and laboratory experiments, shows that the time of payment is an important contingency factor in PWYW pricing. In particular, the authors find that payments after consumption can help to resolve uncertainties about service processes and outcomes, eventually resulting in higher voluntary payments by buyers and higher profitability of the PWYW mechanism.

**Strategic Considerations/Reputational Models of Finitely Repeated Games with Incomplete Information**
The duration as well as how the duration of a PWYW offer is communicated to potential buyers is another factor that can influence the effectiveness of the PWYW mechanism. Regarding the latter, depending on whether a seller presents PWYW as a short-term price promotion (vs. a long-term pricing mechanism), buyers may have less (more) of an incentive to pay positive prices voluntarily. Since promotions typically attract price-conscious buyers, communicating PWYW as a short-term price promotion may result in lower voluntary payments (Natter and Kaufmann 2015).

Furthermore, framing the PWYW mechanism as a temporary price promotion may affect buyers' strategic considerations and their beliefs about what constitutes an appropriate price to pay. More specifically, buyers might justify lower payments under a PWYW price promotion with the belief that prices during price promotions are always lower (Kim *et al.* 2014a). If, however, buyers are aware that a seller is committed to using PWYW as a long-term pricing mechanism, strategic considerations to keep the seller in the market or to encourage the seller's future provision of the participative pricing mechanism may be more important.

A few empirical papers use observational data (in some cases combined with survey data) to examine the evolution and long-term effects of

PWYW pricing. Payment dynamics and long-term effects in PWYW have been studied mainly in gastronomy. Kim *et al.* (2010) describe the case of a Persian restaurant in Frankfurt am Main, Germany, that adopted PWYW for its lunch buffet. The results from an initial testing period and after about 12 months showed that revenues improved significantly. While the average price paid was significantly lower than the previous posted price, the increased number of unit sales (i.e., buyers) rendered the total effect positive. Furthermore, the average price and revenues were even higher after the first year compared to the testing period benchmark. Schons *et al.* (2014) study the dynamics of voluntary payments over multiple transactions of customers in an outdoor coffee bar on an individual buyer level. Conversely to the results by Kim *et al.* (2010), Schons *et al.* (2014) find during an eight-week observation period that repetition negatively affects buyers' voluntarily paid prices. However, decreases in payments are declining and buyers' individual preferences for fairness and satisfaction have an attenuating effect on these decreases. Riener and Traxler (2012) report results from the Vienna-based restaurant "Wiener Deewan". The restaurant offers self-service, buffet-style Pakistani food (lunch and dinner) and is, according to the authors, considered one of the best curry huts in the city. Whereas drinks are sold at posted prices, restaurant guests may pay what they want for the food. Before leaving the restaurant, restaurant guests pay for their drinks plus a voluntary PWYW payment for their food. The payment process involves a personal interaction with the restaurant staff at the counter. Fairly consistent with the findings by Kim *et al.* (2010), the transactional data from two years reveal that payments are positive (albeit slightly declining) and the number of daily guests increasing, leading to a substantial increase in total revenues. The authors explain the observed long-term payment behavior through a social norms framework and show that short-term fluctuations in average payments are caused by weather-induced changes in mood.

## *Signaling*

Regarding signaling motives in PWYW, prosocial incentives and relationship distance are important factors influencing the effectiveness of the participative pricing mechanism. For instance, PWYW can be combined with a charitable component so that every voluntary payment not only benefits the seller but also a charitable partner. Conducting a large-scale field experiment in an amusement park, Gneezy *et al.* (2010, 2012) find that the

PWYW mechanism is much more profitable in conjunction with a charitable component (in which every voluntary payment benefits both the seller and a charitable partner) than without it. Instead, combining a charitable component with a traditional posted-price strategy leads to only slightly higher demand. The authors reasoning is that PWYW allows buyers to better express their self-identification with the seller and the charitable cause via their payment, thus making PWYW more effective. Importantly, while payments in the *PWYW + charity* condition were significantly higher (compared to the plain PWYW condition), fewer people opted to actually make a purchase. The authors explain this result through image concerns. People with low valuations rather refrain from purchasing the product than pay a low price, as paying a low price would send a bad signal and might jeopardize their positive image. Jung *et al.* (2017) replicate these insights in two field experiments. People's purchase likelihood under shared social responsibility (SSR; a percentage of each voluntary payment supports a charitable cause) is significantly lower, but conditional on purchase, payments are significantly higher. In addition, the two experiments demonstrate that people care whether any part of their payment goes to a charitable cause, but they are largely unaffected by the magnitude of this fraction.

In the context of signaling motives, relationship distance is discussed as a further key factor influencing voluntary payments in PWYW settings. However, it is necessary to distinguish between a relationship distance that is induced by a payment method or context and the individual relationship between buyer and seller (Natter and Kaufmann 2015). With respect to the former, PWYW researchers examined the effects of whether payments are made anonymously or not. In their restaurant experiment, Gneezy *et al.* (2012) manipulated buyer anonymity by having buyers make their payments either directly to a person ("observed") or by putting their payment in an envelope ("anonymous"), which also contained 20 EUR in change, enabling buyers to pay their desired amount without being forced to ask the staff for change. Their results reveal that buyers paid more when they were anonymous, which may be explained by self-image considerations on part of the buyers. Relatedly, Kim *et al.* (2014a) study the effect of relationship distance in an online experiment and in a field experiment. In their online study, the authors document higher payments of participants in the observed (vs. the anonymous) payment setting, but they cannot replicate this result in their field experiment. Also, Jung *et al.* (2017), in a more recent field experiment, did not find an effect of payment anonymity on buyers' voluntary payments.

Another crucial aspect to account for in deciding whether PWYW payments are to be made anonymously or not is that there may exist relevant interactions between self-image and social-image considerations. While both mechanisms might work in the same direction, Gneezy *et al.* (2012) provide evidence that is consistent with the idea that payments in the public sphere crowd out the self-signaling value of buyers' voluntary payments. This

**Table 2.**   PWYW design implications organized by the three theoretical accounts.

| Theoretical account | Design aspect | Operationalization (Examples) |
|---|---|---|
| Outcome-based theories of social preferences | Information cues regarding fair price | • External reference prices (e.g., regular posted price)<br>• Payment norms (e.g., "what others were paying on average", "suggested price")<br>• Cost information (e.g., seller's costs)<br>• Pre-selected price points as PWYW price options (optional with a default) |
| | Structural characteristics | • Discount/reduction relative to an anchor price |
| Intention-based models of reciprocity | Structural characteristics | • Pay It Forward (i.e., "your product was paid by someone else, you pay for someone else") |
| | Timing of payment | • PWYW payment before consumption (e.g., higher payment to receive better service)<br>• PWYW payment after consumption (e.g., higher payment to reciprocate for product quality) |
| Strategic considerations | Duration of PWYW offering | • Communicate PWYW as permanent mechanism rather than short-term promotion |
| Self-signaling | Prosocial incentives | • Percentage of PWYW payment donated to charity |
| Self-signaling social signaling | Anonymity of payment | • Anonymous payments can lead to higher (self-signaling) or lower (social signaling) prices paid |
| Social signaling | Relationship between buyer and seller | • Personal connection and/or loyal customer base increase payments |

suggests that if buyers are strongly motivated by self-image concerns, sellers might be better off by designing the payment process in an anonymous way. With respect to the relationship between buyer and seller, prior research found that buyer loyalty positively influences payments in PWYW settings (Kim *et al.* 2014a; Kim *et al.* 2010; Kim *et al.* 2009). If buyers have a personal connection to a seller, for example, because the seller is chatting regularly with them, this may translate into higher voluntary payments as buyers know whom they are paying (e.g., Kim *et al.* 2009). The case of Radiohead, with many of their *loyal* fans paying for the digital download of the album *In Rainbows*, provides additional anecdotal evidence in this direction (e.g., Chen *et al.* 2017).

Table 2 summarizes implications for PWYW design and effectiveness organized by the three theoretical accounts.

## Opportunities for Research and Practice

Research on PWYW is largely concerned with whether, why, and how much buyers are paying to PWYW sellers voluntarily. Studies commonly find that many buyers indeed pay positive prices despite not being forced to do so. The existing body of research on PWYW pricing provides numerous case studies from various industries (e.g., gastronomy, entertainment, and culture) in which PWYW has been applied successfully, in some cases in the long run. Prior research has identified and examined a variety of drivers (e.g., social preferences, strategic considerations, and image motivation) that determine the success and viability of PWYW as a pricing model. Yet, buyer (and seller) behavior under PWYW is not completely understood and several open questions remain that provide avenues for future research.

First, despite many people paying positive prices, profit results are sometimes mixed and the application of PWYW is not always found to be a (lasting) success. However, the circumstances and conditions under which PWYW is going to fail have not been systematically explored so far. In this regard, other candidate drivers of buyer behavior such as social influence or physical context, which have not been considered in the literature yet, may contribute in explaining these cases.

Second, the motivation of buyers to participate in the PWYW pricing format requires future research. Some studies report of buyers opting to shop with a posted-price seller when given the choice to buy the same product from a PWYW seller (e.g., Schmidt *et al.* 2015). However, the underlying forces driving this behavior remain unclear. The psychological processes behind the decision of buyers for a voluntary payment amount may provide an explanation for this observation that necessitates better understanding.

Third, prior research on PWYW has focused much on buyer behavior under PWYW pricing, but not on the downstream consequences of participating in pricing. For example, such empowered buyers may become more engaged with the seller or product because, compared to accepting a posted-price offer, they invest more effort (e.g., thinking costs) into acquiring the product. Thus, analyzing whether and how being involved in a pricing decision affects customer satisfaction, repeat purchases, or word-of-mouth activities are relevant questions for sellers using or contemplating to use PWYW. In fact, the downstream consequences of participative pricing mechanisms may be a motivational force for sellers to delegate pricing power in the first place.

Eventually, PWYW appears to be mainly employed in the domain of experiential products (i.e., money spent on doing) and for the sale of digital products (e.g., music, software) in business-to-consumer contexts. However, the empirical literature provides only limited evidence on whether PWYW can be employed for (material) products of higher cost. Likewise, studying PWYW in business-to-business relationships seems like a fruitful avenue for future research. These relationships are often characterized by repeated interaction between buyer and seller and high levels of trust, potentially altering behavior and outcomes observed in other settings.

For practice, promising opportunities loom, for example, in further exploring PWYW as a price promotion instrument. While prior research is suggestive in that sellers may expect lower payments if the PWYW mechanism is framed as a temporary price promotion (vs. a permanent pricing model), PWYW may yet be a valuable alternative to price reductions or free sampling (e.g., Kim *et al.* 2014b). In this study, Kim *et al.* (2014b) conduct two field experiments to compare PWYW to free samples and large discounts as a promotional tool for men's razors and portrait prints at a photographer's studio. They find that the entertaining and innovative character of PWYW can induce consumers to try the products and may yield a higher repeat purchase rate of new customers. Further, sellers using PWYW can benefit from higher word-of-mouth behavior and yield higher promotional revenues. Consequently, PWYW may be an interesting promotional tool for a wide range of companies.

By using PWYW initially as a price promotion only, sellers can gain experience with the pricing mechanism and learn about the behavior of their customers. Besides payment behavior of buyers, relevant performance metrics for sellers in this context include word-of-mouth behavior and promotional revenues.

Evidently, PWYW can be employed more readily for products that are characterized by rather low marginal cost of production (i.e., digital goods and services). Higher marginal cost entails a greater risk for the seller. By making informed design decisions, sellers can systematically influence the effectiveness and profitability of the PWYW pricing mechanism by adapting the implementation to their individual situation. These design decisions include whether, which, and when to provide what kind of information cues, whether the mechanism should be combined with prosocial incentives (e.g., donation to charity), and if so, what proportion of payments should go to charity, whether payments are observable by others or not, at which point in time payments are to be collected (e.g., prior or after consumption), and what kind of relationship is sought with customers.

# Conclusions

Pay-What-You-Want pricing will remain a niche *and* a novel pricing mechanism. Owing to the counter-intuitive approach of delegating full price-setting control to buyers, the application will remain an "eye-catcher" and source of attention via private and public word-of-mouth (e.g., through journalists or bloggers) in the future. The majority of applications is still offline, presumably driven by concerns that anonymity is detrimental to prices paid. However, prior research found that anonymous PWYW payments need not be lower. Further, the low marginal cost of digital goods or digitally mediated services greatly reduce the risk of PWYW prices below cost. Therefore, applying carefully designed PWYW mechanisms for digital products appears to provide great potential for Internet-based business models and research on this phenomenon alike.

# References

Andreoni, J. and J. Miller (2002), Giving according to Garp: An experimental test of the consistency of preferences for altruism, *Econometrica*, 70(2), 737–753.

Ariely, D., A. Bracha, and S. Meier (2009), Doing good or doing well? Image motivation and monetary incentives in behaving prosocially, *American Economic Review*, 99(1), 544–555.

Ariely, D., U. Gneezy, and E. Haruvy (2018), Social norms and the price of zero, *Journal of Consumer Psychology*, 28(2), 180–191.

Atlas, S. (2015), Rebate-what-you-want, in *Advances in Consumer Research*, Vol. 43, K. Diehl and C. Yoon, eds., Duluth, MN, USA: Association for Consumer Research.

Bénabou, R. and J. Tirole (2011), Identity, morals, and taboos: Beliefs as asset, *Quarterly Journal of Economics*, 126(2), 805–855.

Bernheim, B. D. (1994), A theory of conformity, *Journal of Political Economy*, 102(5), 841–877.

Bertini, M. and O. Koenigsberg (2014), When customers help set prices, *MIT Sloan Management Review*, 55(4), 57–64.

Bochet, O., T. Page, and L. Putterman (2006), Communication and punishment in voluntary contribution experiments, *Journal of Economic Behavior & Organization*, 60(1), 11–26.

Carpenter, J. P. (2007), Punishing free-riders: How group size affects mutual monitoring and the provision of public goods, *Games and Economic Behavior*, 60(1), 31–51.

Chen, Y., O. Koenigsberg, and Z. J. Zhang (2017), Pay-as-you-wish pricing, *Marketing Science*, 36(5), 645–812.

Croson, R. T. and M. B. Marks (2000), Step returns in threshold public goods: A meta-and experimental analysis, *Experimental Economics*, 2(3), 239–259.

Dana, J., D. M. Cain, and R. M. Dawes (2006), What you don't know won't hurt me: Costly (but quiet) exit in dictator games, *Organizational Behavior and Human Decision Processes*, 100(2), 193–201.

Dubé, J.-P. H., X. Luo, and Z. Fang (2017), Self-signaling and prosocial behavior: A cause marketing experiment, *Marketing Science*, 36(2), 161–186.

Dufwenberg, M. and G. Kirchsteiger (2004), A theory of sequential reciprocity, *Games and Economic Behavior*, 47(2), 268–298.

Falk, A. and U. Fischbacher (2006), A theory of reciprocity, *Games and Economic Behavior*, 54(2), 293–315.

Fehr, E. and U. Fischbacher (2003), The nature of human altruism, *Nature*, 425, 785–791.

Fehr, E. and K. M. Schmidt (2006), The economics of fairness, reciprocity and altruism — Experimental evidence and new theories, in *Handbook of the Economics of Giving, Altruism and Reciprocity*, Vol. 1, S.-C. Kolm and J. M. Ythier, eds., Amsterdam: Elsevier.

Fehr, E. and K. M. Schmidt (1999), A theory of fairness, competition, and cooperation, *Quarterly Journal of Economics*, 114(3), 817–868.

Feldhaus, C., T. Sobotta, and P. Werner (2019), Norm uncertainty and voluntary payments in the field, *Management Science*, 65(4), 1855–1866.

Frederick, S. (2012), Overestimating others' willingness to pay, *Journal of Consumer Research*, 39(1), 1–21.

Gautier, P. A. and B. van der Klaauw (2012), Selection in a field experiment with voluntary participation, *Journal of Applied Econometrics*, 27(1), 63–84.

Gerpott, T. J. (2016), A review of the empirical literature on pay-what-you-want price setting, *Management & Marketing*, 11(4), 566–596.

Gneezy, A., U. Gneezy, L. D. Nelson, and A. Brown (2010), Shared social responsibility: A field experiment in pay-what-you-want pricing and charitable giving, *Science*, 329(5989), 325–327.

Gneezy, A., U. Gneezy, G. Riener, and L. D. Nelson (2012), Pay-what-you-want, identity, and self-signaling in markets, *Proceedings of the National Academy of Sciences*, 109(19), 7236–7240.

Isaac, M. R. and J. M. Walker (1988), Group size effects in public goods provision: The voluntary contributions mechanism, *Quarterly Journal of Economics*, 103(1), 179–199.

Jang, H. and W. Chu (2012), Are consumers acting fairly toward companies? An examination of pay-what-you-want pricing, *Journal of Macromarketing*, 32(4), 348–360.

Johnson, J. W. and A. P. Cui (2013), To influence or not to influence: External reference price strategies in pay-what-you-want pricing, *Journal of Business Research*, 66(2), 275–281.

Jung, M. H., L. D. Nelson, A. Gneezy, and U. Gneezy (2014), Paying more when paying for others, *Journal of Personality and Social Psychology*, 107(3), 414–431.

Jung, M. H., L. D. Nelson, U. Gneezy, and A. Gneezy (2017), Signaling virtue: Charitable behavior under consumer elective pricing, *Marketing Science*, 36(2), 187–194.

Kim, J.-Y., K. Kaufmann, and M. Stegemann (2014a), The impact of buyer–seller relationships and reference prices on the effectiveness of the pay what you want pricing mechanism, *Marketing Letters*, 25(4), 409–423.

Kim, J.-Y., M. Natter, and M. Spann (2010), Kish: Where customers pay as they wish, *Review of Marketing Science*, 8(2), Article 3.

Kim, J.-Y., M. Natter, and M. Spann (2009), Pay what you want: A new participative pricing mechanism, *Journal of Marketing*, 73(1), 44–58.

Kim, J.-Y., M. Natter, and M. Spann (2014b), Sampling, discounts or pay-what-you-want: Two field experiments, *International Journal of Research in Marketing*, 31(3), 327–334.

Krämer, F., K. M. Schmidt, M. Spann, and L. Stich (2017), Delegating pricing power to customers: Pay what you want or name your own price? *Journal of Economic Behavior & Organization*, 136, 125–140.

Kreps, D. M., P. Milgrom, J. Roberts, and R. Wilson (1982), Rational cooperation in the finitely repeated prisoners' dilemma, *Journal of Economic Theory*, 27(2), 245–252.

Kreps, D. M. and R. Wilson (1982), Reputation and imperfect information, *Journal of Economic Theory*, 27(2), 253–279.

Kunter, M. (2015), Exploring the pay-what-you-want payment motivation, *Journal of Business Research*, 68(11), 2347–2357.

Mak, V., R. Zwick, A. R. Rao, and J. A. Pattaratanakun (2015), "Pay what you want" as threshold public good provision, *Organizational Behavior and Human Decision Processes*, 127, 30–43.

Masclet, D., C. Noussair, S. Tucker, and M.-C. Villeval (2003), Monetary and nonmonetary punishment in the voluntary contributions mechanism, *American Economic Review*, 93(1), 366–380.

Natter, M. and K. Kaufmann (2015), Voluntary market payments: Underlying motives, success drivers and success potentials, *Journal of Behavioral and Experimental Economics*, 57, 149–157.

Rabin, M. (1993), Incorporating fairness into game theory and economics, *American Economic Review*, 83(5), 1281–1302.

Regner, T. (2014), Social preferences? Google answers! *Games and Economic Behavior*, 85, 188–209.

Regner, T. (2015), Why consumers pay voluntarily: Evidence from online music, *Journal of Behavioral and Experimental Economics*, 57, 205–214.

Regner, T. and J. A. Barria (2009), Do consumers pay voluntarily? The case of online music, *Journal of Economic Behavior & Organization*, 71(2), 395–406.

Riener, G. and C. Traxler (2012), Norms, moods, and free lunch: Longitudinal evidence on payments from a pay-what-you-want restaurant, *Journal of Socio-Economics*, 41(4), 476–483.

Santana, S. and V. G. Morwitz (2011), Buying what you can get for free: How self-presentation motives influence payment decisions in pay-what-you-want contexts, in *Advances in Consumer Research*, Vol. 39, R. Ahluwalia, T. L. Chartrand and R. K. Ratner, eds., Duluth, MN, USA: Association for Consumer Research.

Schmidt, K. M., M. Spann, and R. Zeithammer (2015), Pay what you want as a marketing strategy in monopolistic and competitive markets, *Management Science*, 61(6), 1217–1236.

Schons, L. M., M. Rese, J. Wieseke, W. Rasmussen, D. Weber, and W.-C. Strotmann (2014), There is nothing permanent except change — Analyzing individual price dynamics in "pay-what-you-want" situations, *Marketing Letters*, 25(1), 25–36.

Schröder, M., A. Lüer, and A. Sadrieh (2015), Pay-what-you-want or mark-off-your-own-price — A framing effect in customer-selected pricing, *Journal of Behavioral and Experimental Economics*, 57, 200–204.

Soule, C. A. A. and R. Madrigal (2015), Anchors and norms in anonymous pay-what-you-want pricing contexts, *Journal of Behavioral and Experimental Economics*, 57, 167–175.

Spann, M., G. Häubl, B. Skiera, and M. Bernhardt (2012), Bid-elicitation interfaces and bidding behavior in retail interactive pricing, *Journal of Retailing*, 88(1), 131–144.

Spann, M., L. Stich, and K. M. Schmidt (2017), Pay what you want as a pricing model for open access publishing? *Communications of the ACM*, 60(11), 29–31.

Spann, M., R. Zeithammer, M. Bertini, E. Haruvy, S. D. Jap, O. Koenigsberg, V. Mak, P. T. L. Popkowski Leszczyc, B. Skiera, and M. Thomas (2018), Beyond posted prices: The past, present, and future of participative pricing mechanisms, *Customer Needs and Solutions*, 5(1–2), 121–136.

Viglia, G., Maras, M., Schumann, J., and Navarro-Martinez, D. (2019), Paying before or paying after? Timing and uncertainty in pay-what-you-want pricing. *Journal of Service Research*, 22(3), 272–284. https://doi.org/10.1177/1094670519835308.

# Chapter 6

# How Does Partitioning Prices Influence Consumer Responses?*

Ajay T. Abraham and Rebecca W. Hamilton

Consumers often encounter mandatory surcharges and fees (e.g., taxes, shipping for online purchases). For example, when purchasing a book online, the consumer may pay one price to purchase the book and another price to ship it. This chapter uses the framework of partitioned pricing (Morwitz *et al.* 1998) to analyze the effect of such mandatory surcharges on consumer responses by identifying three mechanisms — *encoding*, *attentional*, and *appraisal* — by which the effects of partitioned pricing versus all-inclusive pricing influence consumer responses. The chapter reports a meta-analysis of the existing academic literature in this domain

---

*In *New Directions in Behavioral Pricing*, Chezy Ofir Ed., 2024, World Scientific Publishing Company. This chapter is based on research reported in Abraham, A. T. and R. W. Hamilton (2018), When does partitioned pricing lead to more favorable consumer preferences? Meta-analytic evidence, *Journal of Marketing Research*, 55 (October), 686–703.
Ajay T. Abraham, Albers School of Business and Economics, Seattle University, Seattle, WA, USA (abrahama@seattleu.edu); Rebecca W. Hamilton, McDonough School of Business, Georgetown University, Washington, DC, USA (rebecca.hamilton@george-town.edu).

to investigate the relative strength of these three mechanisms. The findings of this meta-analysis indicate the strongest evidence for the *appraisal* mechanism, followed by the *encoding* mechanism, and then the *attentional* mechanism. The chapter concludes by highlighting insights based on the meta-analysis and fruitful avenues for future research in this domain.

Consumers often encounter mandatory surcharges and fees, such as when paying taxes included on cell phone bills or shipping surcharges as part of online purchases. These surcharges are often proposed as an innovative method for service providers to increase their bottom-lines by charging consumers fees for services that they previously took for granted (Mayer 2002), especially if consumers do not fully account for these surcharges and fees when estimating the price they will pay for products or services (Bigda *et al.* 2006).

For example, although consumers might now be familiar with checking account fees in the banking industry and checked baggage fees or leg-room fees on airlines, the airline industry has also added carry-on baggage fees (Carey 2011) and breathing taxes (Pardo 2014), and it has even considered lavatory fees (Mackey 2009). In the wireless telecommunications industry, mandatory surcharges including excise taxes and 911 services add 17% on average to consumers' bills (Goldman 2013). Similarly, consumers have seen a recent proliferation of mandatory resort fees and duty fees in the travel industry (Hobica 2013).

Although these surcharges and fees appear to help recoup some operating costs in the short run, negative consumer responses may limit revenue, so it is not clear whether adding these surcharges and fees — rather than simply increasing prices — improves firm outcomes (Hamilton *et al.* 2010). Considering that the U.S. airline, wireless telecommunications, and lodging industries have or were forecasted to have annual revenues of 185 billion (First Research 2018), 272 billion (Statista 2018), and 208 billion dollars (Statista 2016), respectively, in recent years, differences in consumers' responses to small surcharges can have a relatively large economic impact. Given the potentially significant revenue implications for marketers, it is important for managers to understand when surcharges lead to more favorable consumer responses and when they lead to less favorable consumer responses, as well as the mechanisms by which surcharges influence consumer responses.

Complementing a recently published meta-analysis of the partitioned pricing literature (Abraham and Hamilton 2018), this chapter highlights and tests three mechanisms that have been proposed in prior research on partitioned pricing and identifies fruitful avenues for future research in this domain.

# The Framework of Partitioned Pricing

This chapter uses the framework of *partitioned pricing* (Morwitz *et al.* 1998) to analyze the effect of mandatory surcharges and fees on consumer responses to prices for goods and services. A partitioned price is defined as a price presentation format in which the total price of a product or service is presented in two or more mandatory parts — a *base price*, which is associated with the *focal component*, and one or more *surcharges*, which are associated with *secondary components*. In the case of purchasing a book online, a partitioned price would include the base price of the book as well as separate prices for "Shipping" and "Taxes" as surcharges. We compare the consumer's response to a partitioned price, such as this one, with an all-inclusive price for the book, shipping, and taxes.

The principle of description invariance (Tversky *et al.* 1988) suggests that the consumer's preferences for an offer should not depend on how the price is presented as long as the total price remains the same. However, prior research shows that even when the total price of a product or a service is held constant, the format in which the price is presented (partitioned pricing versus all-inclusive pricing) influences consumers' evaluations of offers and their purchase intentions (e.g., Morwitz *et al.* 1998).

## *Prior research on partitioned pricing*

Although the initial research in the domain of partitioned pricing suggested that how the prices are presented (e.g., currency format versus percentage format for a shipping fee) influenced consumer responses by biasing price recall (e.g., Morwitz *et al.* 1998; Xia and Monroe 2004), subsequent research suggests that additional mechanisms also may be at work. For example, the magnitude of the prices involved (e.g., high shipping fee versus low shipping fee) can moderate consumer responses to partitioned pricing (e.g., Cheema 2008). Research also suggests that contextual factors that drive consumer appraisals of surcharges (e.g., high perceived benefit versus low perceived benefit derived from a shipping surcharge) can moderate consumer responses to partitioned pricing (e.g., Hamilton and Srivastava 2008).

Several articles have reviewed academic research on partitioned pricing. In a recent article, Greenleaf *et al.* (2016) proposed that partitioned pricing operates across a series of six interrelated stages: attention to partitioned pricing components; attitude toward surcharges and the use of partitioned pricing; combining price components to determine a perception of total price or cost; attention to, and evaluation of, product benefits; overall evaluation of the product offer; and the impact of partitioned pricing on post-purchase perceptions and behavior. In another recent article, Voester *et al.* (2017) integrate findings from the existing empirical literature on partitioned pricing to suggest some managerial implications about when and how to use partitioned pricing. However, neither of these articles directly tested the proposed underlying mechanisms that underpin the effects of partitioned pricing versus all-inclusive pricing on consumer responses.

Abraham and Hamilton (2018) added to this research by conducting a meta-analysis of research comparing the effect of partitioned prices and all-inclusive prices on consumer preference. Although individual papers in the literature have investigated some of the underlying mechanisms for partitioned pricing in isolation, prior research has not investigated these different mechanisms in parallel. In this chapter, we test the relative strengths of three different mechanisms for partitioned pricing that overlap with the three categories of moderators that were identified in the meta-analysis by Abraham and Hamilton (2018), and we draw out implications for managers and future research based on their relative strengths.

## Gaps in prior research on partitioned pricing

Prior research investigating the effects of partitioned pricing versus all-inclusive pricing on consumer responses has generally focused on one or two moderators at a time. An advantage of meta-analysis is that it allows us to investigate the influences of multiple moderators from the existing academic literature at the same time. Such an integrated approach is important for marketers who have to decide on levels of not just one or two moderators, but several at the same time. For example, will partitioning shipping surcharges result in more favorable consumer responses because consumers encode and recall a lower price, or will it call attention to the shipping surcharges that they dislike paying for (e.g., Schindler *et al.* 2005), resulting in less favorable consumer responses? Will the intensity of more favorable or less favorable consumer responses depend more on appraisals of the numerical magnitude of the shipping fee, or will it depend more on appraisals of the product category of the focal component?

Considering that marketing managers often require answers to questions like these, an examination of the underlying mechanisms for partitioned pricing effects is of interest. By identifying the most influential mechanisms that are responsible for the effects of partitioned pricing versus all-inclusive pricing on consumer responses, managers can make trade-offs between the advantages of manipulating moderators that operate through those mechanisms and the disadvantages of manipulating moderators that are less amenable to managerial intervention (e.g., the product category of the focal component).

In order to better understand these issues, this chapter first provides an overview of the framework of partitioned pricing, followed by a discussion of how the effects of partitioned pricing versus all-inclusive pricing influence consumer responses. We then identify three distinct mechanisms by which the effects of partitioned pricing operate, and we undertake a meta-analysis of the existing academic literature in the domain of partitioned pricing to investigate the relative strengths of these three distinct mechanisms. The chapter concludes with a focus on insights based on the findings of the meta-analysis, and highlights some fruitful avenues for future research in this domain.

# How Does Partitioning Prices Influence Consumer Responses?

## How does partitioned pricing operate?

Before proceeding further, it is important to clarify the difference between partitioned pricing and bundling. Stremersch and Tellis (2002) state that bundling is the sale of two or more separate products in a package. Although Greenleaf *et al.* (2016) also state that partitioned pricing deals with two or more components, they restrict their definition to include only those situations in which both types of components of a purchase (focal product and secondary component) are mandatory but cannot be purchased as standalone products (e.g. shipping or taxes for an online book purchase).

In their article introducing the framework of partitioned pricing, Morwitz *et al.* (1998) demonstrated that partitioned pricing often leads to favorable consumer responses by biasing price recall. Consumers who observed partitioned prices tended to ignore surcharges and recall lower total prices than those who observed all-inclusive prices. The mechanism suggested by these authors was that, when consumers were presented with a partitioned price, they anchored on the base price and did not completely process the surcharge information. Past research on anchoring has demonstrated that the magnitude of adjustment is usually insufficient (Tversky and Kahneman 1974); analogously, consumers adjust the base price by an amount smaller than the magnitude of the surcharge, leading to a lower recalled total price than in the case of all-inclusive prices. The lower recalled total price then manifests itself in the form of higher demand and purchase intentions.

## Mechanisms for partitioned pricing

Although the initial research on partitioned pricing demonstrated that surcharges could be beneficial to marketers, 20 years of follow-up research has found both beneficial and detrimental effects of partitioned pricing, leaving managerial recommendations unclear. For example, research has demonstrated that the effect of partitioned pricing may be less favorable when consumers appraise the surcharge as providing low rather than high value (e.g., Bertini and Wathieu 2008) or when the surcharge is represented as a currency amount rather than as a percentage of the total price, thereby facilitating encoding and price recall (e.g., Kim 2006). To better understand the drivers that lead to partitioned pricing having a more favorable effect on consumer responses than all-inclusive pricing, we conducted a meta-analysis of the existing academic research in the domain of partitioned pricing, with a particular focus on the underlying mechanisms that might be able to explain when partitioned pricing (versus all-inclusive pricing) leads to more favorable or less favorable consumer responses. We first propose a classification that reflects three underlying mechanisms by which the effects of partitioned pricing operate, and we report additional analyses to test the relative importance of these mechanisms.

Based on our detailed review of the partitioned pricing literature, we identified three mechanisms underlying partitioned pricing effects in the existing research. The first mechanism is an *encoding* mechanism that operates through the incomplete processing and encoding of surcharge information. For example, the total price might be present at the time of committing to the purchase decision or the total price might be absent, and the surcharge might be priced in currency terms or expressed as a percentage of the base price. The initial findings in the domain of partitioned pricing were obtained in studies that were run with the total price absent (Morwitz *et al.* 1998), indicating that these effects of partitioned pricing versus all-inclusive pricing on consumer responses were driven by the incomplete processing and encoding of surcharge information. Similarly, when the surcharge is priced in currency terms (e.g., dollars), consumers might find this surcharge information easier to process than when the surcharge is priced in percentage terms, and they are therefore likely to more completely process and encode currency format surcharge information than percentage format surcharge information, resulting in a lower recalled total price (e.g., Morwitz *et al.* 1998).

The second mechanism is an *attentional* mechanism that operates through the attention that is paid to the surcharge. For example, the total price level (including both the base price and the surcharge) might be low or it might be high, and the surcharge magnitude might be low or it might be high. When the price level decreases, the same surcharge appears larger relative to the base price, increasing the salience of the surcharge, and drawing more attention to it (Berlyne 1960). Similarly, as the surcharge magnitude increases, the salience of the surcharge also increases, drawing more attention to it (Berlyne 1960).

Finally, the third mechanism is an *appraisal* mechanism that operates through consumer appraisals of the different components or consumer appraisals of the seller characteristics. For example, the seller's control over the surcharge might be perceived to be low or high, and the surcharge might be perceived to provide a low level of consumer benefit or a high level of consumer benefit. When the seller's control over the surcharge is perceived to be high (e.g., service charges), consumers might believe that these surcharges are being included in order to add to marketers' profits (Folkes 1988), resulting in lower consumer appraisals of the secondary component (e.g., Schindler *et al.* 2005) than when the seller's control over the surcharge is perceived to be low (e.g., taxes). Additionally, when the surcharge is perceived to provide a low level of consumer benefit (e.g., one sitcom episode and refreshments as in Bertini and Wathieu (2008)), this is likely to result in lower consumer appraisals of the secondary component than when the surcharge is perceived to provide a high level of consumer benefit (e.g., six movie channels and a full-service meal as in Bertini and Wathieu (2008)). Similar arguments can be made for how the moderating influences of hedonic versus utilitarian category, seller reputation, and typicality of partitioning operate through consumer appraisals of the different components or consumer appraisals of the seller characteristics.

The three categories of moderators identified in Abraham and Hamilton (2018) — *price presentation* moderators, *magnitude* moderators, and *contextual* moderators — focus on how managers can leverage the different moderators that belong to each category. The three mechanisms we test here — *encoding*, *attention*, and *appraisal* — focus more on how we believe these three categories of moderators are operating from the consumer's perspective. The *encoding* mechanism is triggered by *price presentation* moderators, which managers can control by manipulating how the price is conveyed to consumers. Similarly, the *attentional* mechanism is triggered by *magnitude* moderators, which managers can control by manipulating the actual prices charged for the different components. Finally, the *appraisal* mechanism is triggered by *contextual* moderators, which managers can control by manipulating the non-price characteristics of a transaction.

# Meta-Analysis of the Effects of Partitioned Pricing versus All-Inclusive Pricing on Preference

## Overview of the meta-analysis

We examined the relative strength of these three mechanisms — *encoding*, *attentional*, and *appraisal* – by meta-analyzing 17 years of partitioned pricing research that examines 149 contrasts between partitioned pricing and all-inclusive pricing across 43 studies from 27 papers ($N = 12,878$; Abraham and Hamilton 2018). Abraham and Hamilton (2018) meta-analyzed these data at two different levels of aggregation: (1) testing the overall effect of partitioned pricing versus all-inclusive pricing on consumer preference, and (2) testing the parallel effects of nine individual moderators (presence of the total price, surcharge format, price level, surcharge magnitude, hedonic versus utilitarian category, seller control-lability, seller reputation, surcharge benefit, and typicality of partitioning) on the relationship between partitioned pricing versus all-inclusive pricing and consumer preference. In this chapter, we focus on the intermediate level of aggregation, in which we test the role of the *encoding, attentional,* and *appraisal* mechanisms in parallel in the relationship between partitioned pricing versus all-inclusive pricing and consumer preference. That is, we aggregate the individual moderators into groupings based on the three hypothesized mechanisms they represent.

A lot of the common methodological information for meta-analyzing the parallel roles of these mechanisms (e.g., identification of observations to include in the analysis, coding of the moderators and the standard control variables, information about the model that was used for the analysis), as well as the findings for the overall effect and the individual moderators, are reported in the meta-analysis of moderators in Abraham and Hamilton (2018). Therefore, we briefly review these results but do not repeat all of the details here; we direct readers interested in these aspects to that article. Instead, in this chapter, we focus on the intermediate level of aggregation, which we did not report in Abraham and Hamilton (2018): meta-analysis based on the three underlying mechanisms by which the effects of partitioned pricing versus all-inclusive pricing influence consumer responses.

## *Meta-analysis of the role of the three mechanisms*

We reasoned that, if each moderator in the partitioned pricing literature influences consumers' responses to partitioned pricing versus all-inclusive pricing through one of the three proposed underlying mechanisms, the corresponding mechanism would be activated when each of the moderators was relatively high or relatively low. Therefore, in order to test the relative strength of the three proposed mechanisms — *encoding, attentional,* and *appraisal* — for the effects of partitioned pricing versus all-inclusive pricing on consumer responses, we created mechanism variables by combining the moderator variables corresponding to each of these mechanisms. In other words, if a moderator was *not* expected to influence the effects of partitioned pricing versus all-inclusive pricing on consumer responses through a particular mechanism, it contributed nothing to the corresponding mechanism variable. On the other hand, if a moderator was expected to influence the effects of partitioned pricing versus all-inclusive pricing on consumer responses through a particular mechanism, the corresponding mechanism variable was incremented by one when higher levels of the moderator were predicted to result in more favorable consumer preference for partitioned pricing over all-inclusive pricing. Similarly, the corresponding mechanism variable was decremented by one when higher levels of the moderator were predicted to result in less favorable consumer preference for partitioned pricing over all-inclusive pricing.

In this manner, the ENCODING mechanism variable was computed as [(–Presence of the Total Price) + Surcharge Format], and it ranged from –2 to +2. Similarly, the APPRAISAL mechanism variable was computed as [Hedonic Versus Utilitarian Category + (–Seller Controllability) + Seller Reputation + Surcharge Benefit + Typicality of Partitioning], and it ranged from –5 to +5. To compute the ATTENTIONAL mechanism variable, Price Level and Relative Surcharge Magnitude were first recoded as –1, 0, or +1, respectively, if they were below, at, or above their respective medians in our dataset. Because the existing literature contains evidence for both positive and negative effects of surcharge magnitude, we computed two ATTENTIONAL mechanism variables, ATTENTIONAL_1 and ATTENTIONAL_2, which we computed as [Price Level + Relative Surcharge Magnitude] and [Price Level + (–Relative Surcharge Magnitude)], respectively. The ATTENTIONAL_1 and ATTENTIONAL_2 mechanism variables ranged from –2 to +2.

We then ran two separate hierarchical linear models (HLMs) — the first one with the ENCODING, APPRAISAL, and ATTENTIONAL_1 mechanism variables and the standard control variables as predictors, and the second one with the ENCODING, APPRAISAL, and ATTENTIONAL_2 mechanism variables and the standard control variables as predictors. We used HLMs to account for correlations between non-independent observations from the same study. The dependent measure for the HLMs was Cohen's $d$ effect size measure (Cohen 1977) for the effect of partitioned pricing versus all-inclusive pricing on preference.

For robustness, we also transformed these four mechanism variables (a) by averaging so that all three variables ranged from –1 to +1 (a simple rescaling), (b) by recoding all negative values as –1 and all positive values as +1, and (c) by recoding the variable as –1 only if all the constituent variables were –1 or 0, as +1 only if all constituent variables were +1 or 0, and as 0 otherwise. The first variable transformation was performed in order to ensure that each of the mechanism variables ranged from the same lower bound to the same upper bound. Otherwise, the APPRAISAL mechanism variable would have had a different range than the other two mechanism variables, and any results might be attributable to these differential ranges rather than to differences in the underlying mechanisms. The second and third transformations contributed to relatively conservative tests of the underlying mechanisms because they were, respectively, a dichotomization of more granular variables and a multiplicative recoding. After each of these three transformations, we again ran the two separate HLMs with each of these three sets of recoded mechanism variables. Figure 1 contains a graphical representation of the framework for our meta-analysis of these three mechanisms.

Across the eight HLMs that we ran, we observed positive and significant coefficients for the APPRAISAL mechanism variable in all eight models, suggesting that this mechanism is likely the strongest route by which the effects of partitioned pricing versus all-inclusive pricing influence consumer responses. We also observed positive and marginally significant coefficients for the ENCODING mechanism variable in five out of the eight models and a directionally positive coefficient ($p = .10$) in one model, suggesting that this mechanism is also influential but less so than

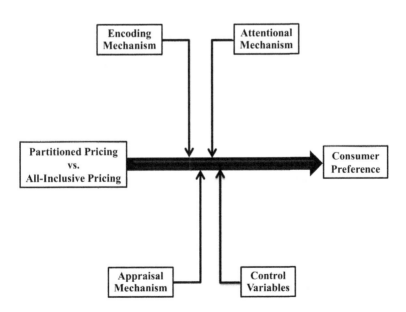

Figure 1.   Conceptual framework.

the APPRAISAL mechanism. The coefficients for the ATTENTIONAL_1 and ATTENTIONAL_2 mechanism variables were not significant in any of the eight models, suggesting that this mechanism is likely the weakest route by which the effects of partitioned pricing versus all-inclusive pricing influence consumer responses. Table 1 contains the coefficients and significance levels of the mechanism variables in these eight models.

Table 1.  Coefficients and significance levels of the mechanism variables in the eight models.

| Model | Findings | ENCODING mechanism | APPRAISAL mechanism | ATTENTIONAL_1 mechanism | ATTENTIONAL_2 mechanism |
|---|---|---|---|---|---|
| 1 | Coefficient | **.14** | **.14** | .04 | NA |
|   | *p*-value | **.07** | **.0003** | .20 | |
| 2 | Coefficient | **.14** | **.15** | NA | .03 |
|   | *p*-value | **.07** | **.0001** | | .39 |
| 3 | Coefficient | **.28** | **.69** | .12 | NA |
|   | *p*-value | **.07** | **.0003** | .20 | |
| 4 | Coefficient | **.28** | **.73** | NA | .09 |
|   | *p*-value | **.07** | **.0001** | | .39 |
| 5 | Coefficient | **.24** | **.23** | .07 | NA |
|   | *p*-value | **.10** | **.009** | .16 | |
| 6 | Coefficient | **.25** | **.25** | NA | .06 |
|   | *p*-value | **.098** | **.005** | | .32 |
| 7 | Coefficient | −.07 | **.23** | .09 | NA |
|   | *p*-value | .64 | **.01** | .40 | |
| 8 | Coefficient | −.06 | **.23** | NA | .02 |
|   | *p*-value | .71 | **.01** | | .88 |

*Notes:*
(a) Significant, marginally significant, and directional coefficients are in bold.
(b) The mechanism variables that were included in each of the models are as follows:
  • *Models 1, 3, 5, and 7*: ENCODING, APPRAISAL, and ATTENTIONAL_1, or transformed versions of these three variables.
  • *Models 2, 4, 6, and 8*: ENCODING, APPRAISAL, and ATTENTIONAL_2, or transformed versions of these three variables.
  • *Model 1*: ENCODING, APPRAISAL, and ATTENTIONAL_1.
  • *Model 2*: ENCODING, APPRAISAL, and ATTENTIONAL_2.
  • *Models 3 and 4*: Mechanism variables were averaged to rescale them from −1 to +1.
  • *Models 5 and 6*: Mechanism variables were recoded with all negative values as −1 and all positive values as +1.
  • *Models 7 and 8*: Mechanism variables were recoded as −1 and +1 only if all constituent variables were −1 or 0 and +1 or 0, respectively.

# Insights and Opportunities for Future Research

## Insights based on the meta-analysis of mechanisms

The meta-analysis of individual moderators reported by Abraham and Hamilton (2018) demonstrated that the overall effect of partitioned pricing versus all-inclusive pricing on consumer preference was .08 and was directionally significant ($p = .10$). This result demonstrates that, consistent with the initial work in this area by Morwitz *et al.* (1998) and Lee and Han (2002), consumer responses to partitioned pricing tend to be more favorable than consumer responses to all-inclusive pricing. In addition to this main effect of partitioned pricing versus all-inclusive pricing on preference, Abraham and Hamilton (2018) also demonstrated the influence of specific moderating variables that nuance the interpretation of this main effect. Specifically, their meta-analysis of individual moderators showed that consumer responses to partitioned pricing were more favorable than consumer responses to all-inclusive pricing "when the total price is absent, as the price level increases, when the surcharges are typical for the product category, when the surcharges are perceived as offering high benefit, and when the product category is utilitarian" (see Abraham and Hamilton 2018, p. 686).

From the perspective of the current chapter, the meta-analysis of individual moderators conducted by Abraham and Hamilton (2018) provided evidence for the efficacy of at least one moderator in each of the three moderator categories — *price presentation, magnitude,* and *contextual* — that correspond to our three mechanisms that we proposed in this chapter — *encoding, attentional,* and *appraisal.* Notably, this suggests that the single construct of partitioned pricing that is often referred to in the literature actually reflects multiple mechanisms.

The goal of the meta-analysis of the three mechanisms reported in the current chapter was to test whether, at a more aggregate level, the effect of partitioned pricing versus all-inclusive pricing on consumer responses seems to be one effect or multiple effects. By virtue of their significant coefficients in our meta-analytic models, our findings provide supporting evidence for two distinct mechanisms, the *appraisal* and *encoding* mechanisms, suggesting that partitioned pricing is a complex and multi-dimensional phenomenon.

Additionally, our meta-analysis of mechanisms reported in this chapter attempted to determine the relative strengths of the three mechanisms. The findings demonstrated that the coefficient corresponding to the *appraisal* mechanism was the strongest, considering that it was significant in all of our eight models. Furthermore, the coefficient corresponding to the *encoding* mechanism was the next strongest, considering that it was significant in five of our eight models and directionally positive in another one of the eight models. Taken together, these findings demonstrate that the evidence is stronger for the *appraisal* and *encoding* mechanisms, and weaker for the *attentional* mechanism, for which the corresponding coefficient was not significant in any of the eight models. Therefore, although partitioned pricing is a complex and multi-dimensional phenomenon, managers may want to prioritize moderators that activate stronger mechanisms.

The finding that the *appraisal* mechanism is the strongest underlying driver for the influence of partitioned pricing versus all-inclusive pricing on consumer preference is consistent with the existing literature in this domain, which has found significant effects for multiple moderators that activate this particular mechanism. For example, Baghi *et al.* (2010) demonstrated that, for hedonic products such as an MP3 player or a digital camera, partitioned pricing resulted in diminished product attractiveness as compared to all-inclusive pricing, suggesting the role that appraisals of attractiveness had to play as an underlying mechanism. On the other hand, for utilitarian products such as a microwave oven or a laser printer, there was no difference in appraisals of product attractiveness between the partitioned pricing condition and the all-inclusive condition.

Similarly, previous research has demonstrated that, for high-reputation sellers, partitioned pricing results in a positive effect on price fairness and purchase intentions as compared to all-inclusive pricing (Carlson and Weathers 2008), and a null effect on service sign-up likelihood as compared to all-inclusive pricing (Cheema 2008). On the other hand, for low-reputation sellers, there was no difference between partitioned pricing and all-inclusive pricing on price fairness and purchase intentions (Carlson and Weathers 2008), and a negative effect of partitioned pricing versus all-inclusive pricing on service sign-up likelihood (Cheema 2008). These findings again suggest the role of appraisals as an underlying mechanism by which evaluations of the seller's characteristics — such as reputation — were ostensibly transferred to appraisals of the overall partitioned pricing presentation versus all-inclusive pricing presentation.

Along similar lines, the evidence that we found for the *appraisal* mechanism is also consistent with the existing literature that has documented how consumers appraise partitioned components or partitioned prices more favorably when they are not under a marketer's control (Bambauer-Sachse and Mangold 2010), when partitioned components offer relatively high benefit rather than relatively low benefit (Hamilton and Srivastava 2008), and when components are typically partitioned (Redden *et al.* 2007). Taken together, our findings complement the existing literature with respect to moderators that activate the *appraisal* mechanism, and suggest that managers who are looking to activate the *appraisal* mechanism have multiple moderators that they can manipulate in order to influence the effect of partitioned pricing versus all-inclusive pricing on consumer responses.

The finding that the *encoding* mechanism is also a relatively strong underlying driver for the influence of partitioned pricing versus all-inclusive pricing on consumer preference is consistent with the earliest research in this domain (Morwitz *et al.* 1998). These researchers demonstrated that partitioned pricing resulted in a price recall bias because consumers recalled lower total prices as compared to all-inclusive pricing, suggesting the role of the incomplete processing and encoding of surcharge information as the underlying mechanism. Importantly, the experimental stimuli that were used by these researchers contained partitioned prices for which the total price was not present, suggesting that the role of the *encoding* mechanism is especially important under these circumstances.

On the other hand, Hamilton and Srivastava (2008) demonstrated that, even when the total price was explicitly provided, thereby attenuating the role of the underlying *encoding* mechanism, consumers appraised high-benefit components more favorably than low-benefit components, thereby suggesting the activation of the underlying *appraisal* mechanism. These findings provide further evidence that partitioned pricing is a complex and multi-dimensional phenomenon. At the same time, as in Hamilton and Srivastava (2008), even when one underlying mechanism (*encoding*) for the effect of partitioned pricing on consumer responses is controlled for, another underlying mechanism (*appraisal*) can be activated. Alternatively, even when the *encoding* mechanism is controlled for by means of the total price being present, this mechanism can be activated by the manipulation of the surcharge format as currency versus percentage, suggesting that, just like with the *appraisal* mechanism, managers can manipulate multiple moderators in order to activate the *encoding* mechanism as well.

Although our findings suggest that managers should prioritize certain moderators that activate the *appraisal* and *encoding* mechanisms, moderators such as hedonic versus utilitarian category, surcharge benefit, and typicality of partitioning — which were significant in the meta-analysis of individual moderators (Abraham and Hamilton 2018), and which operate through the *appraisal* mechanism — are not always particularly easy for managers to control. For example, managers are unlikely to always have a choice of product categories in which to market their products and services, especially if they are tasked with marketing in a particular product category. Additionally, for a given combination of focal component and secondary component, consumer perceptions of surcharge benefit and typicality of partitioning are likely to be less malleable to managerial actions than to pre-existing influences.

However, even with the combination of a given focal component and secondary component at a given price, managers have the flexibility to control moderators such as presence (versus absence) of the total price. Presence (versus absence) of the total price was marginally significant in our meta-analysis of individual moderators (Abraham and Hamilton 2018), and it operates through the *encoding* mechanism, one of the relatively stronger mechanisms based on the findings of our meta-analysis. At the same time, although managers might have the option of not providing the total price when consumers are committing to their purchase decision, this approach can lead to ethical concerns, warranting interest from regulators (e.g., U.S. Federal Trade Commission 2012). Therefore, in addition to the prioritization of *appraisal* and *encoding* moderators as mentioned earlier on the basis of the findings from our meta-analysis of mechanisms, managers should also consider the practicalities such as which moderators are under their control and which moderators are less subject to ethical concerns and regulatory scrutiny.

Furthermore, although the *attentional* mechanism demonstrated the weakest findings from our meta-analysis of mechanisms, this is perhaps because the meta-analysis statistically controlled for the other mechanisms, which demonstrated stronger influences. Despite the weak evidence for the *attentional* mechanism, it is still conceivable that the influence of partitioned pricing versus all-inclusive pricing on consumer responses operates through the attentional route. Along these lines, in marketplace environments wherein managers might have already activated the other mechanisms by manipulating the corresponding moderators, they might still find incremental moderating influences of moderators such as price level, which activate the *attentional* mechanism. Therefore, managers should carefully consider the circumstances in which they are marketing their products or services before ruling out the manipulation of moderators, such as price level, that activate the *attentional* mechanism.

## Opportunities for future research

Abraham and Hamilton's (2018) meta-analysis of individual moderators found either significant or marginally significant results for at least one moderator from each of their three categories of moderators: *price presentation* moderators, *magnitude* moderators, and *contextual* moderators. Although these three categories of moderators were linked with distinct managerial actions, that meta-analysis did not directly investigate whether these individual moderators influenced partitioned pricing by means of one or more of the distinct mechanisms that we proposed in this chapter: *encoding, attentional,* and *appraisal* mechanisms. Given the results reported here, which suggest that partitioned pricing may operate through both the appraisal and encoding mechanisms, one fertile area for future research involves a more explicit investigation of these two mechanisms by which partitioned pricing operates. Such an investigation will require experimental studies that focus on recording process measures to investigate the roles of the corresponding mechanisms. Specifically, in order to investigate the role of attention as a mechanism, especially when manipulating individual moderators such as price level and surcharge magnitude, researchers could consider the use of eye-tracking techniques.

Another interesting avenue for future research may be to examine possible sequences of mechanisms. Greenleaf *et al.* (2016) propose that partitioned pricing works through the cumulative impact of a series of six interrelated stages that may occur concurrently and also influence each other. Thus, future research could investigate the relationship between each of these six interrelated stages and the three mechanisms that we proposed in our research. Multi-method research involving surveys, verbal protocols, eye-tracking, and other neurological methods might be especially fruitful to investigate these relationships as well as to further investigate the multi-stage sequence proposed by Greenleaf *et al.* (2016). Research could also identify when our underlying mechanisms — *encoding, attentional,* and *appraisal* — as well as the stages in Greenleaf *et al.* (2016) occur in parallel and when they occur sequentially. Given the nature of our data, we found evidence for the parallel nature of the influences of the underlying mechanisms on preference. However, these parallel influences do not rule out an underlying sequential process between partitioned pricing and downstream outcomes. For example, it is conceivable that a moderator such as surcharge magnitude initially activates the *attentional* mechanism, which consequently influences the *encoding* of price information, which then influences the *appraisal* of the different components. Therefore, it is important to identify the sequence by which these mechanisms operate, perhaps by means of multi-stage experiments.

One of the primary advantages of experimental studies is experimental control, but the disadvantage is diminished ecological validity. Therefore, future research should consider validating some of the findings from our meta-analysis as well as previous literature in this domain by running field experiments or other field studies. Although there have already been some field studies that use eBay as the data collection environment (e.g., Cheema 2008; Hossain and Morgan 2006), these studies only investigate the role of surcharge magnitude. Our conceptualization of the three mechanisms suggests that surcharge magnitude activates the *attentional* mechanism, which is the weakest of the three mechanisms based on our meta-analytic findings. Therefore, more research is needed to investigate other relationships and the corresponding stronger mechanisms — *appraisal* and *encoding* — in this domain that have not yet been investigated in more ecologically valid environments.

In addition to these opportunities for future investigations, researchers could consider investigating the role of existing moderators that have not yet been studied in greater detail in the field of partitioned pricing, as well as new moderators that are beginning to be studied in the field of partitioned pricing. For example, in the meta-analysis of individual moderators that was reported in Abraham and Hamilton (2018), the meta-analysis was limited to only those moderators that had been manipulated in two or more papers, so that the results would not be based only on the effects that were reported in a single paper, which would have limited generalizability. By using this criterion, moderators such as "need for cognition (Cheema 2008), recall-versus stimulus-driven information (Kim 2006), construal level (Albinsson *et al.* 2010), and the number of surcharges (Xia and Monroe 2004)" were not investigated in the Abraham and Hamilton (2018, p. 689) meta-analysis or in this chapter. More recent research in the field of partitioned pricing has also studied the role of moderators such as independent versus interdependent self-construal (Das and Roy 2019), new versus used products (Crosno and Cui 2018), and temporal distance (Choi *et al.* 2019). Future research could examine these moderators either experimentally, or if new papers appear, using meta-analysis. In addition to confirming or disconfirming existing findings, new experimental studies will increase the number of moderators that can be meta-analyzed, which will help add to our ability to generalize implications from the findings of a moderator meta-analysis in the field of partitioned pricing.

Furthermore, future meta-analyses that investigate the three mechanisms that underlie partitioned pricing can build upon the meta-analysis of mechanisms that was reported in this chapter to recode the four corresponding mechanism variables — ENCODING, APPRAISAL, ATTENTIONAL_1, and ATTENTIONAL_2 — after taking into account how moderators not included in this meta-analysis map onto these mechanism variables. This will result in a more comprehensive and generalizable meta-analysis of mechanisms, which can be used to analyze the influence of more moderators on each of the three mechanisms, rather than just those moderators that have thus far been manipulated in two or more papers.

# Summary

As mentioned in the introduction to this chapter, consumers often encounter mandatory surcharges for a variety of transactions, and they are increasingly exposed to more innovative types of surcharges as marketers attempt to increase their profits. This chapter presents *partitioned pricing* (Morwitz *et al.* 1998) — in which the total price of a product or service is presented in two or more mandatory parts (a *base price* and one or more *surcharges*) — as an appropriate framework with which to investigate the effects of surcharges and fees on consumer responses. Managers can use insights from the partitioned pricing literature in order to design and implement their marketing tactics. Specifically, these insights can help managers identify conditions under which partitioned pricing (as opposed to all-inclusive pricing) leads to consumer responses that are more favorable or less favorable.

Although partitioned pricing might appear to be very similar to bundling (Stremersch and Tellis 2002), this chapter clarifies that the major conceptual difference between these two constructs is that bundling is undertaken by including two standalone products or services in a single package, whereas partitioned pricing involves two or more components that cannot be purchased separately. The chapter also explains the process by which partitioned pricing operates, as well as identifies three mechanisms — *encoding, attentional,* and *appraisal* — by which the effects of partitioned pricing versus all-inclusive pricing on consumer responses occur. For each of these three mechanisms, this chapter then discussed how some relevant moderators of partitioned pricing versus all-inclusive pricing are likely to activate the corresponding mechanism. The chapter also discussed the overlap between these three mechanisms and the three categories of moderators that were identified in Abraham and Hamilton (2018).

We undertook two meta-analyses of the existing academic literature in the domain of partitioned pricing by investigating 149 effect sizes that represented differences between partitioned pricing and all-inclusive pricing from 43 studies in 27 published and unpublished papers ($N = 12,878$). The first meta-analysis focused on the moderating influences of individual moderators on the effects of partitioned pricing versus all-inclusive pricing on preference (reported in Abraham and Hamilton 2018), and the second meta-analysis (reported in this chapter) focused on the role of the three mechanisms in the effects of partitioned pricing versus all-inclusive pricing on preference. Across multiple models that represented various robustness checks, the meta-analysis of the mechanisms demonstrated positive and significant coefficients for the *appraisal* mechanism in all eight models, as well as positive and marginally significant coefficients for the *encoding* mechanism in five out of eight models along with a directionally positive coefficient in one model. The coefficients for the *attentional* mechanism were not significant in any of the eight models.

Based on the findings from our meta-analysis, this chapter also discussed some helpful insights for researchers and managers. First and foremost, partitioned pricing is a complex and multi-dimensional phenomenon. Additionally, managers should prioritize moderators that activate the strongest underlying mechanisms — *appraisal* and *encoding*. The relative strength of the *appraisal* and *encoding* mechanisms is consistent with the existing literature that has demonstrated evidence for multiple moderators that ostensibly activate these mechanisms, suggesting that managers who are looking to activate either of these mechanisms have multiple moderators that they can manipulate in order to influence the effect of partitioned pricing versus all-inclusive pricing on consumer responses. Moreover, even if managers might not always be able to activate certain mechanisms by manipulating the corresponding moderators, they still have the option of activating other mechanisms by manipulating different moderators. Furthermore, even if managers are attempting to prioritize some moderators over others, they should also consider the practicalities such as which moderators are more amenable to managerial intervention and less subject to ethical concerns and regulatory scrutiny. Finally, although the *attentional* mechanism was not significant in our analysis, managers might still be able to activate this mechanism by the incremental moderating influences of moderators such as price level.

This chapter also identified some promising avenues for future research that relate to an investigation of the multiple mechanisms by which partitioned pricing might operate, including the potential use of eye-tracking techniques to investigate the role of attention. This chapter also identified other potential avenues for future research in the form of investigating (a) relationships between the six interrelated stages involved in partitioned pricing (Greenleaf *et al.* 2016) and our three mechanisms, (b) whether our three mechanisms always operate in parallel or whether there is also scope for them to operate sequentially, (c) the ecological validity of findings from the existing academic literature in this domain, (d) the role of recent moderators (which researchers have only just begun to explore) and other moderators that have been manipulated in only one paper each thus far, and (e) how these moderators map onto the mechanism variables that were reported in this chapter.

In summary, we hope that this chapter will be helpful for managers who are considering the use of partitioned pricing, and who seek to better understand the mechanisms by which certain moderators may lead to more favorable consumer responses. We also hope that this chapter will be helpful for researchers who might be interested in further investigating some of the open avenues that we identified for future research in this domain.

# References

Abraham, A. T. and R. W. Hamilton (2018), When does partitioned pricing lead to more favorable consumer preferences? Meta-analytic evidence, *Journal of Marketing Research*, 55(October), 686–703.

Albinsson, P. A., B. Burman, and N. Das (2010), Price surcharge and the effects of construal level, *Journal of Applied Business and Economics*, 11(4), 56–69.

Baghi, I., E. Rubaltelli, and M. Tedeschi (2010), Mental accounting and cause related marketing strategies, *International Review on Public and Nonprofit Marketing*, 7(2), 145–156.

Bambauer-Sachse, S. and S. Mangold (2010), Does a marketer's responsibility for a surcharge moderate price partitioning effects?, in *Advances in Consumer Research*, Vol. 37, M. C. Campbell, J. Inman, and R. Pieters, eds., Duluth, MN: Association for Consumer Research, pp. 333–339.

Berlyne, D. E. (1960), *Conflict, Arousal and Curiosity*, New York: McGraw-Hill.

Bertini, M. and L. Wathieu (2008), Attention arousal through price partitioning, *Marketing Science*, 27(2), 236–246.

Bigda, C., K. Nugent, D. Rosato, and C. Weisser (2006), The most outrageous fees of 2010, https://money.cnn.com/galleries/2006/moneymag/0612/gallery.outrageous.fees/index.html (accessed December 19, 2018).

Carey, S. (2011), Airlines to load on more fees, http://online.wsj.com/article/SB10001424052748704728004576176521453253668.html (accessed December 19, 2018).

Carlson, J. P. and D. Weathers (2008), Examining differences in consumer reactions to partitioned prices with a variable number of price components, *Journal of Business Research*, 61(7), 724–731.

Cheema, A. (2008), Surcharges and seller reputation, *Journal of Consumer Research*, 35(1), 167–177.

Choi, J., D. E. Bolton, and M. Grishin (2019), The moderating effect of temporal distance on partitioned vs combined pricing, *Journal of Consumer Marketing*, 36(5), 529–538. https://doi.org/10.1108/JCM-06-2017-2243.

Cohen, J. (1977), *Statistical Power Analysis for the Behavioral Sciences*, rev. ed., New York: Academic Press.

Crosno, J. L. and A. P. Cui (2018), Something old, something new: The role of partitioned pricing in consumers' preference for new versus used products, *Journal of Consumer Marketing*, 35(4), 353–365.

Das, G. and R. Roy (2019), How self-construal guides preference for partitioned versus combined pricing, *Journal of Business Research*, 101(August), 152–160.

First Research (2018), Airlines industry profile, http://www.firstresearch.com/Industry-Research/Airlines.html (accessed December 19, 2018).

Folkes, V. S. (1988), Recent attribution research in consumer behavior: A review and new directions, *Journal of Consumer Research*, 14(4), 548–565.

Goldman, D. (2013), The hidden 17% tax: Your cell phone bill, http://money.cnn.com/2013/07/10/technology/mobile/wireless-taxes/index.html?hpt=hp_t3 (accessed December 19, 2018).

Greenleaf, E. A., E. J. Johnson, V. G. Morwitz, and E. Shalev (2016), The price does not include additional taxes, fees, and surcharges: A review of research on partitioned pricing, *Journal of Consumer Psychology*, 26(1), 105–124.

Hamilton, R. W. and J. Srivastava (2008), When 2 + 2 is not the same as 1 + 3: Variations in price sensitivity across components of partitioned prices, *Journal of Marketing Research*, 45(4), 450–461.

Hamilton, R. W., J. Srivastava, and A. T. Abraham (2010), When should you nickel and dime your customers? A manager's guide to benefits-based price partitioning, *MIT Sloan Management Review*, 52(1), 59–67.

Hobica, G. (2013), 8 'Gotcha' travel fees and how to avoid them, http://www.usatoday.com/story/travel/columnist/hobica/2013/08/13/travel-fees-how-to-avoid/2644311 (accessed December 19, 2018).

Hossain, T. and J. Morgan (2006), …Plus shipping and handling: Revenue (non) equivalence in field experiments on eBay, *Advances in Economic Analysis and Policy*, 5(2), 1–27.

Kim, H.-M. (2006), The effect of salience on mental accounting: How integration versus segregation of payment influences purchase decisions, *Journal of Behavioral Decision Making*, 19(4), 381–391.

Lee, Y. H. and C. Y. Han (2002), Partitioned pricing in advertising: Effects on brand and retailer attitudes, *Marketing Letters*, 13(1), 27–40.

Mackey, R. (2009), Budget airline to charge for toilet use, http://thelede.blogs.nytimes.com/2009/06/03/budget-airline-to-charge-for-toilet-use (accessed December 19, 2018).

Mayer, C. E. (2002), Add-ons can add up for consumers, http://articles.chicagotribune.com/2002-12-03/business/0212030117_1_universal-service-fee-add-ons-long-distance-bills (accessed December 19, 2018).

Morwitz, V. G., E. Greenleaf, and E. Johnson (1998), Divide and prosper: Consumers' reactions to partitioned prices, *Journal of Marketing Research*, 35(4), 453–463.

Pardo, D. (2014), Venezuela's airport 'breathing' tax, https://www.bbc.com/news/blogs-trending-28227198 (accessed December 13, 2018).

Redden, J. P., G. Fitzsimons, and P. Williams (2007), Marketing norms as a moderator of consumer responses to price partitioning, Working Paper, Carlson School of Management, University of Minnesota.

Schindler, R. M., M. Morrin, and N. Bechwati (2005), Shipping charges and shipping-charge skepticism: Implications for direct marketers' pricing formats, *Journal of Interactive Marketing*, 19(1), 41–53.

Statista (2016), Statistics & facts on the hotel and lodging industry, https://www.statista.com/topics/1102/hotels (accessed December 19, 2018).

Statista (2018), Revenue of wireless telecommunication carriers in the United States from 2007 to 2021 (in billion U.S. dollars), http://statista.com/statistics/293490/revenue-of-wireless-telecommunication-carriers-in-the-us (accessed December 19, 2018).

Stremersch, S. and G. J. Tellis (2002), Strategic bundling of products and prices: A new synthesis for marketing, *Journal of Marketing*, 66(January), 55–72.

Tversky, A. and D. Kahneman (1974), Judgment under uncertainty: Heuristics and biases, *Science*, 185(4157), 1124–1131.

Tversky, A., S. Sattath, and P. Slovic (1988), Contingent weighting in judgment and choice, *Psychological Review*, 95(3), 371–384.

U.S. Federal Trade Commission (2012), A conference on the economics of drip pricing, https://www.ftc.gov/news-events/events-calendar/2012/05/economics-drip-pricing (accessed December 19, 2018).

Voester, J., B. Ivens, and A. Leischnig. (2017), Partitioned pricing: Review of the literature and directions for further research, *Review of Managerial Science*, 11, 879–931.

Xia, L. and K. B. Monroe (2004), Price partitioning on the internet, *Journal of Interactive Marketing*, 18(4), 63–73.

Chapter 7

# Crossing the Efficiency Frontier: A Framework for Understanding Consumers' Responses to Bargains*

## Aner Sela

Consumers frequently face potential opportunities, such as products on sale, loyalty programs, rebate offers, and other promotions. Opportunities are a powerful driver of action, and consumers often spend much time and effort to obtain them — sometimes more than seems justifiable by the magnitude of the saving (Blattberg and Neslin 1989; Darke and Dahl 2003; Schindler 1989; Thaler 1985). However, the mere fact that a marketing offer is presented as a potential bargain is often not enough to make consumers see the offer as representing above-normal value for them. In fact, people are usually quite selective in pursuing purported bargains and often forgo them regardless of their resource limitations. Despite the allure of apparent bargains, consumers' perceptions of idiosyncratic value remain elusive.

---

*In *New Directions in Behavioral Pricing*, Chezy Ofir Ed., 2024, World Scientific Publishing Company. This chapter is based on the author's dissertation at Stanford University and contains ideas similar to those published later in Sela, Aner, Itamar Simonson, and Ran Kivetz (2013), Beating the Market: The Allure of Unintended Value, *Journal of Marketing Research*, 50 (December), 691–705.
Aner Sela, University of Florida, Warrington College of Business, Gainesville, FL 32611, United States (aner.sela@warrington.ufl.edu).

How are these subjective perceptions formed, given consumers' difficulty assessing offers based on absolute values (Bettman *et al.* 1998)? In this chapter, I discuss a framework for understanding consumers' responses to marketing offers and the cues they use as indicators of idiosyncratic value or lack thereof.

# Beating the Market: Opportunities as Idiosyncratic Deviations from a Perceived Efficiency Frontier

When do we feel we got a bargain? According to economic theory, people buy when the price of the good is lower than the maximum price they agree to pay, or their reservation price. For example, a consumer may agree to spend $250 on a digital camera. When a desired camera costs $200, the consumer has a $50 surplus, making this deal satisfactory. When the camera's price is significantly lower than consumers' reservation price, economics would suggest they have an "above normal" surplus and consumers may feel they found a bargain.

Unfortunately, research suggests consumers often do not know their reservation price. Instead, they construct their preferences on the fly, based on accessible cues, when the need to decide arises (Bettman *et al.* 1998; Schwarz 2007). For example, a "25% off" tag may indicate the deal is attractive (Thaler 1985; Winer 1986). In many cases, however, merely labeling a marketing offer as a bargain is not enough to evoke consumers' perception that the offer represents a bargain (or has above normal value) for them.

I argue that the allure of marketing offers is determined, in large part, by consumers' perception of the offer's idiosyncratic value (i.e., "How much of a deal is it *for me*?"). In particular, the extent to which the offer appears more valuable to them than presumably intended by the marketer. When the offer appears valuable due to individual circumstances or preferences the marketer has not taken into account, consumers often perceive it as a bargain.

This proposition is based on the notion that consumers' perceptions of value are influenced by their theories about marketplace economics (Agarwal and Ratchford 1980; Rosen 1974). Consumers understand marketers are profit-maximizers (Campbell and Kirmani 2000; Friestad and Wright 1994, 1995; Kirmani and Campbell 2004) and they generally understand marketers offer discounts for a reason (e.g., as a persuasion tactic, in response to seasonal demands, or because some options are less attractive than others). In other words, consumers can often explain promotions to themselves in ways that reduce the offer's attractiveness (Raghubir and Corfman 1999).

I argue that the lay-belief in marketers' profit-maximizing motives leads people to view offers as *designed* by sellers to provide the target consumer with the minimum surplus necessary to generate a transaction. One may say that consumers believe marketing offers reside on an efficiency frontier of sorts, representing a tradeoff between cost and utility. Of course, the efficiency frontier is used here figuratively, to conceptualize the common wisdom that it is usually hard to "beat the market".

I propose that consumers are attracted to offers they perceive as deviating, due to idiosyncratic circumstances or preferences unbeknownst to the marketer, from this normal or market-efficient state of affairs. Assuming marketers design offers to provide minimal surplus for their intended targets, offers that appear to deviate from this "efficiency frontier" due to factors unaccounted for by the marketer are likely to be seen as bargains.

Several predictions arise from this proposition. Specifically, marketing offers should be more attractive from a value perspective when they appear to fit the consumer's preference by accident rather than by design, when they seem accidental or nonobvious rather than predictable or obvious, and when they arise from what looks like a random combination of individual and situational factors. Next, I report five studies examining these predictions.

# Study 1: The Effect of Offer Targeting on Bargain Perception

Study 1 tests the prediction that a marketing offer can be more attractive when it appears to fit the consumer's preference by accident than by design. Participants ($N = 173$) completed a questionnaire about their preferences for different products (e.g., jazz music, hybrid cars) and content areas (e.g., news reports, business, science, nature, fashion, gastronomy), allegedly as part of a market research conducted on behalf of an online vendor to assess demand for different types of magazines. They were told that they would later have the option to take advantage of an offer from the company selling those magazines at the end of the study if their name was drawn in a lottery. The questionnaire included questions such as "How much do you enjoy reading about economic and business affairs, relative to the average consumer?"; "How much do you enjoy fashion magazines, relative to the average consumer?". Response scales were anchored on 1 = "Much less than average people", 2 = "Somewhat less than average people", 3 = "About average", 4 = "Somewhat more than average people", and 5 = "Much more than average people". Based on this questionnaire, participants were classified as having either an above-average (>3) or an average/below-average (<4) preference for economic and business magazines, thereby forming a 2 (Relative Preference: high versus low) × 2 (Framing: for average versus classic readers) between-subjects design.

At the end of the session, participants were asked if they wanted to take advantage of a special promotion, as an additional token of appreciation for their participation. They saw one of two versions of an offer to buy a subscription to *The Economist* magazine. The first version was described as "intended to get the average reader excited about *The Economist* magazine". It included an offer to subscribe for *The Economist* at 25% off the regular student price ($44 instead of $59). The second version was described as "intended for the classic reader of *The Economist* magazine". It included an offer to subscribe at 30% off the regular student price ($41 instead of $59). Participants indicated whether they would rather take advantage of the offer or receive $5 in cash, instead of the offer. Their responses served as the main dependent variable.

As predicted, participants who believed they liked economic magazines more than the average were more likely to take advantage of the offer when it was framed as intended for the average reader (27%) than for "classic" readers (11%; $\chi^2(1) = 4.09$, $p < .05$). There was no significant effect of framing among participants who believed they liked economic magazines less than or as much as the average (4% versus 7%, respectively; $\chi^2(1) < .5$, $ns$). Looking at the data another way, participants who liked economic magazines more than the average were more likely to take advantage of the offer than those who liked it less than or as much as the average, but only when the offer was framed as intended for average people (27% versus 4%, respectively; $\chi^2(1) = 9.25$, $p < .005$). This difference disappeared when the offer was framed as intended for "classic" readers (11% versus 7%, respectively; $\chi^2(1) < 1$, $ns$).

These results support the suggestion that consumers may find a bargain offer particularly attractive when they believe the offer happens to be more valuable for them than for the offer's hypothetical target. One might intuitively expect that framing an offer as intended "for the classic reader" should make the offer more appealing than framing it as intended for "average" readers, especially among those who are likely to consider themselves as "classic". However, the results suggest the reverse in this case.

The next study extends these findings to a situation where the offer is directly customized by the marketer based on individual consumers' stated preferences. In addition, the next study examines whether the effect of customization on choice is mediated by perceptions of above-normal value and tests an alternative explanation based on psychological reactance (Brehm 1966; Fitzsimons and Lehman 2004; Kivetz 2005).

## Study 2: The Effect of Explicit Offer Customization

Study 2 was very similar to study 1. After completing the same preferences questionnaire described above, participants ($N = 176$) could opt to buy a subscription to *The Economist* magazine. Different from study 1, participants in the non-explicit customization condition learned that "The company selling these products is offering you to buy a 6-month subscription for *The Economist* magazine at 30% off the regular subscription price ($41 instead of $59), if you are selected in the lottery at the end of this study." In the explicit customization condition, participants were told that "Based on your answers on the previous pages, the company selling these products is offering you to buy a 6-month subscription for *The Economist* magazine at 30% off the regular subscription price ($41 instead of $59)". As in study 1, participants indicated whether they would rather take advantage of the offer or get $5 in cash, instead of the offer, if they won the lottery. Their decision on this measure served as the main dependent variable.

To gain further insight into the process underlying people's choices, participants then indicated to what extent the value of the offer they received seemed "different from what someone like you could normally get" (1 = Not at all different; 7 = Very different). Finally, following a filler task from an unrelated study, participants completed the 11-item psychological reactance scale (Hong and Faedda 1996) by rating their agreement with each statement on a five-point scale (e.g., "I resist the attempts of others to influence me," "I consider advice from others to be an intrusion," and "It irritates me when someone points out things which are obvious to me"). The responses were averaged to form an individual reactance score ($\alpha = .84$). The reactance score was not influenced by the customization manipulation ($F < 1$, *ns*).

Consistent with study 1 and extending it, participants who indicated they liked economic magazines better than the average person were more likely to buy the subscription in the absence of explicit customization (23%) than when the offer was said to be customized for them based on their preferences (3%; $\chi^2(1) = 5.17$, $p < .05$). Purchase likelihood among consumers who indicated they liked economic magazines less than or as much as the average person was not affected by the customization manipulation (1% versus 4%, respectively), ($\chi^2(1) < 2$, *ns*). Looking at the data another way, participants who indicated they liked economic magazines more than the average were more likely to buy the subscription, in the absence of explicit customization, than those who indicated they liked those magazines as much as or less than the average ($\chi^2(1) = 13.98$, $p < .001$). However, the difference disappeared when the offer was said to be customized based on participants' individual preferences ($\chi^2(1) < .1$, *ns*).

A mediation analysis (Baron and Kenny 1986), focusing on those participants who indicated a higher-than-average preference for economic magazines, indicated that the effect of explicit customization on choice was mediated by the extent to which the offer's value seemed different from what people could normally obtain. Specifically, a linear regression model suggested that explicit customization significantly reduced the extent to which participants believed the value of the offer was different from what someone like them could normally get ($\beta = -1.71$, $SE = .44$; $t = 3.89$, $p < .001$). A second model, with explicit customization and perceptions of above-normal value as the independent variables and purchase likelihood as the dependent variable, indicated that perceptions of above-normal value predicted purchase likelihood ($\beta = 1.38$, $SE = .54$; $t = 2.57$, $p < .05$) whereas the effect of explicit customization was non-significant ($\beta = -1.00$, $t = -.76$, *ns*), ($z = 2.10$, $p < .05$; Sobel 1982). Testing the alternative reverse model suggested that the effect of explicit customization on perceived value was not mediated by purchase likelihood.

If the effect of customization on purchase likelihood is driven by psychological reactance, then it should be stronger among consumers higher in the tendency to experience psychological reactance. A logistic regression on choice, with customization and reactance scores as independent variables, indicated that reactance did not interact with customization to affect choice ($\chi^2(1) < 2$, *ns*). These results cast doubt on the possibility that reactance was driving the observed effect.

## Study 3: Offer Versus Product Customization

Study 3 was based on the same paradigm used in study 2. In addition to the explicit and non-explicit customization conditions, however, this study included a third condition in which only the type of magazine was customized to fit participants' taste (i.e., product customization) but the price was said to be the same for everyone. Participants ($N = 310$) went through the same procedure described in study 2. At the end of the session, they were offered a subscription to *The Economist* at a 30% discount. Participants in the non-explicit and explicit customization conditions saw the same respective offers described in study 2. The third (fixed discount) condition was identical to the explicit customization condition, but participants were told that everyone who participated in the study could benefit from a 30% discount on selected offers.

Consistent with the previous results, among participants who indicated a high preference for economic and world news, 10.5% in the non-explicitly customized condition chose to take advantage of the offer whereas none of those in the explicitly customized condition chose to do so ($\chi^2 = 5.90$, $p < .05$). However, participants in the fixed discount condition were significantly more likely to buy the subscription (12.5%) than in the regular explicit customization condition ($\chi^2 = 6.95$, $p < .01$).

## Studies 1–3: Discussion

The results of studies 1–3 support the proposition that consumers are attracted to offers they perceive as valuable to them in a manner unaccounted for by the marketer. Participants who saw themselves as having an above-average preference for the target option were significantly more likely to take advantage of the offer than those with an average or below-average preference, but only when it was described as designed for typical people (study 1) or when the option was believed to fit their individual preferences by coincidence (studies 2 and 3). When the offer was presented as customized based on consumers' preferences (studies 1 and 3) or simply described as designed for people who are likely to appreciate such an option (study 1), the offer's attractiveness dropped significantly.

Study 3 identifies an important boundary condition for the negative effect of offer customization, suggesting that customization is less likely to undermine the offer's attractiveness when the deal's value (e.g., the magnitude of a discount) is believed to be independent of individual preference. This finding further casts doubt on a psychological reactance alternative account, because reactance should ensue even if only the type of magazine is customized.

An important element of the present conceptualization is the notion that consumers evaluate options as if they are in competition or a zero-sum game with the marketer. Consumers are attracted to offers that they feel just happen to be more valuable to them than intended, which enables them to take advantage of the situation and "beat the market". The lay belief in the competitive or efficient nature of the market implies that if the marketer can anticipate consumers' individual circumstances or preferences and tailor the offer accordingly, the offer is likely to be fairly priced (i.e., provide only minimal surplus) given those circumstances or preferences. The next study tests the role of competitiveness in these effects.

# Study 4: The Effect Priming Competition on Responses to Tailored Offers

Study 4 used a priming manipulation adapted from prior research (Kay *et al.* 2004, study 1) in which half of the participants were exposed to pictorial and verbal representations of everyday objects related to competition and other aspects of self-interested behaviors, whereas the other half were exposed to neutral objects. Specifically, exposure to objects related to business (e.g., a business suit, a boardroom meeting table) was shown to activate a competitive mindset.

Participants ($N = 180$) were randomly assigned to a condition in a 2 (Prime: business-related versus neutral) × 2 (Targeting: coincidental versus targeted offer) between-subject design. After completing an "object recognition" task in which they were exposed to either objects related to business or neutral objects (i.e., the competition priming task), participants moved on to the focal choice task. They were asked to imagine they had been recently shopping around for a new Bose home entertainment system. In the coincidental condition, they read a scenario in which they happened to find in their mailbox a direct mail offer from a nearby electronics store, offering them a Bose home entertainment system at a price of $849.99, presumably reflecting a "special dealer's discount" of 15% over the regular list price of $999.99. In the targeted offer condition, participants read a similar scenario in which they had first visited the electronics store, where they discussed their needs with a salesperson and saw several models. One week after the store visit, they supposedly found in their mailbox a direct mail offer from the same store they had visited, offering them to buy the same home entertainment system, at the same discounted price as in the coincidental condition. As a dependent variable, participants were asked to indicate how likely they would be to take advantage of such an offer (1 = Most likely throw it away; 7 = Most likely use it).

Funnel debriefing indicated that none of the participants thought the object recognition (i.e., priming) task was related to the choice task. An ANOVA on stated purchase likelihood, with offer (coincidental versus targeted) and priming (competition versus neutral) as independent variables, revealed a significant targeting by prime interaction effect ($F(1, 120) = 8.20, p < .005$) and a significant main effect of targeting ($F(1, 120) = 6.58, p < .05$). Specifically, consistent with prior studies, participants in the neutral prime condition were less likely to take advantage of the offer when it was targeted at them by a marketer who presumably knew about their preferences ($M = 4.2$) than when the same offer appeared to match their preferences by coincidence ($M = 5.2$; $F(1, 120) = 3.79, p < .06$). However, this effect increased significantly when participants had been primed with business-related objects ($M = 3.3$ versus $M = 5.3$, respectively; $F(1, 120) = 5.09, p < .05$). Looking at the data another way, participants in the targeted condition said they would be less likely to take advantage of the offer when primed with competition than did participants exposed to the neutral prime ($p < .1$).

These findings suggest that the cognitive accessibility of concepts related to competition increases the negative effect of deliberate offer targeting on offer attractiveness. This supports the notion that the effect of individually tailored offers is driven by consumers' beliefs about the competitive nature of markets.

## Study 5: Contrasting the Effects of Coincidental and Deliberate Circumstances

Study 5 contrasts the effects of coincidental and deliberate circumstances on consumers' response to apparent opportunities. Participants were asked to evaluate a direct mail offer which either had been mailed to them deliberately, by the marketer, or intended for another consumer and mailed to them by mistake (i.e., a coincidence). For half of them, the offer was framed as an opportunity in the form of a price discount whereas for the other half it was not. Participants were expected to find the offer framed as an opportunity more attractive when it resulted from a coincidental mistake. In contrast, consistent with the prior studies, participants were expected to find the opportunity-framed offer less attractive when it resulted from circumstances planned by a marketer. Study 8 also addresses an alternative account based on increased cognitive elaboration for the predicted effect of coincidence.

Method

Participants ($N$ = 124; mean age = 35, range 18–70; 64% females) completed this study online and were randomly assigned to a condition in a 2 (Opportunity Framing: discounted versus non-discounted offer) $\times$ 2 (Circumstances: deliberate versus coincidental) between-subject design. Participants were asked to imagine they had been shopping around for a new home entertainment system and had previously visited an electronics store where they discussed their budget with a salesperson and saw several models. One week after the store visit, they supposedly found in their mailbox a direct mail offer from the same store they had visited, offering a home entertainment system at a priced of $849.99. In the opportunity framing condition, this price represented a 15% discount from the regular list price of $999.99.

At this point, participants in the deliberate condition were asked to rate on a seven-point scale how likely they would be to take advantage of the offer (1 = Most probably throw it away; 7 = Most likely use it). In contrast, participants in the coincidence condition read the following additional message: "When you look again, however, it looks like this direct mail offer was put in your mailbox by mistake. It was actually meant for Erik Walker, who used to be your next-door neighbor. You know for sure that Eric has recently moved to another country, permanently, and cannot be contacted. It says on the back that the offer is transferable, and so you could either use it yourself or throw it away."

Participants were expected to find the opportunity less attractive when it came from the same store they had supposedly visited and was described as a special offer from the dealer, as consistent the findings of Chapter 2. In contrast, participants were expected to find the opportunity more attractive when the offer was put in their mailbox by mistake.

To address an alternative account based on enhanced cognitive processing in the coincidence condition (see what follows), participants were asked to complete two unrelated filler tasks and then to complete the need for cognition scale (Cacioppo *et al.* 1984). Their responses on this measure were averaged and mean-centered (Aiken and West 1991).

## Results and Discussion

The results support the prediction that coincidental circumstances would increase the attractiveness of the opportunity whereas circumstances that had been initiated by the marketer would attenuate it. An ANOVA on stated purchase likelihood, with opportunity framing (discounted versus non-discounted) and circumstances (deliberate versus coincidental) as independent variables, revealed a significant opportunity by circumstances interaction effect on the purchase likelihood ($F(1, 120) = 8.20$, $p < .005$) and a significant main effect of circumstances ($F(1, 120) = 6.58$, $p < .05$). Specifically, consistent with the findings of Chapter 3, participants in the deliberate circumstances condition were less likely to take advantage of the offer when it was framed as an opportunity ($M = 4.2$) than when it was not ($M = 5.2$; $F(1, 120) = 3.79$, $p < .06$). In contrast, participants in the coincidence condition were more likely to take advantage of the offer when it was framed as an opportunity ($M = 6.1$) than when it was not ($M = 5.1$; $F(1, 120) = 4.49$, $p < .05$). Further, participants were significantly more likely to take advantage of the opportunity in the coincidental than in the deliberate condition ($F(1, 120) = 14.79$, $p < .001$).

*Alternative account.* According to the proposed theoretical account, participants are particularly likely to pursue opportunities arising from a coincidence because coincidence is a cue that is consistent with the notion of "true" deviations from the efficiency frontier. However, one could argue that the effect of coincidence is caused by increased cognitive elaboration or attention in response to unexpected circumstances. That is, "surprising" participants with unusual circumstances such as those described in the coincidence condition might increase the cognitive resources they allocate to the evaluation task, resulting in a more pronounced effect of the opportunity framing. Note that, according to this alternative account, the effect of coincidental circumstances on opportunity compulsion should be especially pronounced among people who otherwise would not allocate as much cognitive resources to the task (e.g., those low in need of cognition, Cacioppo and Petty 1982) and less pronounced among people who tend to think effortfully regardless of the circumstances (e.g., those high in need for cognition (NFC)).

To address this alternative account, it was first verified that none of the independent variables influenced participants' need for cognition scores (all $F(1, 120) < 1.8$, *ns*). Then, purchase likelihood was regressed, among participants in the discount condition, on framing (discounted versus non-discounted) and mean-centered need for cognition scores. This analysis revealed a significant framing by NFC interaction effect ($t(64) = 2.73$, $p < .01$) and a marginally significant main effect of framing ($t(64) = 1.67$, $p < .1$), with no main effect of NFC ($t < 1$, *ns*). Specifically, although opportunity framing had the predicted main effect, this effect was stronger among participants high in NFC than among those low in NFC. These results cast doubt on the possibility that cognitive elaboration was driving the effect.

## Conclusions and Implications

The findings reported in this chapter illustrate that presenting marketing offers as promotions is often not enough to make consumers perceive them as bargains. Instead, an offer's attractiveness may depend on the extent to which consumers perceive it as more valuable for them than intended by the marketer.

The findings also underscore that competitiveness underlies these perceptions of opportunity, namely, that consumers often respond to offers as if they are playing a zero-sum game with the marketer where they try to "beat the market". The findings extend the opportunity construct as it relates to consumers' experiences in the marketplace, suggesting that consumers often act based on certain assumptions about marketers' intentions and their ability to price-discriminate.

One way to conceptualize the findings is to say that consumers are attracted to options located beyond what they perceive as an "efficiency frontier". Namely, consumers appear to spontaneously construct a subjective impression of what people like them can obtain under typical circumstances, and they try to take advantage of options that seem better than expected due to circumstances or preferences that the marketer has not factored in. Consequently, offers that appear to fit their preferences better than those of the typical person and coincidental opportunities are more attractive than offers that fit their preferences by design. Believing, for example, that a marketer has tailored an offer for a particular consumer decreases its attractiveness.

Aside from accounting for the current results, the account proposed here provides a unifying framework for understanding a broad array of prior findings, including the moderating effects of scarcity and other restrictions (Inman *et al.* 1997), discount depth (Lalwani and Monroe 2005), and consistency (Raghubir and Corfman 1999) on effectiveness of price discounts. These prior findings can be thought of as reflecting additional factors that influence whether consumers perceive offers as deviating from normal value (or the efficiency frontier). For example, a time-restricted offer (e.g., "valid only today") will *feel* like a bargain when a consumer is interested in the product but happens to be at the store on the critical day, in part because it just *happens* to fit the consumer's circumstances. The current framework provides novel insight into the idiosyncratic fit heuristic (Kivetz and Simonson 2003) and identifies important boundary conditions for this phenomenon. Specifically, it suggests that consumers may be enticed by offers that fit their preferences better than those of typical others not only because these offers help consumers get ahead of others, but also because they provide a cue for above-normal value and enable consumers to "beat the market". Although one might expect customized offers to be even more attractive than non-customized ones, the current findings suggest that idiosyncratically fitting offers may ironically become less attractive when the consumer's idiosyncratic advantage is accounted for by the marketer.

The findings have important practical implications for marketers, especially with regard to customization, targeting, one-to-one marketing, and other marketing practices that are aimed at individual customers. In particular, marketers should consider the tradeoff between two potentially conflicting consequences of making their customization and targeting efforts explicit. On the one hand, explicit customization (e.g., describing offers as designed "especially for you") may enhance the perceived fit between the offer and consumers' individual preferences, which may augment the offer's attractiveness (Kivetz and Simonson 2003; Simonson 2005). On the other hand, making customization explicit introduces the risk of undermining perceptions of bargain and opportunity. This precaution may be particularly important when there is less ambiguity about whether the option matches consumers' preferences and more ambiguity about whether it is a good deal.

# References

Agarwal, M. and B. T. Ratchford (1980), Estimating demand function for product characteristics: The case of automobiles, *Journal of Consumer Research*, 7(December), 249–262.

Aiken, L. S. and S. G. West (1991), *Multiple Regression: Testing and Interpreting Interactions*, Thousand Oaks, CA: Sage.

Bettman, J. R., M. F. Luce, and J. W. Payne (1998), Constructive consumer choice processes, *Journal of Consumer Research*, 25(December), 187–217.

Blattberg, R. C. and S. A. Neslin (1989), Sales promotion: The long and the short of it, *Marketing Letters*, 1(1), 81–97.

Brehm, J. W. (1966), *A Theory of Psychological Reactance*, New York: Academic Press.

Cacioppo, J. T. and R. E. Petty (1982), The need for cognition, *Journal of Personality and Social Psychology*, 42(1), 116–131.

Cacioppo, J. T., R. E. Petty, and C. F. Kao (1984), The efficient assessment of need for cognition, *Journal of Personality Assessment*, 48(3), 306–307.

Campbell, M. C. and A. Kirmani (2000), Consumers' use of persuasion knowledge: The effects of accessibility and cognitive capacity on perceptions of an influence agent, *Journal of Consumer Research*, 27(June), 69–83.

Darke, P. R. and D. W. Dahl (2003), Fairness and discounts: The subjective value of a bargain, *Journal of Consumer Psychology*, 13(3), 328–338.

Friestad, M. and P. Wright (1994), The persuasion knowledge model: How people cope with persuasion attempts, *Journal of Consumer Research*, 21(June), 1–31.

Friestad, M. and P. Wright (1995), Persuasion knowledge: Lay people's and researchers' beliefs about the psychology of advertising, *Journal of Consumer Research*, 22(June), 62–74.

Fitzsimons, G. J. and D. R. Lehmann (2004), Reactance to recommendations: When unsolicited advice yields contrary responses, *Marketing Science*, 23(1), 82–94.

Hong, S.-M. and S. Faedda (1996), Refinement of the Hong Psychological Reactance Scale, *Educational and Psychological Measurement*, 56(1), 173–182.

Kay, A. C., S. C. Wheeler, J. A. Bargh, and L. Ross (2004), Material priming: The influence of mundane physical objects on situational construal and competitive behavioral choice, *Organizational Behavior and Human Decision Processes*, 95(1), 83–96.

Kirmani, A. and M. C. Campbell (2004), Goal seeker and persuasion sentry: How consumer targets respond to interpersonal marketing persuasion, *Journal of Consumer Research*, 31(December), 573–582.

Kivetz, R. (2005), Promotion reactance: The role of effort-reward congruity, *Journal of Consumer Research*, 31(March), 725–736.

Kivetz, R. and I. Simonson (2003), The idiosyncratic fit heuristic: Effort advantage as a determinant of consumer response to loyalty programs, *Journal of Marketing Research*, 40(November), 454–467.

Lalwani, A. K. and K. B. Monroe (2005), A reexamination of frequency-depth effects in consumer price judgments, *Journal of Consumer Research*, 32(December), 480–485.

Priya, R. and K. Corfman (1999), When do price promotions affect pretrial brand evaluations? *Journal of Marketing Research*, 36(May), 211–222.

Rosen, S. (1974), Hedonic prices and implicit markets: Product differentiation in pure competition, *Journal of Political Economy*, 82(January/February), 34–55.

Schindler, R. M. (1989), The excitement of getting a bargain: Some hypotheses concerning the origins and effects of smart-shopper feelings, in *Advances in Consumer Research*, Vol. 16, Thomas K. Srull, ed. Provo, UT: Association for Consumer Research, pp. 447–453.

Schwarz, N. (2007), Attitude construction: Evaluation in context, *Social Cognition*, 25(5), 638–656.

Simonson, I. (2005), Determinants of customers' responses to customized offers: Conceptual framework and research propositions, *Journal of Marketing*, 69(January), 32–45.

Thaler, R. H. (1985), Mental accounting and consumer choice, *Marketing Science*, 4(3), 199–214.

Winer, R. S. (1986), A reference price model of brand choice for frequently purchased products," *Journal of Consumer Research*, 13(September), 250–256.

# Index

**V**

**W**

Printed in the United States
by Baker & Taylor Publisher Services